A MILLENNIUM OF CLASSIC

A MILLENNIUM OF CLASSICAL PERSIAN POETRY

A GUIDE TO THE READING & UNDERSTANDING OF PERSIAN POETRY FROM THE TENTH TO THE TWENTIETH CENTURY

WHEELER M. THACKSTON

Ibex Publishers,
Bethesda, Maryland

A Millennium of Classical Persian Poetry
A Guide to the Reading and Understanding of Persian Poetry
from the Tenth to the Twentieth Century
by Wheeler M. Thackston

ISBN: 978-0-936347-50-9

Cover illustration: calligraphy by Muhammad Husayn al-Katib (late sixteenth century).
Courtesy of the Metropolitan Museum of Art

Manufactured in the United States of America

The paper used in this book meets the minimum requirements of the American National Standard for
Information Services—Permanence of Paper for Printed Library Materials, ANSI Z39.48–1984

Ibex Publishers strives to create books which are as complete and free of errors as possible. Please help
us with future editions by reporting any errors or suggestions for improvement to the address below,
or corrections@ibexpub.com

Ibex Publishers, Inc.
Post Office Box 30087
Bethesda, Maryland 20824
Telephone: 301–718–8188
Facsimile: 301–907–8707
www.ibexpublishers.com

Library of Congress Cataloging-in-Publication Data

Thackston, W.M. (Wheeler Mcintosh), 1944-
A millennium of classical Persian poetry : a guide to the reading and
understanding of Persian poetry from the tenth to the twentieth century/
Wheeler M. Thackston.
p. cm.
English and Persian
Includes bibliographical references (p. 181-186) and index.
ISBN 0-936347-50-3 (alk. paper)
1. Persian poetry—History and criticism. I. Title.
PK6416.T45 1994
891'.551009—dc20 94-6485
CIP

CONTENTS

Poets of the Afshar, Qajar, and Pahlavi Periods in Iran and the Later Mughal Period in India

INTRODUCTION

FOR A THOUSAND YEARS the classical Persian poetic tradition flourished, continuous and uninterrupted. It began in the great urban centers of Central Asia, Bukhara and Samarkand; and for centuries it dominated the high culture of all of Central Asia, Iran, Azerbaijan, Iraq, Anatolia, and the whole of the northern part of the Indian subcontinent. It has been composed by saints and roués, kings and beggars. It has been written in gold, poets have had their mouths stuffed with precious gems for an apt line of poetry, and the uncivilized have measured their progress into civilization by their ability to quote Persian poetry.

Classical Persian poetry, so called here to distinguish it from modern free verse, represents a continuous body of poetry that conformed to one set of forms and one metrical system, both of which were rigidly defined from the very outset and recognized by all, practitioner and audience alike.

Most of the great poets of the classical period were professional poets, and as professionals attached to courts they produced poetry much as other fine craftsmen produced items on demand for the ruler. "Poetry is a craft *(sinâ'at),*" says Nizâmî Arûzî of Samarkand at the beginning of the discourse on poets in his *Chahâr maqâla* (Four Discourses, circa A.D. 1155),

> by means of which the poet arranges in order premises that produce an image in the mind and knits together arguments that lead to a conclusion in such a way that he makes the meaning of an insignificant thing significant and the meaning of a significant thing insignificant, and he displays a beautiful thing in a hideous robe and an ugly thing in a gorgeous raiment. By means of such ambiguousness he stirs up the irascible and concupiscent faculties so that people experience contractive and expansive moods and thereby cause great affairs in the order of the world.[1]

Even if one did not become a poet in order to effect change in the world, obviously poetry was not a calling to be entered into lightly. It also required a long apprenticeship and years of preparation.

> A poet cannot reach such a degree [of effectiveness] unless during his youth he learns twenty thousand lines of the ancients' poetry and passes before his eyes ten thousand lines of the moderns. He must continually peruse the divans of

---

[1] Ahmad ibn 'Umar al-Nizâmî al-'Arûzî al-Samarqandî, *Chahâr maqâla,* ed. Muhammad ibn-i 'Abdu'l-Vahhâb Qazvînî (Berlin: Iranschähr, 1927), p. 30 (translation mine).

the masters and remember how they get themselves into and out of tight spots in poetry."[2]

Because poets were expected, as Nizâmî Arûzî observes, to have read practically the entire corpus of Persian poetry before they ever composed their first poem, and because refinement of existing conventions was valued, not innovation, the tradition is cumulative and builds upon itself. The stereotypes of lover and beloved—miserable, suffering, unrequited lover, and aloof, unconcerned, and inapproachable beloved—and the *topoi*, the conventional metaphors, that typify these relationships, such as the moth and the candle, the nightingale and the rose, Farhâd and Shîrîn, and so forth, all are immutably fixed in the tradition.

The metaphorical language of poetry also developed within the cumulative tradition. What began initially as a simile, lips as red as rubies, for instance, became so commonplace and hackneyed after thousands of repetitions over the decades and centuries that in the end the simile was scrapped, and ruby lips became simply rubies. So also tears that initially rolled down the cheeks like pearls became, in the end, simply pearls, while tears that glistened like stars became stars. A face as round and lovely as the moon similarly became simply the moon. In the twelfth century Nizâmî could write that Layli's mother *mah-râ zi sitâra tawq barbast* (bound a necklace of stars onto the moon) and know that his audience would immediately understand by this that she covered her daughter's face with tears.

In ghazals, particularly those of the fifteenth through the eighteenth centuries, when the bizarre comparison and highly intellectualized metaphor were greatly prized, the logic that underlies many an image can be stated as follows: if A shares any attribute with B, and B shares any attribute with C, then A = C. For instance, when the down on the beloved's lip is called *sabz*, it means dark, but the literal meaning of *sabz* is "green"; parrots are green; therefore, the down on the lip becomes a parrot. The lips are as sweet as sugar and become simply sugar. Parrots are spoken of as sweet of speech (the parrot's irritating voice is beside the point—the tradition so named them); therefore, they are *shikarkhâ* (sugar-chewing). The final stage in this series is to have the parrot of the down chewing the sugar of the beloved's lips. On first encountering such an image, the English reader may be puzzled, if not to say repulsed. It should be remembered that English too has many expressions a Persian speaker would find strange and distasteful. It is necessary to go beyond one's own cultural conditioning to appreciate an alien literary tradition, and since English literature and Persian literature, like European and Oriental music, have virtually no common ground or shared cultural tradition, it is all but impos-

---

[2] Ibid., p. 34.

sible to appreciate the one in terms of the other. Each must be taken on its own terms.

One of the major difficulties Persian poetry poses to the novice reader lies in the pervasion of poetry by mysticism. Fairly early in the game the mystics found that they could "express the ineffable" in poetry much better than in prose. Usurping the whole of the poetic vocabulary that had been built up by that time, they imbued every word with mystical signification. What had begun as liquid wine with alcoholic content became the "wine of union with the godhead" on which the mystic is "eternally drunk." Beautiful young cupbearers with whom one might like to dally became *shâhids*, "bearers of witness" to the dazzling beauty of that-which-truly-exists. After the mystics had wrought their influence on the tradition, every word of the poetic vocabulary had acquired such "clouds" of associated meaning from lyricism and mysticism that the two strains merged into one. Of course, some poets wrote poetry that is overtly and unmistakably mystical and "Sufi." It is much more difficult to identify poetry that is not mystical. It is useless to ask, for instance, whether Hâfiz's poetry is "Sufi poetry" or not. The fact is that in the fourteenth century it was impossible to write a ghazal that did not reverberate with mystical overtones forced on it by the poetic vocabulary itself. When Hâfiz speaks of *ân turk-i shîrâzî* (that Turk of Shiraz, p. 64), it is irrelevant whether the Turk is male or female, really a Turk or not, or a native or Shiraz or not. The "Turk" is the beloved—any beloved, all beloveds—because, by definition within the ghazal, the beloved is cruel and so are the martial Turks: therefore the beloved is a Turk. Turks are also enchantingly beautiful, just as the beloved is irresistibly seductive. (In this particular line Hâfiz also needed an antithesis to the dark "Hindu mole" on the beloved's cheek, and for that purpose nothing suits better than a light-skinned Shirazi Turk who might hail from Samarkand or Bukhara, the two cities mentioned at the end of the line.)

To return to the craft of poetry, some of its techniques, the rhetorical figures, need to be mentioned. Since this is not the place to go into a detailed study of Persian poetical rhetoric, only a few of the more commonly used figures in which every poet was trained will be given.[3] In addition to those so familiar that they need no discussion, like antithesis, hyperbole, simile, and allusion, the following are frequently encountered. *Husn-i ta'lîl* (etiology) is the assigning of a fanciful cause to a naturally occurring phenomenon, as in a line by Hilâlî (p. 76): "That was not dew in the morning during Layli's time:

---

[3]For a fuller discussion, see E. G. Browne, *A Literary History of Persian*, vol. 2 (1906; reprint ed., Cambridge: At the University Press, 1964), pp. 47–76, and E. J. W. Gibb, *A History of Ottoman Poetry*, vol. 1 (1900; reprint ed., London: Luzac and Company, 1958), pp. 111–24. For a good introduction in Persian, see Vahîd Tabrîzî, *Risâla-i jam'-i mukhtasar*, ed. A. E. Bertels (Moscow: Izdatel'stvo Vostochnoy Literatury, 1959).

it was the heaven weeping all night until dawn over Majnun's state." *Îhâm* (amphibology) is the intentional use of an ambiguous word, like Khusraw's use of *nizâm* (both "order" and the first part of Nizâmuddîn Awliyâ's name) and *'ayn* (both "eye" and "the thing itself") on page 52. *Laff u nashr* ("folding and spreading") is the naming of objects and the subsequent naming of their respective attributes, often in reverse order. *Raddu'l-'ajuz 'ala's-sadr* (epanadiplosis) is the repetition in the second hemistich of a word or phrase occurring in the first hemistich, the best employment of which is reckoned as the repetition of the last word of the first hemistich as the first word of the second hemistich, like Rumi's repetition of *bâz* in line 3 on page 42. *Murâ'ât-i nazîr* (maintaining the like) refers to the introduction of things that are naturally associated, like moon, sun, and stars, or hand, foot, and head.

Tajnîs (homonymy, paronomasia, or the pun), with its several subcategories, was employed by all poets. "Perfect" *tajnîs* occurs when two homophonous sequences give very different meanings, as in Nizâmî's *bargrêzân* (autumn) and *zi barg rêzân* (dripping from the leaves) on page 32, Khâqânî's *bar khwân* (on the table) and *bárkhwân* (recite) in line 26 of the qasida on page 30, and Rumi's use of *nîst bâd* (it is not the wind) and *nîst bâd* (may he not exist) in line 9 of the *Masnavî* on page 43. "Imperfect" *tajnîs* involves two words that are almost the same except for an extra letter in one of the two, like *diyâr* and *yâr* on page 24.

The following figures depend upon the Arabic script. *Tajnîs-i muharraf* refers to words that are written the same but read differently, like انگشت *angisht* and انگشت *angusht* in Daqîqî's poem on page 3, Khâqânî's کم ترکو *kamtar gû* and کم ترکو *kam tarakû* on page 30, especially since the k and g were not differentiated in Khâqânî's time, and Qâ'ânî's مرغ زار *murgh-i zâr* and مرغزار *marghzâr* on page 99. *Tajnîs-i khattî* refers to words that have identical letter shapes but different dots, like مست *mast* and مشت *musht*, باد *bâd* and یاد *yâd*.

Much has been written on the unity of a Persian ghazal, but in fact those who composed them did not consider them entities with thematic unity so much as exactly what the term for poetry, *nazm*, implies: a string of ordered pearls—not as Sir William Jones said, "Orient pearls at random strung." Each line within a ghazal is a unity unto itself; it need not—indeed, grammatically it should not—depend upon the preceding or following line. The form, meter, and rhyme unify all the lines of a ghazal; and secondarily there may also be a thematic or modal unity. The myriad of variants and different line orders in manuscript copies of divans show all too well that European notions of thematic unity and logical progression from one line to the next do not necessarily apply to the ghazal.

METRICS AND PROSODY

Because of certain inadequacies inherent to the Arabic script, namely the absence of any indication of most occurrences of the *izâfa* and the orthographic similarity of many verbal tenses (e.g., برد *burd/barad*, ماند *mând/mânad*, آورد *âvurd/âvarad*)—and further complicated by the inversion of normal word order in poetry—no Persian poem can be read safely without first establishing the meter. Although the meter will not solve all problems of understanding the poetry, it will eliminate many of the causes for confusion.

§1 Principles of Transcription. Until the student is completely and comfortably conversant with the scansion process, it is recommended that no attempt be made to scan in the Arabic script. Transcribe every line of poetry to be scanned.

(a) **Consonants.** Digraphs such as *sh, ch, kh, gh,* and *zh* count as one consonant each since they represent only one sound. Doubled (geminate) consonants are necessarily transcribed twice, like بچّه *bachcha* and خرّم *khurram*. One of the two consonants in any word ending in a doubled consonant, like قد *qadd* and دُرّ *durr*, may be deleted (*qad* and *dur*).

(b) **Vowels.** The short vowels are *a, i,* and *u,* as in درد *dard,* دل *dil,* and گل *gul*. These are the vowels that are transcribed from modern Persian as *a, e,* and *o (dard, del, gol)*.

The long vowels are *â, î, ê, ô,* and *û,*[4] as in جانان *jânân,* میبینی *mî-bînî,* پیش *pêsh,* پوش *pôsh,* and پول *pûl*.

The two diphthongs/glides are *aw* and *ay,* as in دولت *dawlat* and میل *mayl,* where the *w* and *y* are counted as full consonants.

(c) **Ambiguous vowels: non-Arabic elements in the system.** The vowels and diphthongs described above are all that exist in Arabic (the Persian vowels *ê* and *ô* do not exist in Arabic, but they were easily incorporated into the system as equivalent to *î* and *û*). When the Arabic system of scansion and prosody was adopted, there were certain elements of Persian that had to be adapted to the system.

The first of these is the word-final short vowel *-a* (the "silent" *h* now pronounced *e* in Iran, as in خانه *khâna* and دیده *dîda,* modern *khâne* and *dide*). This vowel is reckoned as *either long or short* depending upon the exigencies of the meter. It is transcribed as *-ă*.

Also ambiguous is the word-final vowel *-u* in the words *du* "two," *tu* "you," *chu* (poetic contraction of *chun*) "like, when," and the vowel of the enclitic conjunction *-u* "and." It is transcribed as *-ŭ*.

---

[4] For the vowels *ê* and *ô,* see W. M. Thackston, *Introduction to Persian* (Iranbooks: Bethesda, Md., 1993), p. 196, §78.

The third ambiguous vowel is the -*i* of the *izâfa*, and the ambiguity of length in the final short vowels is unaffected by the addition of an enclitic, as خانهٔ *khână-yĭ* and دیده و *dîdă-ŭ*.

Also reckoned as ambiguous is the vowel resulting after the addition of enclitics to words ending in -*û*, like سوی *sŭ-yĭ* and آرزوی *ârzŭ-yĭ*.

When vowel-initial enclitics like -*i* and -*u* are added to words ending in -*î*, like *shâdî*, the final *î* may remain long, as *shâdî-ĭ*, or it may be shortened, as *shâdi-yĭ*.

In all the above ambiguous cases, the meter in use determines which of the possibilities is to be chosen.

§2 Syllabic Shapes. Persian scansion is based on the unit of the syllable, of which there are two types, long and short. A short syllable is defined as one consonant (indicated by "C") followed by one short vowel (indicated by "v̆"). In syllabic division, all syllables begin with one and only one consonant.

$$|C\breve{v}| \text{ as } \text{د } da$$

Long syllables are (1) one consonant plus one short vowel plus one consonant:

$$|C\breve{v}C| \text{ as } \text{بَر } bar$$

or (2) one consonant plus one long vowel:

$$|C\bar{v}| \text{ as } \text{با } bâ \text{ and } \text{بی } bê$$

§3 Anomalous Syllables. The syllables described above (Cv̆, Cv̄, Cv̆C) are the only syllabic shapes admissible in the Arabic system; all syllables not conforming to these three shapes are anomalous and must be resolved by transformation, except in hemistich-final position, where overlong syllables are left unresolved.

The "overlong" syllabic shape |Cv̆CC|, as in *dast*, and its analog |Cv̄C|, as in *dâd*, are both quite common in Persian. When the final consonant of such words cannot be joined by liaison to a following initial vowel (see below, §4), the overlong syllable is divided into two syllables by the addition of an anaptyctic vowel, called *nîm-fatha* and represented in transcription by "ə." The *nîm-fatha* is not pronounced, but its effect can be easily detected in the rhythm of poetic recitation and singing. All syllables created by the addition of the *nîm-fatha* are by definition short. Thus,

$$|C\breve{v}CC| > C\breve{v}C|C\eth, \text{ as } dast > das\text{-}t\eth \ (\bar{\ }\breve{\ })$$
$$|C\bar{v}C| > C\bar{v}|C\eth, \text{ as } d\hat{a}d > d\hat{a}\text{-}d\eth \ (\bar{\ }\breve{\ })$$

The final anomalous syllabic shape is |Cv̄CC|, like *dâsht* and *nîst*, and it needs special consideration. When the final consonant can be joined by liaison to a following vowel-initial word, the resulting anomalous syllable ($|$C$\bar{\text{v}}$C$|$) is then resolved as described above:

$$\text{C}\bar{\text{v}}\text{CC v...} > {}^*\text{C}\bar{\text{v}}\text{C}|\text{Cv...} > \text{C}\bar{\text{v}}|\text{Cə}|\text{Cv...}$$
$$\textit{dâsht û} > {}^*\textit{dâsh-tû} > \textit{dâ-shə-tû}$$

When such a syllable is followed by a word beginning with a consonant, in which case liaison is not possible, a *nîm-fatha* is added to the anomalous syllable, thus separating the final consonant from the original syllable. The resulting anomaly of $|$C$\bar{\text{v}}$C$|$ is ignored and counted as a simple long syllable, as

$$|\text{C}\bar{\text{v}}\text{CC}| > \text{C}\bar{\text{v}}\text{C}|\text{Cə}$$
$$\textit{dâsht} > \textit{dâsh-tə}$$

In effect then it can be said that any given overlong syllable can be "fixed" once and only once. In the example given immediately above, a *nîm-fatha* was added to fix a doubly overlong syllable. Even though the resulting first syllable is still overlong, it cannot be fixed again.

§4 Elidible glottal stop and liaison. Initial glottal stop (*hamza*) may be retained as a normal, regular consonant (in which case transcribe with an apostrophe and scan as any other consonant, e.g., *'âmad*). Otherwise, if the preceding word ends in a consonant, the glottal stop may—according to the exigencies of the meter—be elided, in which case the final consonant of the preceding word joins by liaison with the initial vowel to form a syllable, as

مرد آمد *mardə 'âmad* (⁻ ˘ ⁻ ⁻) or *mar-dâ-mad* (⁻ ⁻ ⁻)

درافتادم *dar 'uftâdam* (⁻ ⁻ ⁻ ⁻) or *da-ruf-tâ-dam* (˘ ⁻ ⁻ ⁻).

Intervocalic and word-internal glottal stops cannot be elided; and although the *'ayn* is pronounced like a glottal stop, it is never subject to elision.

شمع انجمن *sham'-ĭ 'anjuman* (⁻ ˘ ⁻ ˘ ⁻)

§5 N-deletion. Syllable-final n preceded by a long vowel is generally not reckoned in scansion. Formerly this must have resulted in nasalization of the vowel; but it is not done in reciting Persian poetry in Iran today, although the practice is general in the Indian subcontinent. Although n-deletion does not necessarily occur, it almost always happens with *-ân*, generally also with *-în*, but seldom with *-ûn*, although it too is found occasionally.

آنان را *ânân-râ* (⁻ ⁻ ⁻)

§6 Retention of Overlong Syllables. An overlong final syllable of any hemistich remains overlong (i.e., one of the anomalous syllables described in

§3 above) and is left unresolved. An overlong syllable is indicated by the symbol ±.

§7 Contractions.

(a) The conjunctive *vâv* (normally pronounced *-u*) may be contracted before an initial vowel to *v-*. In this case many initial *alifs* are dropped (depending on individual editors), as in the following:

$$-u \hat{\imath}n > \text{وین} \ v\hat{\imath}n$$
$$-u \ \hat{a}n > \text{وان} \ v\hat{a}n$$
$$-u \ az > \text{وز} \ vaz$$
$$-u \ agar > \text{وگر} \ vagar$$

(b) *Vagar* may be further contracted to ور *var*.

(c) دیگر *dîgar* is sometimes contracted to دگر *digar* (always indicated in the spelling).

(d) In any verbal stem the first syllable of which is short and contains the vowel *-i-* or *-u-*, this vowel may be contracted:

بگذریم *buguzarîm* (˘ ˘ ˘ ±) > *bugzarîm* (ˉ ˘ ±)
بنشست *binishast* (˘ ˘ ±) > *binshast* (ˉ ±)

(e) The vowel of کِ *ki* may be contracted before any word beginning with a vowel. In the case of a word beginning with *â*, the *kâf* is annexed directly to the initial *alif* and the *madda* may be dropped or not; in cases of other than initial *â-* the *alif* may be dropped. Examples:

کِ آسمان *ki âsimân* > کاسمان *kâsimân*
کِ او *ki û* > کاو or کو *kû*
کِ ای *ki ay* > کای or کی *kay*
کِ این *ki în* > کاین or کین *kîn*
کِ آن *ki ân* > کآن or کان *kân*
کِ از *ki az* > کز *kaz*
کِ از او *ki az û* > کزو *kazû*

Ki may be contracted to *-k* (this almost always occurs in hemistich-final position):

az ân-ki > زانک *zân-ki* > زانك *zânk*
bídân-ki > بدانك *bídânk*

(f) The enclitic pronouns may be annexed directly to contracted *ki*. This is always indicated by the spelling.

$$ki\text{-}am > \text{کم } kam$$
$$ki\text{-}at > \text{کت } kat$$
$$ki\text{-}ash > \text{کش } kash$$

(g) The vowel of the enclitic pronouns -*at* and -*ash* may be contracted to fit a given meter:

پدرش *pidar-ash* (˘ ˘ ‾) > *pidar'sh* (˘ ±)

جانت آمد *jân-at âmad* (‾ ˘ ‾ ‾) > *jân't âmad* (‾ ‾ ‾)

(h) In all forms containing the sequence -*a-a*-, the second *a* may be elided. This is sometimes indicated by a variant spelling, although such practice is by no means universal.

بوده‌است *bûda-ast* (‾ ˘ ±) > بودست *bûdást* (‾ ±)

سرمه‌ام *surma-am* (‾ ˘ ‾) > سرمم *surmám* (‾ ‾)

(i) All Persian (not Arabic) words ending in -*âh* may be contracted to a short vowel -*ah*. These will always be indicated by a variant spelling; they must not be confused with the resulting homographs:

چاه *châh* > چه *chah* "pit, well"

شاه *shâh* > شه *shah* "king"

کاه *kâh* > که *kah* "straw"

گاه *gâh* > گه *gah* "time"

ماه *mâh* > مه *mah* "moon"

§8 Protractions. A few words admit protracting, or lengthening, a normally short *u*. These are always indicated by a variant spelling:

امید *umêd* (˘ ±) > اومید *ûmêd* (‾ ±)

افتاد *uftâd* (‾ ±) > اوفتاد *ûfətâd* (‾ ˘ ±)

§9 The Silent Vâv. For purposes of scansion, the "silent" *vâv* that occurs after *kh*- is entirely disregarded; thus, خواست *kh^wâst* ("wanted') and خاست *khâst* ("arose") are scanned, as they are pronounced in Iran, exactly alike. For the purposes of rhyme, however, the silent *vâv* must sometimes be reckoned. Long vowels after it are unaffected: *kh^wâb* rhymes with *tâb* and *kh^wêsh* rhymes with *pêsh*. However, where the *vâv* is followed by a short vowel and forms the rhyme, the original form must be taken into consideration. Words such as خوردن ("to eat") and خود ("self"), now pronounced *khurd* and *khud*, were originally pronounced *khward* and *khwad*, and the consonant cluster *khw* was considered one single consonant (similar to the English "qu-" [kw]). The original vowel of these words, -a-, was retained for purposes of rhyme. The cluster represented by *khw* is counted as one consonant. *Khwad* then rhymes with *bad*, and *khward* rhymes with *kard*.

§10 **Sample Scansion.** The scansion of Persian poetry, like any other technical skill, requires a great deal of practice to arrive at any degree of proficiency. If you have mastered the principles of scansion set down in the preceding pages, you are ready to attempt to scan a line. Take this famous line from Sa'di's *Gulistán*:

دل اندر جهان‌آفرین بند و بس   جهان ای برادر نماند بکس

Like every line of Persian, Arabic, Turkish, and Urdu poetry, this "line" is divided into two halves. Each half is called a **hemistich** (مصرع *misra'* or مصراع *misrá'*); the two halves form one **line** (*bayt* pl. *abyát*). The hemistiches of this particular line rhyme in *-as*. In the form of poetry called *masnaví*, of which this is an example, hemistiches rhyme one with another within the line, and all lines are of the same meter. The masnavi can obviously be extended indefinitely, as there are no restrictions on repetition of rhyme, although to repeat the same rhyme in close proximity is not considered good style.

To begin scansion, the first two syllables pose no ambiguity whatsoever. It makes no difference whether the -n in *jahán* is deleted and the *hamza* in *'ay* counted, or whether the -n is elided to the vowel of *ay*; the result is the same: *ja-hán-'ay* (˘ ‾ ‾) = *ja-há-nay* (˘ ‾ ‾). The next word poses no difficulty: *ba-rá-dar* (˘ ‾ ‾).

If you are tempted to read نماند as *namánd*, not an illogical assumption at this point, you will have the following scansion:

˘	‾	‾	˘	‾	‾	˘	‾	˘	˘	‾
ja	há	nay	ba	rá	dar	na	mán	də	ba	kas
1	2	3	4	5	6	7	8	9	10	11

Now try to match the second hemistich to the first. If you are not certain whether or not to join the *l* of *dil* to *andar*, look at the first syllable of the first hemistich: it is unambiguously short. Therefore, *dil andar* is scanned as *di-lan-dar*.

˘	‾	‾
di	lan	dar

Now, if you do not know that *jahán-áfarín* is a compound noun and are tempted to put an *izáfa* on *jahán*, syllables 7 and 8 will not match:

—	—	ˇ	—
râ	dar	na	mân

—	ˇ	—	ˇ
hâ	nĭ	'â	fa

If you hesitate to delete the -n in syllable 8, look ahead and see what will happen to syllable 10: the two hemistiches will not have the same number of syllables:

—	ˇ	ˇ	—	
mân	də	ba	kas	

—	ˇ	—	˙	—
rî	nə	ban	du	bas

Now *bas* must rhyme with *kas*, and they must be in the same position. At this point it is often a good idea to begin working backwards from the end to see what could be wrong:

—	ˇ	ˇ	—
mân	də	ba	kas

—	—	ˇ	—
rîn	ban	dŭ	bas

The ninth syllable of the second hemistich does not match what has been derived for the first hemistich. As there can be no doubt that this syllable is long, as shown by the second hemistich, something must be wrong in the first hemistich. If نماند is read *namânad* instead of *namând*, it will fit the meter of the second hemistich.

Now line the two hemistiches up syllable by syllable, the second directly beneath the first:

ˇ	—	—	ˇ	—	—	ˇ	—	—	ˇ	—
ja	hâ	nay	ba	râ	dar	na	mâ	nad	ba	kas
di	lan	dar	ja	hâ	nâ	fa	rîn	ban	dŭ	bas

It is now obvious that the ambiguity of the tenth syllable of the second hemistich has been resolved by its counterpart in the first hemistich and is to be read short. There were no other ambiguities in these two hemistiches. This sequence can be found in the Table of Meters below, N° 17, *mutaqârib mahzûf*.

The meter of this particular poem can be derived from only two hemistiches. This is, however, not particularly representative, for many poems need far more than two hemistiches scanned before the meter can be derived because multiple ambiguities in the same position or positions mask the meter. With perseverance the ambiguities resolve themselves, and with practice the process becomes easier and easier. Once the meter has been derived, every line of the poem must be checked against the meter to ascertain the correct reading. Of course, ambiguities will remain, but the meter will show where most instances of the *iẓâfa* go and where they do not belong.

Before the meters are listed, a word is in order on the distinction between metrical theory and practice. Since the theoretical underpinnings of Persian metrics were adopted wholesale from Arabic, the theoretical definition of all meters is couched in terms of the Arabic meters. Arabic metrics, however, are as different in practice from Persian as anything imaginable, and although the Arabic system describes well and gives a name to each of the sequences of long and short syllables that constitute the Persian meters, the division into metrical feet occasionally fails to reflect the reality of Persian. The regular meters (those composed of one foot repeated a given number of times, often with an apocopated final foot, like *mutaqârib* ˘ ¯ ¯/˘ ¯ ¯/˘ ¯ ¯/˘ ¯, and *ramal* ¯ ˘ ¯ ¯/¯ ˘ ˘ ¯/ ¯ ˘ ¯) are perfectly well described by the Arabic system, but certain others are not. For instance, the meter *haẓaj akhrab maqbûẓ mahẓûf* (¯ ¯ ˘/˘ ¯ ˘ ˘/¯/˘ ¯ ¯), the meter of Niẓâmî's *Laylî u Majnûn*, is divided into three feet as shown above because that is how the Arabic system forces the division. The natural rhythm of the line, however, is ¯ ˘ ˘ ˘ ¯/ ˘ ¯ ˘ ˘ ¯, and it is one of the most lilting and melodic of all the Persian meters. In short, it is best to think of the meters, without reference to the foot-divisions, as a set sequence, regular or irregular, of long and short syllables. Only in giving a meter a name are the foot-divisions of great consequence.

TABLE OF METERS

The following arrangement gives the foot-divisions within a hemistich and the name of the meter once the sequence of short and long syllables has been determined by scansion. The meters are arranged below without regard to foot-division. In any given position, short syllables precede long, i.e., the sequence ¯ ˘ ˘ ˘ ¯ precedes ¯ ¯ ˘ ˘ ˘ ¯, which precedes ¯ ¯ ˘ ˘ ¯. The symbol ± indicates an overlong syllable. In practice a long syllable and an overlong syllable in hemistich-final position are equivalent.

Note that in meters where two adjacent short syllables are produced, regardless of foot boundaries, one long syllable may always be used as equivalent to the two shorts. The reverse is not true: two short syllables may not substitute for a long syllable.

Hexameter *(musaddas)* and octameter *(musamman)* meters are measured by the line, not the hemistich. Number one below, with four feet to the hemistich, has eight feet in the line; therefore, it is octameter. Number seven, with three feet to the hemistich, has six feet in the line; therefore, it is hexameter.

1. ˘ ˘ ¯ ˘|˘ ˘ ¯ ˘|˘ ˘ ¯ ˘|˘ ˘ ¯ ˘   Ramal mashkûl

2. ˘ ˘ ¯ ˘|˘ ˘ ¯ ¯|˘ ˘ ¯ ˘|˘ ¯ ¯   Ramal mashkûl makhbûn

3. ˘ ˘ ¯|˘ ˘ ¯|˘ ˘ ¯|˘ ˘ ¯   Mutadârik makhbûn

4. ˘ ˘ ¯ ¯ ˘|¯ ˘ ˘ ¯|˘ ˘ ˘ ˘|¯ ˘ ˘ ¯   Ramal mashkûl sâlim

   ˘ ˘ ¯ ¯ (this is the *ramal makhbûn* foot: it may replace the normal *ramal*
                 foot, ¯ ˘ ¯ ¯, wherever it occurs)

5. ˘ ˘ ¯ ¯ ¯|˘ ˘ ¯ ¯ ¯|˘ ˘ ¯ ¯ ¯|˘ ˘ ±   Ramal makhbûn maqsûr

6. ˘ ˘ ¯ ¯ ¯|˘ ˘ ¯ ¯ ¯|˘ ¯ ¯ ¯   Gharîb makhbûn

7. ˘ ˘ ¯ ¯ ¯|˘ ¯ ¯ ˘ ¯|˘ ˘ ±   Khafîf makhbûn maqsûr

8. ˘ ˘ ¯ ¯ ¯|˘ ¯ ¯ ˘ ¯|˘ ˘ ¯ ¯ ˘ ¯   Khafîf makhbûn

9. ˘ ¯ ˘ ¯ ¯|˘ ˘ ¯ ¯|˘ ˘ ˘ ¯|˘ ˘ ¯   Mujtass makhbûn makhbûn
                                                    mahzûf

10. ˘ ¯ ˘ ¯ ¯|˘ ˘ ˘ ¯|˘ ˘ ˘ ¯|˘ ˘ ¯   Mujtass makhbûn mahzûf

11. ˘ ¯ ˘ ¯ ¯|˘ ˘ ˘ ¯|˘ ˘ ˘ ¯|˘ ˘ ˘ ¯   Mujtass makhbûn

12. ˘ ˘ ˘ ¯ ¯|˘ ˘ ˘ ¯|˘ ˘ ˘ ¯|˘ ¯   Mujtass makhbûn aslam

13. ˘ ˘ ˘ ¯ ¯|˘ ˘ ˘ ¯|˘ ˘ ˘ ¯|˘ ˘ ˘ ±   Hazaj maqbûz musabbagh

14. ˘ ¯ ¯ ˘ ¯|˘ ˘ ˘ ¯|˘ ˘ ˘ ¯|˘ ˘ ˘ ¯   Rajaz makhbûn matvî

15. ˘ ¯ ¯ ¯ ˘|¯ ˘ ¯ ˘|¯ ˘ ¯ ˘|¯ ˘ ¯   Hazaj makfûf mahzûf

16. ˘ ¯ ¯ ¯ ˘|¯ ˘ ±|˘ ¯ ¯ ¯ ˘|¯ ˘ ±   Muzâri' makfûf maqsûr

17. ˘ ¯ ¯ ¯|˘ ¯ ¯ ¯|˘ ¯ ¯|˘ ¯   Mutaqârib mahzûf

18. ˘ ¯ ¯ ¯|˘ ¯ ¯ ¯|˘ ¯ ¯ ¯|˘ ¯ ¯   Mutaqârib sâlim

19. ˘ ¯ ¯ ¯ ¯|˘ ¯ ¯ ¯|˘ ¯ ¯ ¯|˘ ¯ ¯   Hazaj sâlim mahzûf

20. ˘ ¯ ¯ ¯ ¯|˘ ¯ ¯ ¯   Hazaj sâlim (murabba')

21. ˘ ¯ ¯ ¯ ¯|˘ ¯ ¯ ¯ ¯|˘ ¯ ¯   Hazaj mahzûf

22. ˘ ¯ ¯ ¯ ¯|˘ ¯ ¯ ¯ ¯|˘ ¯ ¯ ¯   Hazaj sâlim (musaddas)

23. ˘ ¯ ¯ ¯ ¯|˘ ¯ ¯ ¯ ¯|˘ ¯ ¯ ¯ ¯|˘ ¯ ¯ ¯   Hazaj sâlim (musamman)

24. ˘ ¯ ¯ ¯ ¯|˘ ¯ ¯ ¯ ¯|˘ ¯ ˘ ¯ ¯   Qarîb sâlim

25. ˘ ¯ ¯ ¯ ¯|˘ ˘ ¯ ¯ ¯|˘ ¯ ¯ ¯|˘ ˘ ¯ ¯   Muzâri' sâlim

26. ¯ ˘ ˘ ¯ ¯|˘ ˘ ˘ ¯ ¯|˘ ˘ ˘ ¯ ¯|˘ ˘ ˘ ¯   Rajaz matvî makhbûn

27. ¯ ˘ ˘ ¯ ¯|˘ ˘ ˘ ¯ ¯|˘ ˘ ˘ ¯ ¯|˘ ˘ ˘ ¯   Rajaz matvî

28. ¯ ˘ ˘ ¯ ¯|˘ ˘ ˘ ¯ ¯|˘ ¯ ¯   Sarî' matvî makshûf

29. ‾ ˘ ˘ ‾|‾ ˘ ˘ ˘|‾ ˘ ˘ ‾|‾ Mujtass matvî makfûf majhûf

30. ‾ ˘ ˘ ‾|‾ ˘ ‾|‾ ˘ ˘ ‾|˘ ‾ Munsarih matvî makshûf

31. ‾ ˘ ˘ ‾|‾ ˘ ±|‾ ˘ ˘ ‾|˘ ± Munsarih matvî mawqûf

32. ‾ ˘ ˘ ‾|‾ ˘ ‾|‾ ˘ ˘ ‾|± Munsarih matvî mawqûf majdû'

33. ‾ ˘ ‾ ˘|˘ ‾ ‾ ˘|‾ ˘ ± Mushâkil makfûf maqsûr

34. ‾ ˘ ‾ ˘|‾ ˘ ˘ ‾ Muqtazab matvî

35. ‾ ˘ ‾ ˘|‾ ˘ ˘ ˘ ‾|‾ ˘ ˘ ˘|‾ ˘ ˘ ‾ Muqtazab matvî (musamman)

36. ‾ ˘ ‾|˘ ‾ ‾ ‾|˘ ˘ ‾|˘ ‾ ‾ Hazaj ashtar mahzûf

37. ‾ ˘ ‾|˘ ‾ ‾ ‾|˘ ‾ ‾|˘ ‾ ‾ ‾ Hazaj ashtar sâlim

‾ ˘ ‾ ‾ (the *ramal* foot, wherever it occurs, may be reduced to ˘ ˘ ‾ ‾, ad libitum)

38. ‾ ˘ ‾ ‾|˘ ˘ ‾ ‾|˘ ˘ ‾ ‾|˘ ˘ ‾ Ramal sâlim makhbûn mahzûf

39. ‾ ˘ ‾ ‾|˘ ˘ ‾ ‾|˘ ˘ ‾ ‾|‾ Ramal sâlim makhbûn majhûf

40. ‾ ˘ ‾ ‾|˘ ˘ ‾ ‾|˘ ˘ ‾ Khafîf sâlim makhbûn

41. ‾ ˘ ‾ ‾|˘ ˘ ˘ ‾|‾ ± Khafîf sâlim makhbûn aslam musabbagh

42. ‾ ˘ ‾|‾ ˘ ˘ ‾|‾ ˘ ‾|‾ ˘ ˘ Mutadârik sâlim

43. ‾ ˘ ˘ ‾|˘ ˘ ˘ ‾|˘ ˘ ‾ Mushâkil mahzûf

44. ‾ ˘ ˘ ‾|˘ ˘ ˘ ‾|˘ ˘ ˘ ‾ Mushâkil sâlim

45. ‾ ˘ ˘ ‾|‾ ˘ ˘ ‾ Ramal sâlim (murabba')

46. ‾ ˘ ˘ ‾ ‾|˘ ˘ ‾|‾ ˘ ˘ ‾|˘ ‾ Madîd sâlim

47. ‾ ˘ ˘ ‾ ‾|˘ ˘ ˘ ‾|˘ ˘ ‾ Ramal mahzûf (musaddas)

48. ‾ ˘ ˘ ‾ ‾|˘ ˘ ˘ ‾|˘ ˘ ˘ Ramal sâlim (musaddas)

49. ‾ ˘ ˘ ‾ ‾|˘ ˘ ˘ ‾|˘ ˘ ˘ ‾|˘ ˘ Ramal mahzûf (musamman)

50. ‾ ˘ ˘ ‾|˘ ˘ ˘ ‾|˘ ˘ ˘ ‾|‾ ˘ ˘ ˘ Ramal sâlim (musamman)

51. ‾ ˘ ˘ ‾|‾ ˘ ˘ ‾|‾ ˘ ˘ ‾ Gharîb sâlim

52. ‾ ˘ ˘ ‾|‾ ˘ ˘ ‾|˘ ˘ ˘ ‾|‾ ˘ ˘ ‾ Khafîf sâlim

53. ‾ ‾ ˘|‾ ˘ ˘ ˘ ‾|˘ ‾ ‾ ‾ Hazaj akhrab maqbûz mahzûf

54. ‾ ‾ ˘|‾ ˘ ˘ ˘ ‾|˘ ˘ ˘ ‾|± Hazaj akhrab maqbûz sâlim azall

55. ⁻ ⁻ ˘|˘ ⁻ ⁻ ˘|˘ ⁻ ⁻ ˘|˘ ⁻ ⁻	Hazaj akhrab makfûf mahzûf
56. ⁻ ⁻ ˘|˘ ⁻ ⁻ ˘|⁻ ˘ ⁻ ⁻	Qarîb akhrab makfûf sâlim
57. ⁻ ⁻ ˘|˘ ⁻ ⁻ ⁻|⁻ ˘ ˘|˘ ⁻ ⁻ ⁻	Hazaj akhrab sâlim
58. ⁻ ⁻ ˘ ⁻|˘ ˘ ⁻ ⁻|˘ ⁻ ˘ ⁻|˘ ˘ ⁻	Mujtass sâlim makhbûn makh- bûn maqsûr
59. ⁻ ⁻ ˘|⁻ ˘ ˘ ˘|˘ ⁻ ⁻ ˘|⁻ ˘ ⁻	Muzâriʿ akhrab makfûf mahzûf
60. ⁻ ⁻ ˘|⁻ ˘ ˘ ˘|˘ ⁻ ⁻ ⁻	Muzâriʿ akhrab makfûf sâlim
61. ⁻ ⁻ ˘ ˘|˘ ˘ ⁻ ⁻|˘ ˘ ⁻ ˘|⁻ ˘ ⁻ ⁻	Muzâriʿ akhrab sâlim makfûf sâlim
62. ⁻ ⁻ ˘ ˘|⁻ ˘ ⁻ ⁻|⁻ ˘ ˘|⁻ ˘ ⁻ ⁻	Muzâriʿ akhrab sâlim
63. ⁻ ⁻ ˘ ⁻|⁻ ˘ ⁻|⁻ ˘ ˘ ⁻|⁻ ˘ ⁻	Basît sâlim
64. ⁻ ⁻ ˘ ⁻|⁻ ˘ ˘ ⁻|⁻ ˘ ˘ ˘|⁻ ˘ ⁻ ⁻	Mujtass sâlim
65. ⁻ ⁻ ˘ ⁻|⁻ ˘ ˘ ˘ ±	Rajaz muzâl (murabbaʿ)
66. ⁻ ⁻ ˘ ⁻|⁻ ˘ ˘ ˘|⁻ ⁻ ˘ ⁻	Rajaz sâlim (musaddas)
67. ⁻ ⁻ ˘ ⁻|⁻ ˘ ˘ ˘|⁻ ˘ ˘ ⁻|⁻ ˘ ˘ ⁻	Rajaz sâlim (musamman)
68. ⁻ ⁻ ˘ ⁻|⁻ ˘ ˘ ˘|⁻ ⁻ ⁻ ˘	Sarîʿ sâlim
69. ⁻ ⁻|˘ ⁻ ⁻|⁻ ⁻ ˘|⁻ ⁻	Mutaqârib aslam sâlim
70. ⁻ ⁻ ˘ ⁻|⁻ ⁻ ⁻ ˘|⁻ ˘ ˘ ⁻|⁻ ⁻ ⁻ ˘	Munsarih sâlim

THE METER OF THE RUBÂʿÎ

The meters of the *rubâʿî* are all variants of *hazaj*; however, unlike all other poetic forms, where, with the sole exception of the *ramal* foot (˘ ⁻ ⁻ ⁻ → ˘ ˘ ⁻ ⁻ ad libitum), internal changes of the established meter are not allowed, in the *rubâʿî*, once either *akhram* or *akhrab* is established, any variant may be used in any of the four hemistiches of the *rubâʿî*.

Akhram: ⁻ ⁻ ⁻   ⁻ ⁻ ⁻   ⁻ ⁻ ˘   ˘ ⁻
           ⁻ ⁻ ⁻   ⁻ ⁻ ⁻   ⁻
           ⁻ ⁻ ˘   ⁻ ⁻ ˘   ⁻
           ⁻ ⁻ ˘   ˘ ⁻ ⁻ ˘   ˘ ⁻
           ⁻ ˘ ⁻   ˘ ⁻ ⁻ ˘   ˘ ⁻
           ⁻ ˘ ⁻   ˘ ⁻ ⁻ ⁻   ⁻

Akhrab: ⁻ ⁻ ˘   ˘ ⁻ ⁻ ⁻   ⁻ ⁻ ˘   ˘ ⁻
                        ˘ ⁻ ⁻ ⁻   ⁻ ⁻ ⁻   ⁻

```
˘ – – ˘        ˘ – – –        –
˘ – – ˘        ˘ – – ˘        ˘ –
˘ – ˘ –        ˘ – – –        –
˘ – ˘ –        ˘ – – ˘        ˘ –
```

SYNOPSIS OF POETICAL FORMS AND RHYME

Definitions

بیت	*bayt*	stich, verse, line
فرد	*fard*	one detached hemistich
مصرع	*misra‘*	hemistich, half-verse, half-line
مطلع	*matla‘*	first stich of a *qasîda* or *ghazal*
مقطع	*maqta‘*	last stich of a *qasîda* or *ghazal*
تخلص	*takhallus*	pen name (often included in the *maqta‘* of a ghazal)

Multiple-rhyme Form:

Masnavî مثنوی	Rhyme scheme:	…a/…a …b/…b …c/…c …n/…n	Length: unrestricted; topic: unrestricted, narrative ("n" indicates any length)

Monorhyme Forms:

Qasîda قصیده	Rhyme scheme:	…a/…a …x/…a …n/…a	Length: 10 to 100+ lines; topic: enco-miastic, eulogistic, elegiac (*marsiya*)
Ghazal غزل	Rhyme scheme:	…a/…a …x/…a …n/…a	Length: 2–15 lines; topic: erotic, lyric
Qit‘a قطعه	Rhyme scheme:	…x/…a …x/…a	Length: 2–15 lines; topic: unrestricted
Rubâ‘î رباعی	Rhyme scheme:	…a/…a …x/…a	Length: 2 lines; topic: unrestricted

Strophic forms are ghazals, which form stanzas, separated one from an-
other by two rhyming hemistiches. In a *tarkîb-band* the rhyming hemistiches
are different between every two stanzas; in a *tarjî'-band* the rhyming hemistiches
are a refrain repeated between every two stanzas.

Tarkîb-band:	...a/ ...a	*Tarjî'-band:*	...a/ ...a
	...x/ ...a		...x/ ...a
	...n/ ...a		...n/ ...a
	...b/ ...b		...b/ ...b
	...c/ ...c		...c/ ...c
	...x/ ...c		...x/ ...c
	...n/ ...c		...n/ ...c
	...d/ ...d		...b/ ...b

The *mukhammas* consists of five hemistiches per strophe, the fifth hemistich
serving as a refrain. It has the following rhyme scheme:

...a/ ...a
...a/ ...a
...a
...b/ ...b
...b/ ...b
...a

Rhyme (*qâfiya*) technically consists of one vowel, long or short, plus one
or more consonants. Rhyme may be masculine or feminine. An example of
masculine rhyme is the rhyme in the second selection on page 1, *darâz* and *bâz*.
An example of feminine rhyme is the rhyme in the first line of the first selec-
tion on page 1, *sazâvârî* and *bârî*, where the rhyme is -*âr*. Anything extra that
follows the rhyme itself is loosely termed *radîf*, like the final î in the last ex-
ample. The *radîf* can be extended indefinitely, and a good example is the
ghazal by Ghâlib on page 98, in which the rhyme is -*ar*. The *radîf*, necessarily
repeated whenever the rhyme comes, is *natavân guft*.

In the texts of the poems, grammatical points of early New Persian that differ
from modern Persian are noted, and references are keyed to my *Introduction
to Persian* (Bethesda, Md.: Iranbooks, 1993). Allusions deemed unfamiliar to
American students are also explained in the notes. The vocabulary in the back
is intended to be a vocabulary for this book, not a dictionary. In a few instances
the basic meaning of a word never occurred in the poetry, so the meanings
given all reflect secondary or extended meanings. On the other hand, since the

poetic lexicon of Persian is fairly small, this vocabulary probably represents most of the words one is likely to encounter in poetry at large.

One of the most notable features of classical Persian is its conservatism, not only in terms of the literary tradition, but also linguistically. With only one major grammatical change (the function of -râ, for which see *Introduction to Persian*, p. 197, §82), the language of the poetry, even of a thousand years ago, is so close to today's living language that it can be easily read and understood by any educated speaker of Persian. In contrast, the English contemporary with Rûdakî is more alien to us than German or Dutch and has to be learned like any other foreign language. The earliest poem the editors of *The Oxford Book of English Verse* could find that bears any resemblance to the language we speak dates from the thirteenth century, but the first pages of the *Oxford Book* can be read only with many more glosses and annotations than are necessary for the non-native learner to read Persian poetry from the tenth century.

The flow of classical Persian, particularly poetry, does not readily lend itself to European-style punctuation. Traditionally, of course, Persian had no punctuation of any sort—no question marks, commas, periods, or quotation marks. A certain amount of punctuation, however, is helpful, particularly question and quotation marks, and these have been introduced into the text here. It should be noted that the punctuation does not affect the scansion in any way, i.e., liaison occurs across any and all marks of punctuation.

This book is intended as a learner's introduction to Persian poetry. It is not intended as an anthology, although I hope it may serve both functions. I have chosen poems that seem representative of each poet, and usually they are also coincidentally among each poet's best. Excluded on principle, however, are poems that contain lines too difficult or obscure for the learner. By and large I have tried to resist the temptation to include poems that contain one or two "great lines" everybody knows, the rest falling into the so-so category. It is no coincidence, however, that the first lines of many poems are obviously superior to the rest, for, in accordance with the rhetorical principle of *husn-i matla'*, the first line should be catchy and memorable. Many of the poems included here have been taken from Dr. Zabîhullâh Safâ's anthology, *Ganj-i sukhan: Shâ'irân-i buzurg-i pârsîgûy u muntakhab-i âsâr-i ânân*, 3 volumes (4th revised ed., Tehran: Ibn-i Sînâ, 1969). Other good anthologies are Mazâhir Musaffâ, *Qand-i Pârsî: Nimûnahâ-yi shi'r-i darî* (Tehran: Safî Alî Shâh, 1348/1970), and 'Abdul-Rafî' Haqîqat, *Nigîn-i sukhan*, 6 vols. (Tehran: Âftâb-i Haqîqat, 1363–67).

I would like to take this opportunity to thank the many students with whom I have read Persian poetry over the last twenty years at Harvard. Their comments and questions have formed the basis of this book.

❋

POETS OF THE SAMANID AND GHAZNAVID PERIODS

RÛDAKÎ
رودکی

Originally from Rûdak near Samarkand, Abu-Abdullâh Ja'far Rûdakî (d. 940) was attached to the court of the Samanid Nasr b. Ahmad (r. 864–892) at Bukhara and was one of the first to handle with facility various themes and genres of New Persian poetry. He versified the Indian Bidpai fables, known to the Islamic world as *Kalila and Dimna*, but only fragments of his rendition exist today. He also versified a *Sindbâd-nâma*, of which only isolated lines remain.

In the first two poems Rudaki moralizes on the transitory nature of this life, its pleasures and sorrows, and the folly of reliance on material wealth. In the third poem, his most famous, the poet addresses the prince, attempting to entice him to return to Bukhara.

واندر نهان سرشك همی باری	ای آنکه غمگنی و سزاواری
بود آنچه بود ، خیره چه غم داری؟	رفت آنکه رفت و آمد آنك آمد
گیتیست ، کی پذیرد همواری؟	هموار کرد خواهی گیتی را؟
زاری مکن که نشنود او زاری	مستی مکن که نشنود او مستی
کی رفته را به زاری باز آری؟	شو¹ تا قیامت آید زاری کن
گر تو بهر بهانه بیازاری	آزار بیش بینی زین گردون
بر هر که تو بر او دل بگماری	گوئی گماشتست بلائی او
بگرفت ماه و گشت جهان تاری	ابری پدید نی و کسوفی نی
بر خویشتن ظفر ندهی باری	فرمان کنی ویا نکنی ، ترسم
فر و بزرگمردی و سالاری	اندر بلای سخت پدید آید

*

نه بآخر بمرد² باید باز؟	زندگانی چه کوته وچه دراز ،

---

¹See *shudan* in the vocabulary.

²*Bimurd: murd* is the short infinitive, complement to *bâyad*; for the perfective prefix *bi-*, see ITP §84.

1

این رسن را¹ اگرچه هست دراز   هم بچنبر گذار خواهد بود

خواهی اندر امان بنعمت و ناز   خواهی اندر عنا و شدت زی²

خواهی از ری بگیر تا بطراز   خواهی اندکتر از جهان بپذیر

خواب را حکم³ نی مگر بمجاز   اینهمه باد و بود⁴ تو خواب است

نشناسی ز یکدگرشان باز؟   اینهمه روز مرگ یکسانند

*

یاد یار مهربان آید همی   بوی جوی مولیان⁵ آید همی

زیر پایم پرنیان آید همی   ریگ آموی و درشتیهای او

خنگ مارا تا میان آید همی   آب جیحون از نشاط روی دوست

میر زی تو میهمان آید همی   ای بخارا، شاد باش و دیر زی

ماه سوی آسمان آید همی   میر ماه است و بخارا آسمان

سرو سوی بوستان آید همی   میر سروست و بخارا بوستان

DAQÎQÎ

دقیقی

Abu-Mansûr Muhammad Daqîqî (d. 978) served at the Samanid court during the reigns of Mansûr b. Nûh (r. 961–76) and Nûh II b. Mansûr (r. 976–97) and also at the Chaghanian court. Well known for his *qasîdas* and *ghazals*, he began a versified history of Iran but was killed after completing about a thousand lines. What he had composed Firdawsî later incorporated into the *Shâhnâma*.

سپید روز به پاکی رخان تو ماند   شب سیاه بدان زلفکان تو ماند⁶

گر آبدار بود با لبان تو ماند   عقیق را چو بسایند نیک سوده گران

گل شکفته برخسارکان تو ماند   ببوستان ملوکان هزار گشتم بیش

دو چشم آهو و دو نرگس شکفته ببار   درست و راست بدان چشمکان تو ماند

---

¹*Ín rasan-râ: râ* marks the possessive dative (ITP §82); it goes with *guzâr*.

²*Zî*, imperative of *zístan*. Read "[*Agar*] *khwâhî, zí*...."

³*Khwâb-râ hukm* is the dative construction, equivalent to the modern Persian *hukm-i khwâb*. Here the entire construction *khwâb-râ hukm ní* is equivalent to the modern Persian *khwâb hukm nadârad*.

⁴*Bâd-u-búd* are taken together as a doublet, like *girift-u-gír* and *guft-u-gú*.

⁵*Mûliyân*, a canal in Bukhara.

⁶See *mânistan* in the vocabulary.

كمان بابليان ديدم و ترازی تير٢   كه بركشيده بود بابروان١ تو ماند

ترا بسرو اين بالا٣ قياس نتوان كرد   كه سرورا قد و بالا بدان تو ماند

٭

برخيز و برافروز هلا قبلۀ زردشت   بنشين و برافكن شكم قاتم بر پشت

بس كس كه ز زردشت بگرديد و دگر بار   ناچار كند رو بسوی قبلۀ زردشت٤

من سرد نيابم كه مرا ز آتش هجران آتشكده گشتست دل و ديده چو چرخشت

گر دست بدل بر نهم از سوختن دل   انگشت شود بی‌شك در دست من انگشت

ای روی تو چون باغ وهمه باغ بنفشه خواهم كه بنفشه چنم٥ از زلف تو يك مشت

آنكس‌كه مرا كشت، مرا كشت و ترا زاد

وانكس‌كه ترا زاد، ترا زاد و مرا كشت

MUNJĪK
منجيك

A poet at the court of the princes of Chaghanian (in modern Tajikistan), Abu'l-Hasan Alî Munjîk of Termez (mid-tenth century) was known for his criticism and parody. His collected works are lost, and his poetry is known only from the fragments that were preserved in collections.

ای خوبتر ز پيكر ديبای ارمنی   ای پاكتر ز قطرۀ باران بهمنی

وآنجا كه روی تو، همه كشور بروشنی   آنجا كه موی تو، همه برزن بزير مشك

واندر بهار حسنم تا تو بر منی   اندر فرات غرقم تا ديده با منست

ور ياسمين‌بری تو، بدل چونكه٦ آهنی؟   ار انگبين‌لبی، سخن تلخ مر چراست؟

مگذر بباغ، سرو سهی پاك بشكنی   منگر٧ بماه، نورش تيره شود ز رشك

لاه‌رخ و بنفشه‌خط و ياسمن‌تنی   خرّم بهار خواند عاشق ترا كه تو

ای صبر بر فراق بتان نيك جوشنی   مارا جگر بتير فراق تو خسته گشت

---

[1]For the meter, read *b' abruân* for *ba abruân*.

[2]*Tarâzî tîr*: the inverted adjectival construction, with the adjective preceding the noun it modifies, is fairly common in early New Persian and continues in poetry long after it ceased to be used in prose.

[3]*Turâ...în bâlâ*, "this stature of yours."

[4]*Qibla-i Zardusht*: "Zoroaster's kiblah" is fire.

[5]*Chinam* for *chînam*, for metrical exigence.

[6]*Chunki* here means "why."

[7]For the meter, read *man'gar*. See §7d of the Introduction.

KASÂ'Î
کسانی

Abu'l-Hasan Majduddîn Kasâ'î was born in Merv in 952 and lived into
the reign of Sultan Mahmud of Ghazna (r. 998–1030).

چون تیغ آبداده و یاقوت آبدار   نیلوفر کبود نگ کن میان آب

زردیش بر میانه چو ماه ده و چهار[1]   همرنگ آسمان و بکردار آسمان

وز مطرف کبود ردا کرده و ازار   چون راهبی که دو رخ او سال و ماه زد

مردم کریمتر شود اندر نعیم گل   گل نعمتیست هدیه فرستاده از بهشت

وز گل عزیزتر چه ستانی بسیم گل؟   ای گلفروش ، گل چه فروشی بجای سیم؟[2]

بر چشمکان آن صنم خلخی‌نژاد   نرگس نگر ، چگونه همی عاشقی کند

انگشت زرد کرد و بکافور بر نهاد   گوئی مگر کسی بشد از آب زعفران

FIRDAWSÎ
فردوسی

It is scarcely possible to overrate the place of importance Abu'l-Qâsim
Firdawsî's *Shâhnâma* (completed in 1010) has held throughout the
Iranian world for almost a thousand years. This epic of Iranian king-
ship and the victories of the Iranians over their perennial enemies, the
Turanians, includes epic cycles from various parts of Greater Iran, such
as the Mazanderan and Seistan cycles and the Alexander romance, and
has been accurately called the last great work of pre-Islamic Iran, glorify-
ing the memory of the heroes and the legitimate line of succession of
kings down to the "national catastrophe" of the Arab invasion. The
Shâhnâma has represented a "national epic" for all who consider
themselves Iranian, whether by virtue of descent, race, or geography, or
by conscious choice through the adoption of the Persian ethic and cul-
ture (as with the Turks, who, although geographically "Turanians" and
ethnically by no means Persians, identified themselves as Iranians and
heirs to the old Iranian kingship.

---

[1]The moon on the fourteenth night is full.
[2]*Chi furôshî*, "why do you sell"; *ba jây-i sîm* means "for money."

Rustam and Suhrâb

In this selection is described the final in a series of encounters between Rustam, the Iranian champion, and Suhrâb, the champion warrior of Turan. Suhrâb is actually Rustam's son, but Rustam is unaware of Suhrâb's existence and sees in him only an enemy he has to overcome. Suhrâb, on the other hand, has spent his life searching for his father but does not know that the man with whom he is doing combat is Rustam.

بسان یکی کوه پولاد گشت   چو رستم ز چنگ وی¹ آزاد گشت

چو جان رفته کو باز یابد روان   خرامان بشد سوی آب روان

به پیش جهان آفرین شد نخست   بخورد آب و روی و سر و تن بشست

نبود آگه از بخش خورشید و ماه   همی خواست پیروزی و دستگاه

۵   بخواهد ربودن کلاه از سرش   که چون رفت خواهد سپهر از برش

چنان یافت نیرو ز پروردگار   شنیدم که رستم ز آغاز کار

همی هر دو پایش بدو در² شدی   که گر سنگ را او بسر بر شدی

دل او از آن آرزو دور بود   از آن زور پیوسته رنجور بود

بزاری همی آرزو کرد آن   بنالید بر کردگار جهان

۱۰   که رفتن بره بر³ تواند همی   که لختی ز زورش ستاند همی

ز نیروی آن کوه پیکر بکاست   بدانسان که از پاک یزدان بخواست

دل از بیم سهراب ریش آمدش   چو باز آنچنان کار پیش آمدش

بدین کار این بنده را پاس دار   بیزدان بنالید «کای⁴ کردگار

مرا دادی ای پاک پروردگار»   همان زور خواهم کز آغاز کار

۱۵   بیفزود در تن هر آنچش⁵ بکاست   بدو باز داد آنچنان کش بخواست

پر اندیشه بودش دل و روی زرد   وز آن آبخور شد بجای نبرد

کمندی ببازو، کمانی بدست   همی تاخت سهراب چون پیل مست

---

¹Suhrâb.

²Sang-râ ba-sar bar = bar sar-i sang (see ITP §83); badû dar = dar û (see ITP §79)

³Ba rah bar: see ITP §83.

⁴K'ay: the k' (or ki) here and elsewhere is a spoken quotation mark. Strictly speaking, it does not belong inside the quotation mark, but there is nowhere else to put it. Classical Persian had no quotation marks, of course—or any other marks of punctuation.

⁵Har ancha'sh for har ancha-ash.

گرازان و چون شیر نعره‌زنان — سمندش جهان و جهان را کنان

بر آن گونه رستم چو اورا بدید — عجب ماند و در وی همی بنگرید

غمین گشت و زو ماند اندر شگفت — ز پیکارش اندازه‌ها برگرفت ۲۰

چو سهراب باز آمد ، اورا بدید — ز باد جوانی دلش بردمید

چنین گفت «کای رسته از چنگ شیر — چرا آمدی باز نزدم دلیر؟»

دگر باره اسبان ببستند سخت — بسر بر همی گشت بدخواه بخت

هر آنگه که خشم آورد بخت شوم — شود سنگ خارا بکردار موم

بکشتی گرفتن نهادند سر — گرفتند هر دو دوال کمر ۲۵

سپهدار سهراب آن زوردست — تو گفتی که چرخ بلندش ببست[1]

غمین گشت رستم، بیازید چنگ — گرفت آن سر و یال جنگی پلنگ

خم آورد پشت دلاور جوان — زمانه سرآمد ، نبودش توان

زدش بر زمین بر بکردار شیر — بدانست کو هم نماند بزیر

سبک تیغ تیز از میان برکشید — بر پورِ بیدار دل بردرید ۳۰

(هر آنگه که تو تشنه گشتی بخون — بیالودی این خنجر آبگون[2]

زمانه بخون تو تشنه شود — بر اندام تو موی دشنه شود)

بپیچید ، از آن پس یکی آه کرد — ز نیک و بد اندیشه کوتاه کرد

بدو گفت «کاین[4] بر من از من رسید — زمانه بدست تو دادم کلید[3]

تو زین بیگناهی که این گوژپشت — مرا برکشید و بزودی بکشت ۳۵

ببازی بگویند همسال من — بخاک اندر آمد چنین یال من

نشان داد مادر مرا از پدر — ز مهر اندر آمد روانم بسر

همی جستمش تا ببوسمش روی[5] — چنین جان بدادم درین آرزوی

دریغا که رنجم نیامد بسر — ندیدم درین رنج روی پدر

کنون گر تو در آب ماهی شوی — ویا چون شب اندر سیاهی شوی ۴۰

وگر چون ستاره شوی بر سپهر — ببری ز روی زمین پاک مهر

بخواهد هم از تو پدر کین من — چو بیند که خشت است بالین من

از آن نامداران گردنکشان — کسی هم برد نزد رستم نشان

---

[1] Typically heroes are described as so mighty and lofty that only the celestial spheres could gird their loins.

[2] This and the next line are a moralizing interjection by the poet; they do not continue the narrative.

[3] *Dâd-am kilîd = dâd kilîd-am.*

[4] *K'în,* contracted form of *ki în.*

[5] For the meter, read *bibôsam'sh rûy* for *bibôsam rûy-ash.*

که سهراب کشتست و افکنده خوار   همی خواست کردن ترا خواستار»

چو بشنید رستم، سرش خیره گشت   جهان پیش چشم اندرش خیره گشت ٤٥

همی بی‌تن و تاب و بی‌توش گشت   بیفتاد از پای و بی‌هوش گشت

بپرسید از آن پس که آمد بهوش   بدو گفت با ناله و با خروش

«بگو تا چه داری ز رستم نشان؟   که گم باد نامش ز گردنکشان

که رستم منم، کم مماناد نام!»²   نشیناد بر ماتمم پور سام!»¹

بزد نعره و خونش آمد بجوش   همی کند موی و همی زد خروش ٥٠

چو سهراب رستم بدانسان بدید   بیفتاد و هوش از سرش بپرید

بدو گفت «گر زآنکه رستم توی،   بکشتی مرا خیره بر بدخوی

ز هر گونه بودم ترا رهنمای   نجنبید یك ذره مهرت ز جای

کنون بند بگشای از جوشنم   برهنه ببین این تن روشنم

چو برخاست آواز کوس از درم   بیامد پر از خون دو رخ مادرم ٥٥

همی جانش از رفتن من بخست   یکی مهره بر بازوی من ببست

مرا گفت کاین از پدر یادگار   بدار و ببین تا کی آید بکار»

چو بگشاد خفتان و آن مهره دید   همه جامه بر خویشتن بردرید

همی گفت «کای کشته بر دست من   دلیر و ستوده بهر انجمن»

همی ریخت خون و همی کند موی   سرش پر ز خاك و پر از آب روی ٦٠

چو خورشید تابان ز گنبد بگشت   تهمتن³ نیامد بلشکر ز دشت

ز لشکر بیامد هشیوار بیست   که تا اندر آوردگه کار چیست

دو اسپ اندر آن دشت بر پای بود   پر از گرد و رستم دگر جای بود

گو پیلتن⁴را چو بر پشت زین   ندیدند گردان در آن دشت کین

چنین بُد⁶ گمانشان⁵ که او کشته شد   سر نامداران همه گشته شد ٦٥

بکاوس کی⁷ تاختند آگهی   که «تخت مهی شد ز رستم تهی»

ز لشکر برآمد سراسر خروش   برآمد زمانه یکایك بجوش

1"May Sâm's son (i.e., Zâl son of Sâm, Rustam's own father) sit at my funeral," a curse upon himself.

2K'am...nâm = ki nâm-am; for mamânâd see ITP §80.

3Tahamtan, "great in body," an epithet of Rustam.

4Gav-i pîltan, "the elephant-bodied ox," another of Rustam's epithets.

5For metrical exigence, read gumân'shân, for gumân-ishân.

6Bud, a poetically shortened form of bûd.

7Kâûs-Kay (or Kay-Kâûs) is the king of Iran.

چنین گفت سهراب با پیلتن¹

چو آشوب برخاست از انجمن

همه کار ترکان² دگرگونه گشت

که «اکنون چو روز من اندر گذشت

۷۰   سوی جنگ توران نراند سپاه

همه مهربانی بدان کن که شاه

سوی مرز ایران نهادند روی

که ایشان به پشتی من جنگجوی

بسی کرده بودم ز هر در امید

بسی روزرا داده بودم نوید

بگیتی نماند یکی تاجور

بگفتم اگر زنده بینم پدر

که باشد روانم بدست پدر

چه دانستم ای پهلو نامور

۷۵   مکن جز بنیکی دریشان نگاه

نباید که بینند رنجی براه

گرفتار خمّ کمند من است

درین دژ دلیری³ ببند من است

همه بُد خیال تو در دیده‌ام

بسی زو نشان تو پرسیده‌ام

ازو باز ماند تهی جای او

جز آن بود یکسر سخنهای او

شدم لاجرم تیره روز سپید⁴

چو گشتم ز گفتار او ناامید

۸۰   نباید که آید بجانش زیان

ببین تا کدام است از ایرانیان

بدیدم، نبُد دیده باور مرا

نشانی که بُد داده مادر مرا

که من کشته گردم بدست پدر

چنینم نوشته بُد اختر بسر

بمینو مگر بینمت باز شاد»

چو برق آمدم، رفتم اکنون چو باد»

Zâl and Rûdâba

This selection is a romantic interlude describing the meeting between
the hero Zâl, son of King Minûchihr's champion Sâm, and Rûdâba,
daughter of Mihrâb, the king of Kabul. Rûdâba, having heard of Zâl's
heroicism, has arranged a tryst through the agency of her maid. From
the union of Zâl and Rûdâba comes the heroic Rustam.

در حجره بستند و گم شد کلید

چو خورشید تابنده شد ناپدید

که «شد ساخته کار، بگذار گام»

پرستنده شد سوی دستان سام

---

¹Pîltan, as above, one of Rustam's epithets.

²The Turanians, of whom Suhrâb is the leader, are called Turks because in
Firdawsî's day Transoxiana (Turan) was largely Turkish. It had not been Turkified,
of course, at the time of the ancient rivalry between Iran and Turan, two different
branches of the Indo-Iranian peoples.

³Suhrâb has captured the Iranian Huzhîr, from whom he has tried to extract a
description of Rustam. Huzhîr, thinking that Suhrâb wants to kill Rustam, has given
him a false description (line 78).

⁴Shud-am...tîra rôz-i sipêd: "My bright day became dark," i.e., I lost all hope.

چنان چون بود مردم جفت‌جوی	سپهبد سوی کاخ بنهاد روی
چو سرو سهی بر سرش ماه تام	برآمد سیه‌چشم گلرخ ببام
پدید آمد ، آن دختر نامدار[1]	چو از دور دستان سام[2] سوار
که «شاد آمدی ای جوانمرد شاد	دو بیجاده بگشاد و آواز داد
خم چرخ گردان زمین تو باد	درود جهان‌آفرین بر تو باد
چنانی سراپای کاو کرد یاد	پرستنده خرم‌دل و شاد باد
برنجیدت آن خسروانی دو پای»	پیاده بدینسان ز پرده‌سرای
نگه کرد و خورشیدرخ را بدید	سپهبد چو از باره آوا شنید
ز تاب رخش سرخ یاقوت خاك	شده بام ازو گوهر تابناك
درودت ز من ، آفرین از سپهر	چنین داد پاسخ که «ای ماه‌چهر
خروشان بُدم پیش یزدان پاك	چه مایه شبان دیده اندر سماك
نماید بمن رویت اندر نهان	همی خواستم تا خدای جهان
بدین چرب گفتار با ناز تو	کنون شاد گشتم باواز تو
چه باشی تو بر باره و من بکوی؟»	یکی چاره راه دیدار جوی
ز سر شعر شبگون سبك بر گشود	پریچهر گفت و سپهبد شنود
کس از مشك زانسان نپیچد کمند	کمندی گشاد او ز سرو بلند
بر آن غبغبش تار بر تار بر	خم اندر خم و مار بر مار بر
بدل گفت زال این کمندی سره	فرو هشت گیسو ازان کنگره
که «ای پهلوان‌بچه گردزاد	پس از باره رودابه آواز داد
بر شیر بگشای و چنگ کیان	کنون زود بر تاز و بر کش میان
ز بهر تو باید همی گیسوم»	بگیر این سر گیسو از یك سوم[3]
شگفت آمدش ز آنچان گفت و گوی	نگ کرد زال اندر آن ماهروی
که بشنید آواز بوسش عروس	بسائید مشکین کمندش ببوس
بدین روز خورشید روشن مباد	چنین داد پاسخ که «این نیست داد
برین خسته‌دل تیز پیکان زنم»	که من دست را خیره در جان زنم
بیفکند خوار و نزد هیچ دم	کمند از رهی بستد و داد خم
برآمد ز بن تا بسر یکسره	بحلقه درآمد سر کنگره
بیامد پریروی و بردش نماز	چو بر بام آن باره بنشست باز

---

[1] A run-on line: *ân dukhtar* is the subject of the verb *bug'shâd* in the next line. True run-on lines like this are rare in Persian, but they do occur, especially in narrative masnavis.

[2] *Dastân-i Sâm* is Zâl's epithet.

[3] *în sar-i gêsu...am* = *în sar-i gêsu-am*.

گرفت آن زمان دست دستان بدست   برفتند هر دو بکردار مست

فرود آمد از بام کاخ بلند   بدست اندرون دست شاخ بلند

سوی خانهٔ زرنگار آمدند   بدان مجلس شاهوار آمدند

بهشتی بُد آراسته پر ز نور   پرستنده بر پای، بر پیش حور

شگفت اندر و مانده بُد زال زر[1]   بدان روی و آن موی و آن زیب و فر   ۲۵

اَبا[2] یاره و طوق و با گوشوار   ز دیبای و گوهر چو باغ بهار

دو رخساره چون لاله اندر چمن   سر جعد زلفش شکن بر شکن

همان زال با فرّ شاهنشهی   نشسته بر ماه با فرّهی

حمایل یکی دشنه اندر برش   ز یاقوت سرخ افسری بر سرش

ز دیدنش[3] رودابه مینارمید   بدزدیده در وی همی بنگرید   ۴۰

بدان شاخ و یال و بر آن فر و برز   که خارا چو خار آمدی زو بگرز

فروغ رخش را که جان بر فروخت   درو بیش دیدی دلش بیش سوخت

همی بود بوس و کنار و نبید   مگر شیر کو گورا نشکرید؟

سپهبد چنین گفت با ماهروی   که "ای سرو سیمین بر مشکبوی

منوچهر چون بشنود داستان   نباشد برین گفته همداستان[4]   ۴۵

همان سام نیرم برآرد خروش   کف اندازد و بر من آید بجوش

ولیکن نه پرمایه جانست و تن   همان خوار گیرم، بپوشم کفن

پذیرفتم از دادگر داورم   که هرگز ز پیمان تو نگذرم

شوم پیش یزدان ستایش کنم   چو یزدان پرستان نیایش کنم

مگر کو دل سام و شاه زمین   بشوید ز خشم و ز پیکار و کین   ۵۰

جهان آفرین بشنود گفت من   مگر کآشکارا شوی جفت من"

بدو گفت رودابه "من همچنین   پذیرفتم از داور کیش و دین

که بر من نباشد کسی پادشا   جهان آفرین بر زبانم گوا

جز از پهلوان جهان زال زر   که با تاج و گنج است و با نام و فر"

همی مهرشان هر زمان بیش بود   خرد دور بود، آرزو پیش بود   ۵۵

چنین تا سپیده برآمد ز جای   تبیره برآمد ز پرده سرای

---

[1]Zâl was an albino, hence the epithet "golden."

[2]Abâ, archaic/poetic for bâ.

[3]For the meter, read dîdan'sh.

[4]Because Rûdâba's blood is tainted by descent from the monstrous Zahhâk, the scourge of the house of Jamshêd who was finally overthrown by Prince Frêdûn and Kâva the Blacksmith, both Rûdâba and Zâl know that neither Minûchihr nor Sâm will ever agree to their marriage.

تن خویش تار و برش پود کرد   پس آن ماه‌را شاه پدرود کرد

زبان بر کشیدند بر آفتاب   سر مژه کردند هر دو پر آب

نبایست آمد چنین در ستیز   که ای فرّ گیتی یکی لخت نیز

۶۰   فرود آمد از کاخ فرّخ‌همال   ز بالا کمند اندر افکند زال

FARRUKHÎ
فرخی

Abu'l-Hasan Ali Farrukhî of Seistan (d. 1037) was first panegyrist at the court of Chaghanian, and he was later attached to the retinue of Sultan Mahmud of Ghazna and his son, Sultan Mas'ud.

An accomplished singer and musician, Farrukhî was a master of un-forced and elegant rhetorical ornamentation, and most of his lyrics are on love and wine. His elegy on the death of Sultan Mahmud, here given almost in full, has been acclaimed as one of the finest elegies in Persian.

شهر غزنی نه همانست که من دیدم پار

چه فتادست که امسال دگرگون شده کار؟

خانه‌ها بینم پر نوحه و پر بانگ و خروش

نوحه و بانگ و خروشی که کند روح فگار

کویها بینم پر شورش و سرتاسر کوی

همه پر جوش و همه جوشش از خیل سوار

رسته‌ها بینم پر مردم و درهای دکان

همه بریسته و بر در زده هر یک مسمار

۵   مهتران بینم بر روی زنان¹ همچو زنان

چشمها کرده ز خوناب برنگ گلنار

حاجبان بینم خسته‌دل و پوشیده سیه

کله افکنده یکی از سر و دیگر دستار

بانوان بینم بیرون شده از خانه بکوی

بر در میدان گریان و خروشان هموار

خواجگان بینم برداشته از پیشْ دوات

دستها بر سر و سرها زده اندر دیوار

عاملان بینم باز آمده غمگین ز عمل

---

¹Zanân: see ITP §65.3.

کار ناکرده و نارفته بدیوان شمار

مطربان بینم گریان و ده انگشت گزان

رودها بر سر و بر روی زده شیفته‌وار   ۱۰

لشکری بینم سرگشته سراسیمه شده

چشمها پر نم و از حسرت و غم گشته نزار

این همان لشکریانند که من دیدم دی؟

وین همان شهر و زمینست که من دیدم پار؟

مگر امسال ملك باز نیامد ز غزا؟[1]

دشمنی روی نهادست در این شهر و دیار؟

مگر امسال ز هر خانه عزیزی کم شد؟

تا شد از حسرت و غم روز همه چون شب تار

مگر امسال چو پیرار بنالید ملك؟[2]

نی من آشوب از اینگونه ندیدم پیرار   ۱۵

تو نگوئی چه فتادست بگو گر بتوان

من نه بیگانه‌ام این حال ز من باز مدار

این چه شغلست وچه آشوب و چه بانگست و خروش؟

این چه کارست و چه بارست و چه چندین گفتار؟

کاشکی آن شب و آن روز که ترسیدم ازآن

نه فتادستی و شادی نشدستی تیمار

کاشکی چشم بد اندر نرسیدی بامیر

آه ترسم که رسیدست و شده زیر غبار

رفت و مارا همه بیچاره و درمانده بماند[3]

من ندانم که چه درمان کنم آنرا وچه چار   ۲۰

آه و دردا و دریغا که چو محمود ملك

همچو هر خاری در زیر زمین ریزد خوار

آه و دردا که همی لعل بکان باز شود

او میان گل و از گل نشود برخوردار

---

[1]Typically the sultan went on campaign every spring, returning booty-laden in the late autumn, but campaigns to India were waged in the autumn (see line 48 below).

[2]Two years prior to Sultan Mahmud's own death, one of his sons died.

[3]This is the transitive *mándan*; see vocabulary.

آه و دردا که بی‌او هر کس[1] نتواند دید

باغ پیروزی[2] پر لاله و گلهای ببار

آه و دردا که بیکبار تهی بینم ازو

کاخ محمودی و آن خانهٔ پر نقش و نگار

آه و دردا که کنون قرمطیان[3] شاد شوند

ایمنی یابند از سنگِ پراکنده و دار

۲۵

وای و دردا که کنون برهمنان همه هند

جای سازند بتان را دگر از نو به بهار[4]

میر ما خفته بخاک اندر و ما از بر خاک

این چه روزست بدین زاری ، یارب ، زنهار

فال بد چون زنم این حال جز این نیست مگر

زنم آن فال که گیرد دل از آن فال قرار

میر می خورده مگر دی و بخفتست امروز؟

دیر برخاست؟ مگر رنج رسیدش ز خمار؟

دهل و کوس همانا که همی زان نزنند

تا بخسبد خوش وکمتر بودش بر دل بار؟

۲۰

ای امیر همه میران و شهنشاه جهان

خیز و از حجره برون آی که خفتی بسیار

خیز شاها که جهان پر شغب وشور شدست

شور بنشان و شب و روز بشادی بگزار

خیز شاها که رسولان شهان آمده‌اند

هدیه‌ها دارند آورده فراوان و نثار

خیز شاها که امیران بسلام آمده‌اند

بارشان ده که رسیدست همانا گه بار

---

[1]Generally in poetry, *har kas* + negative is taken to mean "nobody."

[2]Pîrôzî ("victory") here is the name of a garden in Ghazna. The same name occurs below in line 50, and also in line 35 as Fîrôzî, a variant of Pîrôzî.

[3]The Qarmatians, a Shiite sect based in Bahrein whose influence had spread throughout the eastern Islamic world. The staunchly Sunni Ghaznavids were implacable enemies of the Qarmatians, as well as of all other Shiite groups.

[4]Farrukhî refers here to Sultan Mahmud's renowned raids on India, which went as deep into Hindu territory as Gujarat, where the temple at Somnath was sacked and its treasures brought back to Ghazni. *Bahâr* can be taken as "spring," but here it is *bihâr*, for the Sanskrit *vihâra*, a Buddhist temple. The inaccuracy of Brahmins in India restoring idols to a Buddhist temple would not have concerned Farrukhî.

خیز شاها که بفیروزی گل باز شدست

بر گل نو قدحی چند می لعل گسار

۲۵

خیز شاها که به چوگانی گرد آمده‌اند

آنکه با ایشان چوگان زده‌ای چندین بار

خیز شاها که چو هر سال بعرض آمده‌اند

از پس کاخ تو و باغ تو پیلی دو هزار

خیز شاها که همه دوخته و ساخته گشت

خلعت۱ لشکر و کردند بیکجا انبار

خیز شاها که بدیدار تو فرزند عزیز

بشتاب آمده، بنمای مر اورا دیدار

که۲ تواند که بر انگیزد زین خواب ترا؟

خفتی آن خفتن کز بانگ نگردی بیدار؟

۴۰

آنچنان خفتی ای شه که نخواهی برخاست

ای خداوند جهان خیز و بفرزند سپار

خفتن بسیار ای خسرو خوی تو نبود

هیچکس خفته ندیدست ترا زین کردار

خوی تو تاختن و شغل سفر بود مدام

بنیاسودی۳ هر چند که بودی بیمار

در سفر بودی تا بودی در کار سفر

تن چون کوه تو از رنج سفر گشته نزار

سفری کان‌را باز آمدن امّید بود

غم او کم بود ارچند که باشد دشوار

۴۵

سفری داری امسال دراز اندر پیش

که مر آن‌را نه کران است پدید و نه کنار

یکدمك باری در خانه ببایست نشست

تا بدیدندی روی تو عزیزان تبار

---

[1] The robes of honor were distributed to commanders at the annual review of troops.

[2] In classical Persian, *ki* ("who," interrogative, modern *ki*) and *ki* ("who," relative, modern *ke)* are spelled the same.

[3] *Binayâsûdî:* for the tense see *ITP* §87; for the perfective aspect prefix *bi-*, see *ITP* §84. When the perfective aspect prefix *bi-* and the negative prefix *na-* occur together, they generally come in the order *bi-na-*, as here.

رفتن تو بخزان بودی هر سال ، شها
چه شتاب آمد کامسال برفتی ببهار؟

مرغ وماهی چو زنان بر تو همه نوحه کنند
همه با ما شده اندر غم و اندوه تو یار

روز وشب بر سر تابوت تو از حسرت تو
۵۰ کاخ پیروزی چون ابر همی گرید زار

بر حصار از فزع و بیم تو رفتند ، شها
تو، شها، از فزع و بیم که رفتی بحصار؟

تو بباغی چو بیابانی دلتنگ شدی
چون گرفتستی در جایگه تنگ قرار؟

٭

چون پرند نیلگون بر روی پوشد مرغزار
پرنیان هفترنگ اندر سر آرد کوهسار

خاکرا چون ناف آهو مشک زاید بیقیاس
بیدرا چون پرّ طوطی برگ روید بیشمار

دوش وقت صبحدم بوی بهار آورد باد
حبّذا باد شمال و خرّما بوی بهار

باد گویی مشک سوده دارد اندر آستین
باغ گویی لعبتان ساده دارد در کنار

ارغوان لعل بدخشی دارد اندر مرسله
نسترن لولوی بیضا دارد اندر گوشوار

تا رباید جامهای سرخرنگ از شاخ گل
پنجههای دست مردم سر فرا کرد از چنار[1]

باغ بوقلمونلباس و شاخ بوقلموننمای
آب مرواریدگون و ابر مرواریدبار

راست پنداری که خلعتهای رنگین یافتند
باغهای پرّ نگار از داغگاه شهریار

داغگاه شهریار اکنون چنان خرّم بود
کاندر او از خرّمی خیره بماند روزگار

---

[1]The leaves of the plane tree have five lobes, for which reason they are often compared to a human hand.

سبزه اندر سبزه بینی چون سپهر اندر سپهر

خیمه اندر خیمه چون سیمین حصار اندر حصار

UNSURÎ

عنصری

Known for the creation of novel metaphors in his qasidas and ghazals, Unsurî (d. 1039) was a court poet for several Ghaznavid rulers, including Sultan Mahmûd and Sultan Mas'ûd.

بگرد ماه بر از غالیه حصار که کرد؟[1]   بروی روز بر از تیره شب نگار که کرد؟

نبود یار بطبع و بجنس ظلمت و نور

بروی خوب تو این هر دو چیز، یار، که کرد؟

ترا که کرد، بتا، از بهارخانه برون؟ جهان بروی تو بر، جان من، بهار که کرد؟

بماه مانی آنگه که تو سوار شوی   چگونه، ای عجبی، ماہرا سوار که کرد؟

اگر ز عشق تو پر نار گشت جان و دلم   مرا بگوی رخ تو برنگ نار که کرد؟

گر استوار نبودی ز دور بر دل من   مرا بمهر تو نزدیك و استوار که کرد؟

✳

بت که بتگر کندش[2] دلبر نیست   دلبری دستبرد بتگر نیست

بت من دل برد که صورت اوست   آزری‌وار و صنع آزر نیست

از بدیعی ببوستان بهشت   جفت بالای او صنوبر نیست

چیست آن جعد سلسله که همی   بوی عنبرده است و عنبر نیست

هیچ مویی شکافته از[3] بالا   زارتر زان میان لاغر نیست

بینی آن چشم پر کرشمه و ناز   که بدان چشم هیچ عبهر نیست

سیم بی‌بار اگرچه پاك بود   چون بناگوش آن سمنبر نیست

گرد روز آن دو زلف دایره‌نیست   نقطهٔ زان دهانش[4] کمتر نیست

بلطیفی دگر چو تو نبود   بکریمی چو میر دیگر نیست

The following poem is on Sada, the Iranian festival of fire celebrated on the tenth of Bahman, fifty days before Nawroz.

---

[1] Ba gird-i mâh bar, see ITP §83. For ki, see page 14, note 2.

[2] Read kunad'sh for kunad-ash for the meter.

[3] For the meter, read shikâf'ta'z.

[4] For the meter, read dahân'sh for dahân-ash.

ز افریدون و از جم یادگارست   سده جشن ملوك نامدارست

کزو نور تجلی آشکارست   زمین امشب تو گویی کوه طورست

گر این روزست، شب خواندش نباید   وگر شب روز شد، خوش روزگارست

که بس پرنور و روحانی دیارست   همانا کاین دیار اندر بهشتست

که وهم هر دو تن در یك شمارست   فلكرا با زمین انبازیی هست

همه اجسام این، اجزای نارست   همه اجرام آن، ارکان نورست

چرا باد هوا بیجاده‌بارست؟   اگر نه کان بیجادست[1] گردون

که برگش اصل و شاخش صدهزارست   چه چیزست آن درخت روشنایی

عقیقین گنبد زرّین‌نگارست   گهی سرو بلندست و گهی باز

چرا تیره‌روش و همرنگ قارست؟   ور ایدون کو بصورت روشن آمد

چرا امشب جهان چون لاله‌زارست؟   گر از فصل زمستانست بهمن

شرار آتش نمرود و نارست[2]   به لاله ماند این لیکن نه لاله است

MINÛCHIHRÎ
منوچهری

Abu'l-Najm Ahmad "Minûchihrî" of Dâmghân (d. 1040) was first at-tached to the court of Minûchihr son of Qâbûs the Daylamite (r. 1012–31), from whom he took his pen name, and then was at the court of Sultan Mas'ud of Ghazna (r. 1030–40).

ای ماهروی، شرم نداری ز روی ما؟   ای با عدوی ما گذرنده ز کوی ما

با هرکسی همی گله کردی ز خوی ما   نامم نهاده بودی بدخوی و جنگجوی

رستی ز خوی ناخوش و از گفتگوی ما   جستی و یافتی دگری بر مراد دل

آن روز شد که آب گذشتی بجوی ما   اکنون بجوی اوست روان آب عاشقی

گرمست آب ما که کهن شد سبوی ما   گویند سردتر بود آب از سبوی نو

چندین بخیره‌خیر چه گردی بکوی ما؟   اکنون یکی بکام دل خویش یافتی

✽

آمد شب و از خواب مرا رنج وعذابست   ای دوست بیار آنچه مرا داروی خوابست

من خواب ز دیده بمی ناب ربایم   آری، عدوی خواب جوانان می نابست

---

[1]For the meter, read *bîjâda 'st* for *bîjâda ast*.

[2]For the meter, read *lâla 'st*. Nimrod was the tyrant king who cast Abraham into a fiery pit, but the angel Gabriel turned the fire into a rose garden.

سختم عجب آید که چگونه بردش خواب   آن‌را که بکاخ اندر[1] یک شیشه شرابست

وین نیز عجب‌تر که خورد بادهٔ بی‌چنگ   بی‌نغمهٔ چنگش بمی ناب شتابست

اسبی که صفیرش نزنی، می‌نخورد آب   نی مرد کم از اسب و نه می کمتر از آبست

در مجلس احرار سه چیزست و فزون به   وان هر سه شرابست و ربابست و کبابست

ما مرد شرابیم و کبابیم و ربابیم   خوشا که شرابست و کبابست و ربابست

✳

جهان ما سگ شوخست مر ترا بگزد   هرآینه تو مر اورا نگیری و نگزی

مدار دل متفکر بفتنهٔ ایام   چرا که فکرت ایام‌را همی نسزی

بیار باده کجا[2] بهترست باده هنوز   که تو بباده ز چنگ زمانه محترزی

_____

[1]The prepositional phrase is *ba kâkh andar*.
[2]*Kujâ = ki.*

POETS OF THE SELJUQ PERIOD TO THE MONGOL INVASION

AZRAQÎ
ازرقی

Abûbakr Zaynuddîn Azraqî (d. circa 1070) served at the Seljuq court in his native Herat. He wrote some of the finest descriptions of nature in Persian. The first poem given here is a description of clouds. The second is a description of the fiery nature and color of wine.

جا بجا ابر سپید اندر هوا بین ، خرد خرد

همچو بچگان¹ حواصل بر سر دریا روان

راست پنداری نعایم بر سر شاخِ درخت

بیضهٔ سیمین نهادست از بر سبزِ آشیان

چون بلورین حقه‌های حقه‌بازان ، جفت جفت

برنهاده لب بلب ، پر کرده از لؤلؤ میان

بی‌گمان گویی کمان‌کردار شاخِ چفته‌نیست

خرد پیکانهای مینارنگ ازو پر ضیمران

طوطیان دارد زمردگون زبان بر شاخِ خویش

کرده از شاخش برون هر یك زمردگونِ زبان

تا بسان بندگان هر یك بشرطِ بندگی

تهنیت گویند خسرورا بجشنِ مهرگان

٭

بنگر³ این ابرِ گران ، یازان بگردون بر² سبك

---

¹For the meter, read *bach'gân*.
²The prepositional phrase is *ba gardûn bar*.
³For the meter, read *bin'gar*.

19

در چنین روزی سبکتر، بادهٔ[1] باید گران

بزم کیکاوس‌وار آرای و در وی برفروز

زانچه سوگند سیاوش[2] را بدو بود امتحان

گوهری کز تفّ او و در ژرفی دریا صدف

سرخ چون مرجان کند دُرّ سپید اندر دهان

برگ او بر خاک ریزان چون بلورین یاسمن

شاخ او در باد یازان چون عقیقین خیزران

از بلورین یاسمینش، خاک پر سیمین سپر

وز عقیقین خیزرانش، باد چون زرّین سنان

بوستانی را همی ماند که عودش ماه دی

ارغوان تازه نو نو بشکفاند هر زمان

بوستانش را گر از عود ارغوان روید همی

ارغوان از عود روید لابد اندر بوستان

چون نمود او ارغوان از عود رسته پیش تو

بادهٔ باید ببوی عود و رنگ ارغوان

چهرهٔ ساقی چو اندر عکس او پیدا شود

راست پنداری پری در شاخ مرجان شد نهان

جام مروارید همچون کان یاقوتست ازو

ورچه اصل او زمردگون برون آید ز کان

نیست ماه و مهر و مشک و بان، وزو یابی همی

رنگ ماه و نور مهر و طبع مشک و بوی بان

HUJJAT

حجت

Abû-Mu'în Nâsir-i Khusraw "Hujjat" of Qubâdîân (modern Kabadian in Tajikistan) was an official in the employ of the Ghaznavids. Attracted to the Isma'ili sect, Nâsir-i Khusraw undertook a seven-year journey from Balkh to Cairo and back again across the Arabian peninsula. Returning to the Ghaznavid realm as a trained missionary, he was forced to retire for safety, after a few years of propagandist activity, to a for-

---

[1]In classical Persian orthography ء indicates both the *izâfa (a-i)* and the nonspecific enclitic *(a-î)*; here باده spells *bâda-î*. The *hamza* above the *h* is also used to spell the second-person singular narrative-tense verb *(bûdaî,* e.g.).

[2]Siyavush's trial was to pass through fire to prove his innocence.

tress in Yumgan in Badakhshan, where he ended his days circa 1075. He left numerous philosophical works and poetry of a philosophical and religious strain. While credited with being the first to use poetry as a vehicle for philosophical and theological thought, he has been criticized on the same count for having versified philosophy devoid of poetry.

The first poem given here describes a night spent in contemplation (lines 1–5), followed by an excursus on the contrasts produced by the dual nature of man, and ending with the resolution of the antagonism of the material and spiritual natures in the birth of a personal religion of salvation. The second selection is on the illusory and transitory nature of this world, and the third is an allegorical piece on the soul.

هیچ نارامید این خاطر روشن‌بین	در دلم تا بسحرگاه شب دوشین
به دو صد چشم درین تیره‌زمین چندین	گفت بنگر که چرا مینگرد گردون
روز تا شام بزراب‌زده زوبین	خاک را کرتهٔ خورشید همی‌دوزد
تا بهنگام سحر روی خود این مسکین	وز که شام بپوشد بسیه‌چادر
آفرین است روان بر اثر نفرین	روز رخشان ز پس تیره‌شبان گوئی
تلخ وشور و بد وخوب و ترُش وشیرین	خاک را شوی همی دو است۱ که می‌زاید
این چنین باید، پورا، و مدان جز این	از دوشویه‌زن بچه بدو لون آید
نه زنی هرگز زادست بدین آئین	کس ندیدست چنین طرفه زناشویی
از چه ماندست چنین بسته درین سجین؟	وین خردمند و سخنگوی۲ بهشتی جان
بر سر خواب جهان خواب دگر مگزین	عمر خود خواب خواب جهانست. چرا خسی؟
سر من جز که سر زانوی من بالین۳	تا سحرگه ز بس اندیشه نجُست از من
شوی جانست و زنش تنت۴ وخرد کابین	ای پسر، جان و تنت شهره زن و شویند
چو همی‌باید دانی که بزاید دین	زین زن و شوی بدین کابین فرزندی

*

باز جهان را جز از شکار چکارست؟	باز جهان تیزپرّ و خلق شکارست
صحبت دیوار پر ز نقش و نگارست	صحبت دنیا بسوی عاقل هشیار

---

[1] For the meter, read du 'st.

[2] Nâsir-i Khusraw uses the Persian sukhangúy jân here as equivalent to the Arabic al-nafs al-nâtiqa, the soul rational (literally, speaking).

[3] "Until dawn, so anxious was I that my head sought no pillow from me save my knee," i.e., my head was on my knees in contemplation all night.

[4] For the meter, read tan't for tan-at.

گرنه دماغت پر از فساد و بخارست   غره چرا گشته‌ای بکار زمانه؟

دستهٔ گل نیست آن که پشتهٔ خارست   دستهٔ گل گر ترا دهد ، تو چنان دانك

جامهٔ اورا نه هیچ پود و نه تارست   میوهٔ اورا نه هیچ بوی و نه رنگست

میوهٔ خوش زو طمع مکن که چنارست   رهبری از وی مدار چشم که دیوست

هیچ بدینها ترا نه جای فخارست   ای شده غره بملك و مال و جوانی،

فخر من و تو بعلم و رای و وقارست   فخر بخوبی و زرّ و سیم زنان‌راست

۞

واندر طلب طعمه پر و بال بیاراست   روزی ز سر سنگ عقابی بهوا خاست

«امروز همه روی جهان زیر پر ماست   بر راستی بال نظر کرد و چنین گفت

می‌بینم اگر ذرّهٔ اندر تك دریاست   بر اوج چو پرواز کنم از نظر تیز

جنبیدن آن پشه عیان در نظر ماست»   گر بر سر خاشاك یکی پشه بجنبد

بنگر که ازین چرخ جفاپیشه چه برخاست   بسیار منی کرد و ز تقدیر نترسید،

تیری ز قضای بد بگشاد برو راست   ناگ ز کمینگاه یکی سخت‌کمانی

وز ابر مر اورا بسوی خاك فرو کاست   بر بال عقاب آمد آن تیر جگردوز

وانگه پر خویش گشاد از چپ و از راست   بر خاك بیفتاد و بغلطید چو ماهی

گفتا «عجبست اینکه ز چوبی و ز آهن

این تیزی و تندی و پریدن ز کجا خاست؟»

زی تیر نگه کرد و پر خویش برو دید

گفتا «ز که نالیم؟ که از ماست که بر ماست

حجت،³ تو منی را ز سر خویش بدر کن

بنگر به عقابی که منی کرد چها خاست

MAS'ÛD-I SA'D-I SALMÂN
مسعود سعد سلمان

A poet of the later Ghaznavid period in the subcontinent who spent a good portion of his life in prison owing to the calumny and treachery of those who were envious of the wealth and power he had both inherited and augmented by virtue of his civil and military talents, Mas'ûd-i Sa'd-i Salmân (1046–1121) is renowned for his *Habsiyyât* (prison po-

---

[1]Here *garna...ast* = *gar...nîst*.

[2]*Zarra-î*: see p. 20, note 1.

[3]Hujjat, Nâsir-i Khusraw's pen name.

ems), one of which is given here. In it can be seen his superb handling of
the Persian poetic language, for which reason his qasidas have remained
exceptionally popular throughout the centuries.

چو یادم آید از دوستان و اهل وطن   چنان بگریم کم¹ دشمنان ببخشایند

ز بهر آنک نشان تنست پیراهن   سحر شوم ز غم و پیرهن بتن بدرم

که راست ناید اگر در خطاب گویم "من"   ز رنج و ضعف بدان جایگه رسید تنم

بخاست آتش ازین دل چو آذر از آهن   صبور گشتم و دل در بر آهنین کردم

جهان بمن بر تاریک چون چه بیژن   بسان بیژن درماندهام ببند بلا

تنم چو سوزن و دل همچو چشمهٔ سوزن   برم ز دستم چون سوزن آژده وشی

نکرد یارم از بیم دشمنان شیون   نبود یارم از شرم دوستان گریان

شبی سیاهتر از روی و رای اهریمن   ز درد و اندهٔ هجران گذشت بر من ز دوش

که شب دراز همیکرد بر هوا دامن   نمیگشاد گریبان صبح را گردون

ز راست فرقد و شعری ز چپ سهیل یمن²   طلایه بر سپه روز کرد لشکر شب

تنی برنج و عذاب و دلی بگرم و حزن   مرا ملال گرفته ز دیر ماندن شب

پگاه ازین شب تیره چه خواهدم زادن   دران تفکر مانده دلم که فردارا

که هاله چون سپری شد چه زاید آبستن   ازانکه هست شب آبستن و نداند کس

فرو نیارست آمد بر من از روزن   گذشت باد سحرگاه و از نهیب فراق

خیال دوست گوای منست و نجم پرن   نخفتهام همه شب دوش و بودهام نالان

چو ماه روی و چو گل عارض و چو سیم ذقن   نشسته بودم کآمد خیال او ناگاه

جوشان دل مرا بیافت چو یک تار موی، نالان تن   مرا بیافت چو یک قطره خون،

یکی چو در ثمین ویکی چو مشک ختن   زبسکه کند دو زلف و زبسکه راندم اشک

ز مشک و لولو یک آستین و یک دامن   مرا و اورا از چشم و زلف³ گرد آمد

بمهر گفتم کز زلف بیش مشک مکن   بناز گفت که "از دیده بیش اشک مریز"

زدوده طلعت بنمود چشمهٔ روشن   درین مناظره بودیم کز سپهر کبود

MU'IZZÎ

معزی

Attached to the Seljuq court, Amîru'sh-shu'arâ (prince of poets) Abu-
Abdullâh Muhammad of Nishapur took his pen name, Mu'izzî, from

---

¹K'am dushmanân = ki dushmanân-am.

²Since Canopus is visible in Mecca and Medina low on the horizon in the direc-
tion of the Yemen, the star is associated with that country.

³Mard u ûrâ az chashm u zulf = az chashm-i man u zulf-i û.

the Seljuq Mu'izzuddîn Malikshâh (r. 1072–92). He died circa 1125 in the service of Sultan Sanjar (r. 1097–1157). A master at the unforced metaphor and simplicity of diction, Mu'izzî adopted and adapted themes from the Arabic qasida (as here, the theme of the caravan) into his Persian poetry.

ای ساربان منزل مکن جز در دیار یار من

تا یک زمان زاری کنم بر رَبع و اطلال و دمن

ربع از دلم پرخون کنم ، خاك دمن گلگون کنم

اطلال را جیحون کنم از آب چشم خویشتن

از روی یار خرگهی ایوان همی بینم تهی

وز قدّ آن سرو سهی خالی همی بینم چمن

بر جای رطل و جام می گوران نهادستند[1] پی

بر جای چنگ و نای و نی آواز زاغست و زغن

از خیمه تا سعدی بشد وز حجره تا سلمی بشد

وز حجله تا لیلی بشد گوئی بشد جانم ز تن

نتوان گذشت از منزلی کآنجا نیفتد مشکلی

از قصۀ سنگین‌دلی نوشین‌لبی سیمین‌ذقن

آنجا که بود آن دلستان با دوستان در بوستان

شد گرگ و روبه را مکان ، شد گور وکرگس را وطن

ابرست بر جای قمر ، زهرست بر جای شکر

سنگست بر جای گهر ، خارست بر جای سمن

آری چو پیش آید قضا مروا شود چون مرغوا

جای شجر گیرد گیا ، جای طرب گیرد شجن

کاخیکه دیدم چون ارم خرّم‌تر از روی صنم

دیوار او بینم بخم ماننده پشت شمن[2]

تمثالهای بلعجب چاك آوریده بی سبب

گوئی دریدند ای عجب بر تن ز حسرت پیرهن

زینسان‌که چرخ نیلگون کرد این سراها را نگون

دیار کی گردد کنون گرد دیار یار من

یاری برخ چون ارغوان ، حوری بتن چون پرنیان

---

[1] Nihâdastand: for the tense, see ITP §90.
[2] The idolater is seen as bent prostrate before his idol.

سروی بلب چون ناردان ، ماهی بقد چون نارون

نیرنگ چشم او فره ، بر سیمش از عنبر زره

زلفش همه بند و گره ، جعدش همه چین و شکن

تا از بر من دور شد دل در برم رنجور شد

مشکم همه کافور شد ، شمشاد من شد نسترن

از هجر او سرگشته‌ام ، تخم صبوری کشته‌ام

مانند مرغی گشته‌ام بریان شده بر بابزن

KHAYYÂM
خیام

Philosopher, mathematician, astronomer, and physician, Abu'l-Fath Umar ibn Ibrâhîm Khayyâmî of Nishapur (d. ?1132) left a collection of *rubâ'îs* that held no great place in Persian literature until Fitzgerald's version became so popular. Khayyâm's original corpus has also gathered so many accretions over the centuries that it is difficult to sort out which quatrains are actually his.

پیش از من و تو لیل و نهاری¹ بودست   گردنده فلك نیز بکاری بودست

هرجا که قدم نهی تو بروی زمین   آن مردمك چشم نگاری بودست

این یك و سه روزه نوبت عمر گذشت   چون آب بجویبار و چون باد بدشت

هرگز غم دو روز مرا یاد نگشت   روزی که نیامدست و روزی که گذشت

در کارگه کوزه‌گری رفتم دوش   دیدم دو هزار کوزه، گویا و خموش

ناگاه یکی کوزه برآورد خروش «کو کوزه‌گر و کوزه‌خر و کوزه‌فروش؟»

SÛZANÎ
سوزنی

Shamsuddîn Muhammad Sûzanî of Samarkand (d. 1166) was panegyrist to Arslan Khan, the ruler of Transoxiana, and to the Seljuq Sultan Mahmud II (r. 1118–31). Known principally for his obscene verse, Sûza-nî also composed ghazals in a disarmingly simple style.

شکسته‌زلفا ، عهد وصال من مشکن   چو زلف خود مکن از بار هجر قامت من

---

¹*Layl u nahâr* (Ar.) "night and day."

ز آب و آتش چشم و دل رمیده مشو   که آب و آتش من ز دوست داند از دشمن

چو سرو و ماه خرامان بنزد من بازآی   که ماه وسرو منی، مشک‌زلف وسیم‌بدن

بتی پری‌رخ و آهن‌دلی و بی رخ تو   دلی پری‌زده‌کردار، شیفتست و شمن

بمن نمای رخ و اندکی بمن دل ده   که با پری‌زده دارند اندکی آهن[1]

*

درین جهان که سرای غمست و تاسه و تاب
چو کاسه بر سر آبیم و تیره‌دل چو سراب

خراب عالم و ما جغدوار، ازین نه عجب
عجب ازانکه نمانند جغدرا بخراب

بخواب غفلت خفتیم و خورده شربت جهل
که تا شدیم ز بیداد فتنه بی خور و خواب

عقاب طاعت ما بازمانده از پرواز
شدیم صیدِ معاصی چو کبکِ صیدِ عقاب

ANVARÎ
انوری

Awhaduddîn Alî Anvarî of Abîvard (d. 1187) has been almost univer-
sally acknowledged as the master of panegyric verse. Exceptionally
learned in the sciences current in his time, especially astrology, he was
patronized by the Seljuq Sultan Sanjar. His poetry has been criticized as
being pervaded with a "superfluity of erudition," but such obscurity
was regarded as an essential ingredient of the court panegyric.

The first qasida given here is addressed to one Imâduddîn Abu'l-
Muzaffar Tûrânî and is a congratulatory ode written on the occasion of
the Ramadan feast, hence the allusions to the new moon of Shawwal,
introducing an imaginary journey through the cosmos.

The second selection, a good example of Anvarî's intricate manipula-
tion of metaphor, is from a qasida on the advent of spring and the reju-
venation of the world.

چو شاه زنگ برآورد لشکر از مکمن   فرو گشاد سراپرده پادشاه ختن[2]

---

[1] An allusion to the practice of restraining madmen in iron chains; the poet asks
his beloved to give him some of his/her "iron" heart.

[2] The king of Zanzibar is the night; the padishah of Khotan, where dwelt (light-
skinned) Turks, is the sun.

چو برکشید شفق دامن از بسیط هوا   شب سیاه فرو هشت خیمه‌را دامن[1]

هلال عید پدید آمد از کنار فلك   منیر چون رخ یار و بخم چو قامت من[2]

نهان و پیدا گفتی که معنییست دقیق   ورای قوت ادراك در لباس سخن

خیال انجم گردون همی بحسن و جمال   چنان نمود که از کشتزار برگ سمن

یکی چو فندق سیم و یکی چو مهرۀ زر

یکی چو لعل بدخشان، یکی چو دُر عدن

بچرخ بر بتعجب همی سفر کردم   بگام فکرت و اندیشه از وطن بوطن

بهیچ منزل و مقصد نیامدم که درو   مجاوری نبُد از اهل آن دیار و دمن

مقیم منزل هفتم، مهندسی[3] دیدم   درازعمر و قوی‌هیکل و بدیع‌بدن

به پیش خویش برای حساب کون و فساد   نهاده تختۀ مینا و خامۀ آهن

وزو فرود یکی خواجۀ ممکن[4] بود   بروی و رای منور، بخُلق و خُلق حسن

خصال خویش چون روی دلبران نیکو   ضمیر پاکش چون رای زیرکان روشن

به پنجم اندر زیشان زمامکش ترکی[5]   که گاه کینه ببندد زمان‌را گردن

بگرز آهنسای و بنیزه صحره‌گداز[6]   بتیر موی‌شکاف و بتیغ شیر اوژن

فرود ازو بدو منزل کنیزکی[7] دیدم   بنفشه‌زلف و سمن‌عارضین و سیم‌ذقن

رخش ز می شده چون لعل و بربطی بکنار که   با نوای حزینش همی‌نماند حزن

وزان سپس بجوانی[8] دگر گذر کردم   که بود در همه فن همچو مردم یكفن

صحیفه نقش همی‌کرد بی‌دوات و قلم   بدیهه شعر همی‌گفت بی‌زبان و دهن

خدنگهای شهاب اندر آن شب شب‌گون   روان چو نور خرد در روان اهریمن

نجوم کرکس واقع بجدی در گفتی   که پیش ِ یك صنمستی بسجده‌در دو شمن[9]

ز بس تزاحم انجم چنان نمود همی   مجره از بر این گوزپشت ِ پشت‌شکن

---

[1]Khayma-râ dâman = dâman-i khayma.

[2]Bakham chu qâmat-i man: poets always speak of themselves as bent over with age, care, anxiety, poverty, &c.

[3]Saturn, planet of the seventh sphere, is the ancient geometer of heaven. As Chronos, he is the personification of time, the principle of generation and corruption (kawn u fasâd).

[4]In the sixth sphere is Jupiter, the mightiest and most auspicious of the planets.

[5]Mars, the planet of war, is in the fifth sphere.

[6]Read ba gurz, âhansây; u ba nayza, sakhragudâz, &c.

[7]The sun occupies the fourth sphere; it is skipped. Venus, the planet of music and entertainment, is in the third sphere.

[8]Mercury, the scribe of the heavens, is the planet of the second sphere. The first sphere is occupied by the moon.

[9]The poet imagines the isosceles triangle formed by Vega, Altair, and Polaris as two idolaters bowing down before an idol.

که² روز بار ز میران و مهتران بزرگ   در سرای و ره بارگاه صدرِ زمن¹

چو طبلِ رحلت روزه همی‌زند مه عید   بشکرِ رزیت او رایتِ نشاط بزن

هزار عید چنین در سرای عمر بمان   هزار بیخِ خلاف از زمینِ ملک بکن

※

باز این چه جوانی و جمالست جهان را؟   وین حال که نو گشت زمین را و زمان را؟

مقدار شب از روز فزون بود و بدل شد   ناقص همه این را شد و زائد همه آن را

هم جمره برآورد فروبرده نفس را   هم فاخته بگشاد فروبسته زبان را

در باغ، چمن ضامن گل گشت ز بلبل   آن روز که آوازه فکندند خزان را³

اکنون چمن باغ گرفتارِ تقاضاست   آری، بدل خصم بگیرند ضمان را

آهو بسر سبزه مگر نافه بینداخت؟   کز خاک چمن آب بشد عنبر و بان را

گر خام نیسته است صبا رنگ ریاحین،   از عکس چرا رنگ دهد آب روان را؟⁴

خوش‌خوش ز نظر گشت نهان راز دل آب   تا خاک همی عرضه دهد راز نهان را

همچون ثمر بید⁵ کند نام و نشان گم   در سایهٔ او روز کنون نام و نشان را

بادام دو مغزست که از خنجر الماس   ناداده لبش بوسه سراپای فسان را

ژاله سپر برف ببُرد از کتف کوه   چون رستم نیسان بخم آورد کمان را

کُه بیضهٔ کافور زیان کرد و گهر سود   بنگر که چه سودست مرین مایه زیان را؟⁶

از غایت تری که هواراست عجب نیست   گر خاصیت ابر دهد طبع دخان را

گر نائرهٔ ابر نشد پاک بریده،   چون هیچ عنان باز نپیچد سیلان را؟

ور ابر نه در دایگی طفل شکوفه است،   یازان سوی ابر از چه گشادست دهان را؟

ور لاله نورسته نه افروخته شمعیست،   روشن ز چه دارد همه اطراف مکان را؟

---

¹Sadr-i zaman, a title of Imâduddîn Abu'l-Muzaffar.

²A run-on line: chunân numûd...majarra...ki... "the Milky Way appeared like...."

³Typically, when autumn approaches and the rose fades, the nightingale becomes distraught. Here the lawn (chaman) has guaranteed the return of the rose in the spring. In the next line the lawn is begging the rose to return.

⁴Here the colors of the herbs are seen to "bleed" into the water in which they are reflected. This, speculates the poet, must be due to the fact that the zephyr did not make the colors dye-fast.

⁵Samar-i bêd: the willow bears no fruit.

⁶When the same word is repeated in a line (as here, sûd), they generally either have different meanings or are two different parts of speech. Here the first is a verb; the second, a noun. Note also the juxtaposition of antonyms, sûd and ziyân.

KHÂQÂNÎ

خاقانی

Afzaluddîn Badîl Khâqânî (d. 1198), a native of Shirvan in the Transcaucasus, imbibed the imagery of both Islam and Christianity. He traveled widely, made two pilgrimages to Mecca, and was involved in Russo-Georgian relations and ecclesiastical embroilments at the Byzantine court in Constantinople.

Reminiscent of the Latin *ubi sunt* genre, the Madayin qasida, which he composed on seeing the ruins of the Sassanian court at Ctesiphon, shows Khâqânî's erudition and the facile manner in which he introduces the most involved metaphor without sacrificing the orderly progression and careful balance of the elements of the classical qasida. In eighteenth-century Iran, when a reaction set in against the prevailing hypercerebralized style, it was to Khâqânî that they looked for classical perfection.

هان ، ای دل عبرت بین ، از دیده نظر کن هان   ایوان مداین را آئینۀ عبرت دان

یکره ز ره دجله منزل بمداین کن   وز دیده دوم دجله بر خاك مداین ران

خود دجله چنان گرید صد دجلۀ خون گوئی كز گرمی خونابش آتش چكد از مژگان

بینی که لب دجله چون کف بدهان آرد   گوئی ز تف آهش لب آبله زد چندان

از آتش حسرت بین بریان جگر دجله   خود آب شنیدستی كآتش كندش بریان؟   ٥

بر دجله گری نونو وز دیده زكوتش ده گرچه لب دریا هست از دجله زكوةستان

گر دجله درآمیزد باد لب و سوز دل   نیمی شود افسرده، نیمی شود آتشدان¹

تا سلسلۀ ایوان بگسست مداین را   در سلسله شد دجله، چون سلسله شد پیچان²

گەگە بزبان اشك آواز ده ایوان را   تا بو³ كه بگوش دل پاسخ شنوی ز ایوان

دندانۀ هر قصری پندی دهدت نو نو   پند سر دندانه بشنو ز بن دندان   ١٠

گوید که تو از خاكی، ما خاك توئیم اكنون   گامی دو سه بر ما نه، اشكی دو سه هم بفشان

---

[1]Although in line 4 the Tigris's sighs are so hot that they cause blisters on the lip, generally the *bâd-i lab* (sigh emerging from the lip) is taken to be cold when it is a sigh of regret.

[2]Note here the three distinct and different uses of *silsila*. The first, *silsila-i ayvân*, is a reference to Anushirvan's Chain of Justice, a golden chain hung outside the palace so that any subject who felt himself wronged could pull it and summon the emperor for redress.

[3]*Tâ baw*, for *tâ buvad*, "in order that it be."

از نوحهٔ جغد² الحق مائیم بدرد سر   از دیده گلابی¹ کن ز درد سر ما بنشان

آری چه عجب داری کاندر چمن گیتی   جغدست پی بلبل، نوحه است پی الحان؟

ما بارگه دادیم، این رفت ستم بر ما   بر قصر ستمکاران تا خود چه رسد خذلان

گوئی که نگون کردست ایوان فلکرش را؟ ۱۵   حکم فلک گردان یا حکم فلک گردان؟

بر دیدهٔ من خندی کاینجا ز چه میگرید؟   خندند بر آن دیده کاینجا نشود گریان

اینست همان ایوان کز نقش رخ مردم   خاك در او بودی دیوار نگارستان

اینست همان درگه کورا ز شهان بودی   دیلم ملك بابل، هندو شه ترکستان³

اینست همان صفّه کز هیبت او بردی   بر شیر فلك حمله شیر تن شادروان⁴

پندار همان عهدست، از دیدهٔ فکرت بین ۲۰   در سلسلة درگه، در کوکبة میدان

از اسب پیاده شو، بر نطع زمین رخ نه   زیر پی پیلش بین شهمات شده نعمان⁵

مستست زمین زیرا خورددست بجای می   در کاس سر هرمز خون دل نوشروان

بس پند که بود آنگه بر تاج سرش پیدا⁶

صد پند نوست اکنون در مغز سرش پنهان

کسری و ترنج زر، پرویز و ترهٔ زرّین⁷   بر باد شده یکسر، با خاك شده یکسان

پرویز بهر خوانی زرین تره گستردی ۲۵   کردی ز بساط زر زرین ترهرا بُستان

پرویز کنون گم شد، زآن گمشده کمتر گو

زرین تره کو بر خوان؟ رو کَمْ تَرَکوا⁸ برخوان

گفتی که کجا رفتند آن تاجوران؟ اینک   ز ایشان شكم خاكست آبستن جاویدان

بس دیر همی زاید آبستن خاک آری   دشوار بود زادن، نطفه ستدن آسان

---

¹Rosewater is a remedy for headache; because of its red color it is likened to (bloody) tears of regret.

²The owl, a bird of ill omen in Persian, inhabits ruins.

³I.e., the emperors were so great that the king of Babylon was no more than a hired soldier to them, and the shah of Turkistan was only a lowly servant.

⁴The *shêr-i falak* (lion of the celestial sphere) is Leo; the canopy over the throne was emblazoned with the lion-and-sun emblem of Persia.

⁵A reference to the Lakhmid king of Hîra, Nu'mân III (circa A.D. 580–602), who was thrown under an elephant's feet for an offence against the Sassanian emperor. Note the chess terms: *asp*, knight; *piyâda*, pawn; *nat'*, chessboard; *rukh*, rook; *pîl*, bishop; *shâhmât*, checkmate.

⁶The Sassanian crown was embellished with the three Zoroastrian principles of good: *pindâr-i nêk* (good thought), *raftâr-i nêk* (good conduct), and *guftâr-i nêk* (good words).

⁷Khusraw Parvez had golden citrons and leeks at his banquet table. See the next line.

⁸Kam *tarakû* (Koran 44:25), "How many [gardens and fountains] did they leave behind them!" Note the puns on *kamtar gú*, *tara kû*, and *kam tarakû*, and on *bar khwân* and *bárkhwân*.

خون دل شیرینست آن می که دهد رزین

ز آب و گل پرویزست این خم که نهد دهقان

٢٠

چندین تنِ جبّاران کاین خاك فرو خوردست

این گرسنه‌چشم آخر هم سیر نشد زیشان

از خون دل طفل سرخاب رخ آمیزد   این زالِ سپید ابرو وین مامِ سیه‌پستان

خاقانی، ازین درگه دریوزهٔ عبرت کن   تا از در تو زین پس دریوزه کند خاقان

اخوان که ز ره آیند آرند ره‌آوردی   این قطعه ره‌آوردیست از بهر دل اخوان

بنگر که در این قطعه چه سحر همی‌راند

معتوه مسیحادل دیوانهٔ عاقل‌جان[1]

NIZÂMÎ
نظامی

The most brilliant composer of the Persian romantic epic, Ilyâs b. Yûsuf Nizâmî (1141–1209) led a quiet life in his native Ganja (modern Gyandzha, formerly Kirovabad, Azerbaijan), far removed from court life, and his lasting fame rests on his five *masnavîs* known collectively as the Quintet *(Khamsa)*.

The first, *Makhzanu'l-asrâr* (Treasure of Mysteries), dating from 1176, is an ethico-philosophical treasure house of maxims and advice somewhat after the manner of Sana'i's *Hadîqa*. With his second masnavi, *Khusraw u Shîrîn* (composed between 1177 and 1181), Nizâmî begins the romance proper; it is the story of an Armenian princess, Shirin, and her royal lover and husband, Khusraw Parvez. Interwoven with Shirin's love and sorrow is the tragic Farhâd, who, desperately in love with Shirin yet spurned by her, is given the Herculean task of carving a milk-channel through Mount Bîsutûn, where he dies of a broken heart.

In *Laylî u Majnûn* (1188), the old Arabian story of the tragic love of Layli and Qays is evolved into epic proportions. Forbidden to marry each other, Layli is wedded to another while Qays goes mad (hence nicknamed Majnûn, "crazy") and wanders through the desert singing

---

[1]The second hemistich contains a chronogram for the date of completion. The first six letters (m = 40, ' = 70, t = 400, w = 6, h = 5, m = 40) add up to 561, the Hegira date. Taking the next part, *sîhâ* to mean 30 *h*'s (*h* = 8, 8 x 30 = 240), an additional 240 is added to 561, giving 801. Adding to this the numerical value of the rest of the hemistich, 365, the total is 1166, the Christian date. Taken literally, "a delirious person with a Christian heart, a madman with a rational soul," the line does not make overmuch sense, but it indicates that a Christian date is to be found embedded therein.

exquisite lyrics to his beloved Layli. The two selections given here are
from this book, the first describing Layli's deathbed, where she con-
fesses her undying love for Majnun and commends her beloved to her
mother. This selection shows Nizâmî's characteristic development of an
extended metaphor, usually drawn from nature, to introduce and set
the mood for the action or plot development that follows.

Nizâmî's other two masnavis are *Haft paykar* (Seven Beauties), dat-
ing from 1197, a potpourri of episodes centered on the idealized Sas-
sanian Bahram Gor and on a framework story of the prince's love for
the seven princesses of the seven climes. The fifth book, in two parts,
Sharafnâma and *Khiradnâma*, deals with the exploits of the idealized
and romanticized Alexander of Pseudo-Callisthenes.

Nizâmî's *Khamsa* ended the chivalric epic tradition of the *Shâh-
nâma* and paved the way for the lyric epic and its subtle psychology to
be adapted by the mystics. Nizâmî's absolute control over the Persian
language and his use of compounds and learned double-entendres
sometimes make his poetry difficult to understand; nonetheless, his im-
agery and power of depiction have been often imitated but seldom ri-
valed.

شرط است که وقت برگریزان	خونابه شود ز برگ ریزان
خونی که بود درونِ هر شاخ	بیرون چکد از مسام سوراخ
قارورهٔ آب سرد گردد ١	رخسارهٔ باغ زرد گردد
شاخ آبله هلاک یابد	زر جوید برگ ، ٢ خاک یابد
نرکس بجمازه بر نهد رخت	شمشاد در افتد از سر تخت　٥
سیمای سمن شکست گیرد	گل نامهٔ غم بدست گیرد
بر فرق چمن کلالهٔ خاک	پیچیده شود چو مار ضحاك
چون باد مخالف آید از دور	افتادنِ برگ هست معذور
کآنان که ز غرقگه گریزند	ز اندیشهٔ باد رخت ریزند
نازك جگرانِ باغ ، رنجور	شیرین نمکانِ تاك ، مخمور　١٠

---

[1]In medieval medicine, the first step in diagnosis was an examination of a urine
specimen. If the examination revealed that the cold nature was predominant, i.e., out
of balance with the hot, wet, and dry natures, it was a very bad sign.

[2]From Nizâmî's time on, it is safe to assume that if the normal word order of
Persian (subject–object–verb) is changed in any way, the subject of the verb will fol-
low the object, as here: *zar jûyad barg*, where *barg* is the subject of *jûyad* and *zar* is
the object. There are, of course, exceptions to this general observation.

انداخته هندوی کدیور
سرهای نهی ز طرهٔ کاخ
سیب از زنخی بدان نگونی
نار از جگر کفیدهٔ خویش
بر پسته که شد دهن‌دریده
در معرکهٔ چنین خزانی

زنگی بچگانِ تاک را سر[1]
آویخته هم بطرهٔ شاخ
بر نار زنخزنان که «چونی؟»
خونابه چکانده بر دل ریش
عناب ز دورِ لب گزیده ۱۵
شد زخم رسیده گلستانی

لیلی ز سریر سربلندی
شد چشم‌زده بهار باغش
آن سر که عصابهای زر بست
گشت آن تن نازک قصب‌پوش
شد بدرِ مهیش چون هلالی
سودای دلش بسر درآمد
گرمای تموز ژاله را برد
تب لرزه شکست پیکرش را
بالین طلبید زاد سروش
افتاد چنانکه دانه از کشت
بر مادر خویش راز بگشاد
«کای مادر مهربان، چه تدبیر؟
در کوچگه اوفتاد رختم
خون میخورم، این چه مهربانیست؟
چندان جگر نهفته خوردم
چون جان ز لبم نفس گشاید
چون پرده ز راز برگرفتم
در گردنم آر دست یکبار
کان لحظه که جان سپرده باشم
سرمم[3] ز غبار دوست درکش
فرقم ز گلابِ اشک تر کن

افتاد بچاه دردمندی
زد باد تپانچه بر چراغش
خود را بعصابه دگر بست[2]
چون تار قصب ضعیف و بی‌توش ۲۰
وآن سروِ سهیش چون خیالی
سرسامِ سرش بدل برآمد
باد آمد و برگ لاله را برد
تبخاله گزیدِ شکرش را
وز سرو فتاده شد تذروش ۲۵
سربند قصب برخ فرو هشت
یکباره در نیاز بگشاد
کآهوبره زهر خورد با شیر
چون سست شدم، مگیر سختم
جان میکنم، این چه زندگانیست؟ ۳۰
کز دل بدهن رسید دردم
گر راز گشاده گشت، شاید
پدرود که راه درگرفتم
خون من و گردنِ تو زنهار
وز دوریِ دوست مرده باشم، ۳۵
نیلم ز نیاز دوست برکش
عطرم ز شمامهٔ جگر کن

---

[1] The sun-burnt "Hindu" farmer has lobbed off the heads of the "Negroid children of the vine," the grapes.

[2] Layli's head, which used to be wound in golden turbans, is now bound in linen bandages.

[3] *Surma-m* for *surma-am*.

برند حنوطم از گل زرد   کافور فشانم از دم سرد

خون کن کفنم که من شهیدم   تا باشد رنگ روز عیدم

آراسته کن عروس وارم¹   بسپار بخاک پرده‌دارم ۴۰

آوارهٔ من² چو گردد آگاه   کآواره شدم من از وطنگاه،

دانم که ز راه سوگواری   آید بسلام این عماری

چون بر سر خاک من نشیند   مه جوید لیک خاک بیند

یاریست، عجب عزیز یاریست   از من ببر تو یادگاریست

بر خاک من آن غریب خاکی   نالد بدریغ و دردناکی ۴۵

از بهر خدا نکوش داری   در وی نکنی نظر بخواری

آن دل که نیابیش بجوئی   وآن قصه که دانیَش بگوئی

من داشته‌ام عزیزوارش   تو نیز چو من عزیز دارش

گو³ لیلی ازین سرای دلگیر   آن لحظه که می‌برید زنجیر

در مهر تو تن بخاک می‌داد   بر یاد تو جان پاک می‌داد ۵۰

در عاشقی تو صادقی کرد   جان در سر کار عاشقی کرد

احوال چه پرسی‌ام که چون رفت   با عشق تو از جهان برون رفت

تا داشت در این جهان شماری   جز با غم تو نداشت کاری

وآن لحظه که در غم تو می‌مرد   غمهای تو راه‌توشه می‌برد

وامروز که در نقاب خاکست   هم در هوس تو دردناکست ۵۵

چون منتظران درین گذرگاه   هست از قبل تو چشم بر راه

می‌پاید تا تو در پی آئی   سربازپس است تا کی آئی

یکره برهان از انتظارش⁴   درخز بخزینهٔ کنارش٥

این گفت و بگریه دیده تر کرد   وآهنگ ولایت دگر کرد

چون راز نهفته بر زبان داد   جانان طلبید و زود جان داد ۶۰

مادر که عروس را چنان دید   گویا که قیامت آن زمان دید

معجر ز سر سپید بگشاد   موی چو سمن بباد برداد

در حسرت روی و موی فرزند   بر میزد و موی و روی می‌کند

هر مویه که بود خواندش از بر   هر موی که داشت کندش از سر

پیران گریست بر جوانیش   خون ریخت بر آب زندگانیش ۶۵

---

¹Ârâsta-kun...am = marâ ârâsta-kun.

²Âvâra-i man, she means Majnun.

³The following words, down through line 58, are the message Layli's mother is to deliver to Majnun.

⁴Birahân...ash = birahân-ash.

كه ريخت سرشك بر سرينش　　كه روى نهاد بر جبينش

چندان ز سرشكهاش خون رُست　　كآن چشمهٔ آب را بخون شست

چندان ز غمش بمهر ناليد　　كز نالهٔ او سپهر ناليد

آن نوحه كه خون شود بدو سنگ　　مى‌كرد بر آن عقيق گلرنگ ١

مهرا ز ستاره طوق بريست　　صندوق جگر هم از جگر بست ٢ ٧٠

آراستش آنچنان كه فرمود　　گل را بگلاب و عنبر آلود

بسپرد بخاك و نامدش باك　　كآسايش خاك هست در خاك

خاتونِ حصار شد حصارى　　آسود غم از خزينه‌دارى

The following selection, also from *Laylî u Majnûn*, is on Majnun's death at Layli's tomb.

انگشت‌كشان ، سخن‌سرايان　　اين قصه چنين برد به پايان

كآن سوخته‌خرمنِ زمانه　　شد خرمنى از سرشك دانه

دستآسِ فلك شكسَت خُردش　　چون خرد شكست ، باز بردش

زآن حال كه بود زارتر گشت　　بى‌زورتر و نزارتر گشت

جانى ز قدم رسيده تا لب ٣　　روزى بستم رسيده تا شب ٥

نالنده ز روى دردناكى　　آمد سوى آن عروسِ خاكى

در حلقهٔ آن حظيره افتاد　　كشتيش در آب تيره افتاد

غلطيد چو مور خسته‌كرده　　پيچيد چو مار زخم‌خورده

بيتى دو سه زار زار برخواند　　اشكى دو سه تلخ تلخ بفشاند ٤

برداشت بسوى آسمان دست　　انگشت گشاد و ديده بريست ١٠

«كاى خالقِ هرچه آفريدست ٥　　سوگند بهرچه برگزيدست

كز محنتِ خويش وا رهانم ٦　　در حضرت يارِ خود رسانم

آزاد كنم ز سخت جانى　　و آباد كنم به سخت رانى»

---

[1]Rose-colored agate = the lip.

[2]The moon is the face; the stars are tears; the liver is the seat of emotions and passion.

[3]*Jân...rasîda tâ lab:* for the soul to be on the lips is a common idiom for imminent death.

[4]For the meter, read *bif'shând.*

[5]For the meter, read *âfarîda 'st* for *âfarîda ast.* The sense here is "is created," not "has created;" and so also *barguzîda 'st* in the next hemistich.

[6]*Vâ-rahân-am:* -am is the direct object of the imperative *vâ-rahân,* and so also *rasân-am* and, in the next line, *âzâd kun-am* and *âbâd kun-am. Khwêsh* and *khwad* in line 12 refer to the speaker and mean "my."

وان تربت‌را گرفت در بر   این گفت و نهاد بر زمین سر

۱۵ «ای دوست» بگفت و جان برآورد   چون تربت دوست در بر آورد

وان کیست که نگذرد برین راه؟   او نیز گذشت ازین گذرگاه،

از آفت قطع او نرستند   راهیست عدم که هرچه هستند

خاریدهٔ ناخن ستم نیست   ریشی نه که^۱ غورگاه غم نیست

از شورگنی نشد نمک‌سود؟   کو زخم که در کباب این دود

۲۰ کهتاب ز روی کهربارنگ   ای چون خر آسیا کهن لنگ

کو دور شد از خلاص مردان   دوری کن ازین خراس گردان

سیل آمد، سیل، خیز، منشین   در خانهٔ سیلریز منشین

زین پل بجهان جمازه بیرون   تا پل نشکست بر تو گردون

آهسته مران که کاروان رفت   بشتاب که راحت از جهان رفت

۲۵ این پیر زنست کاژدها اوست   آن پیرزنی که اژدهاخوست

چون روی نماید، اژدهائیست   تا رخ ننمایدت، همائیست

جوید ز پی گریز راهی   عاقل که رسد به حبسگاهی

ره جوی که راه دانی آخر   در حبسگه جهانی آخر

با طبع مساز کو شراریست   در خاک مپیچ کو غباریست

۳۰ تا بر سر آسمان کنی جای   بر پایهٔ قدر خویش نه^۲ پای

سیلی خور و روی بر مگردان   از سیل چو کوه سر مگردان

هرجا که روی، لطف‌رسان باش   چون آب رونده خوشعنان باش

چون خاک مکن جهان‌پرستی   خاک تو شده جهان هستی

آن‌را مپرست کآن نماند   دایم بتو بر^۳ جهان نماند

۳۵ و افتادن خود بعجز بنمای   از مرکب خواجگی فرود آی

بر عاجزی تو رحمت آرد   تا شیر اجل چو زحمت آرد

---

¹*Rísh-i na ki...* "there is no wound that..."

²The imperative, *nih.*

³The prepositional phrase is *ba tu bar.*

POETS OF DIDACTIC MYSTICISM

SANÂ'Î
سنائی

First in the great triad of Persian mystics is Abu'l-Majd Majdûd Sanâ'î (d. 1130), followed by Attâr and Rûmî. Born in Ghazna or Balkh, Sanâ'î was a panegyrist to the later Ghaznavids until a spiritual conversion led him to devote the rest of his life to mysticism. His divan introduces the ghazal as a vehicle for mystical meditation, an element that permeated the ghazal for centuries after him. He is also responsible for the intro-duction of asceticism and mysticism into the masnavi, a model that at-tained full bloom with Attâr and Rûmî. Sanâ'î's most famous mystical "epic" is the Hadîqatu'l-haqîqat (The Garden of Truth), completed the year of his death. It is a loose collection of parables and excursuses on reason, gnosis, trust in God, love, philosophy, heaven and hell, etc.—in short, on all topics embraced by Sufism. The accolades heaped by con-temporary and later generations of mystics on this book do not accord with the general Western assessment as sloppy and devoid of great po-etical value as a whole, but the Persian reader is not so interested in a tight, controlled structure as in the insights and inspiration that can be gained by perusal of and meditation on a given section.

The first selection, taken from the Hadîqat, is a typical parable, which would be followed by an elaboration of the moral implications and inferences to be drawn. The second selection, from the divan, is a mystically oriented ghazal exhorting the immortal soul to rise above the prison of the material world.

زآن جهان دیدگان پرهنران	قصهٔ یاد دارم از پدران
مهستی نام دختری و سه گاو	داشت زالی بروستای تکاو
گشت روزی ز چشم بد نالان	نوعروسی چو سرو تر بالان
شد جهان پیش پیرزن تاریک	گشت بدرش چو ماه نو باریک
که نیازی جز او نداشت دگر ۵	دلش آتش گرفت و سوخت جگر
«پیش تو باد مردن مادر»[1]	زال گفتی همیشه با دختر

---

[1] For the tense of guftî, see ITP §87. Pêsh-i tu = pêsh az tu.

37

از قضا گاو زالک از پی خورد
پوز روزی بدیگش اندر کرد

ماند چون پای مقعد اندر ریگ
آن سر مرده‌ریگش اندر دیگ

گاو ماند دیوی از دوزخ
سوی آن زال تاخت از مطبخ

زال پنداشت هست عزرائیل
بانگ برداشت از پی تهویل　۱۰

«کای مقلموت، من نه مهستیم
من یکی زالِ پیرِ محنتیم

تن‌درستم من و نِیَم بیمار
تو خدارا مرا بدو مشمار

گر تِرا مهستی همی‌باید،
آنک اورا ببر. مِرا شاید»[1]

تا بدانی که وقت پیچاپیچ
هیچکس مر تِرا نباشد هیچ

✳

بس که شنیدی صفت روم و چین
خیز و بیا، ملک سنائی ببین

تا همه دل بینی بی‌حرص و بخل
تا همه جا بینی بی‌کبر و کین

زر نه و[2] کانِ ملکی زیر دست
جو نه و اسب فلکی زیر زین

پای نه و چرخ به زیر قدم
دست نه و ملک به زیر نگین

رخت کیانی نه و او روح‌وار
تخت برآورده به چرخ برین

سلوت او خلوتی اندر نهان
دعوت او دولتی اندر کمین

بوده چو یوسف به چه و رفته باز
تا فلک از جذبهٔ حبل‌المتین

زیر قدم کرده از اقلیم شک
تا به نهانخانهٔ عین‌الیقین

با نفسش سحرنمایان هند
در هوسش چهره‌گشایان چین[3]

عافیتی دارد و خرسندیی
اینت[4] حقیقت ملک راستین

خشم نبودست بر اعداش هیچ
چشم ندیدست بر ابروش چین

خشم ز دشمن بود و حلم از او
کاین ز اثیر آمده، آن از زمین

ATTÂR
عطار

Following Sanâ'î's venture into the didactic mystical "epic," Farîduddîn Abû-Hâmid Muhammad Attâr (1142–ca. 1220), the druggist of Nisha-pur, elevated this genre to perfection by maintaining a balance of mysti-cism and the polished art of the story-teller. His most famous work,

---

[1]*Marâ shâyad*, "it's all right with me."

[2]*Zar na u*... "no gold, but..."

[3]The "portraitists of China" were renowned as the most extraordinary artists in the world.

[4]For the meter, read *în't* for *în-at.*

Mantiqu't-tayr (Language of the Birds), tells of the birds, who set out under the leadership of the hoopoe to find their king, the fabulous phoenix Sîmurgh. After most of them perish in the hardships of the seven valleys of inner perfection by progressive destruction of the self, thirty of them reach the Sîmurgh's palace only to discover that the Sî-murgh is, in fact, none other than themselves, the *sî murgh* (thirty birds) that remain.

In the *Musîbatnâma*, Attâr again traces the mystical progression of the soul through forty stages of seclusion on the mythic, cosmic, and physical planes. In the *Ilâhînâma* he speaks through a king who shows his six sons how to attain their fondest wishes through perfection of the self.

Attâr's divan abounds in poems that exhibit fervent raptures of ecstasy couched in the developing idiom of mysticism, like the drop subsumed into the ocean in the first ghazal given here.

کم شدم در خود چنان کز خویش ناپیدا شدم
شبنمی بودم ز دریا ، غرقه در دریا شدم

سایه‌ای بودم ز اول ، بر زمین افتاده خوار
راست کآن خورشید پیدا گشت ، ناپیدا شدم

زآمدن بس بی‌نشان و از شدن بس بی‌خبر
گوئیا یك دم برآمد کآمدم من یا شدم

نه ، مپرس از من سخن زیرا که چون پروانهٔ
در فروغ شمعِ رویِ دوست ناپروا شدم

در رهِ عشقش قدم درنه اگر با دانشی
لاجرم در عشق هم نادان و هم دانا شدم

چون همه تن دیده می‌بایست بود و کور گشت
این عجایب بین که چون بینای نابینا شدم

خاك بر فرقم اگر یك ذره دارم آگهی
تا کجاست آنجا که من سرگشته‌دل آنجا شدم

چون دل عطار بیرون دیدم از هر دو جهان
من ز تاثیر دل او بیدل و شیدا شدم

✳

پگه می‌رفت استاد مهینه
کسی گفتش «بسی آهسته‌کاری.

خری می‌برد بارش آبگینه
بدین آهستگی بر خر چه داری؟»

که گر خر می‌بیفتد ، هیچ دارم»	«چه دارم؟» گفت «دل پر پیچ دارم
ببین کاین هیچ‌را صد گونه پیچ‌ست	چو پی بر باد دارد عمر، هیچست
چو مرگ آید بجان تو که بادست	چنین عمری کزو جان تو شادست

❈

از پای در افتادم و خون شد جگر من	ای همنفسان تا اجل آمد بسر من
نه هست امیدم که کس آید ببر من	رفتم نه چنان کآمدنم روی بود ، نیز
وز خاک بپرسند نشان و خبر من	یا چون ز پس مرگ من آیند زمانی
چه سود؟ که یک ذره نیابند اثر من	گر خاک زمین جمله بغربال ببیزند
جز من که بداند که چه آمد بسر من؟ ٥	من دانم و من حال خود اندر لحد تنگ
رستند کنون از من و از درد سر من	بسیار ز من درد دل و رنج کشیدند
تا روز شمار این همه غم در شمر من	غمهای دلم بر که شمارم؟ که نیاید
بردند بتاراج همه سیم و زر من	من دست تهی با دل پر درد برفتم
نه شام پدیدست کنون، نه سحر من	در ناز بسی شام و سحر خوردم و خفتم
بربندد اجل نیز شمارا کمر من ١٠	غافل منشینید چنین زانک یکی روز
تا روز قیامت که درآید ز در من؟	بر من همه درها چو فرو بست اجل سخت
بی‌مرکب و بی‌زاد ، دریغا سفر من	در بادیه‌ای ماندم تا روز قیامت
دم می‌توان زد ز ره پرخطر من	از بسکه خطر هست درین راه مرا پیش
امروز فرو ریخت همه بال و پر من	دی تازه تذروی بُدم اندر چمن لطف
تابوت شد امروز مقام و مقر من ١٥	دی در مقر عزّ بصد ناز نشسته
یک ذره خبر از من و از خیر و شر من	دردا و دریغا که درین درد ندانید
آن دیدهٔ بینا و دل راهبر من	دردا و دریغا که ندانم که کجا شد
در پرده شد آوازِ خوش پرده‌درِ من	دردا و دریغا که ز آهنگ فرو ماند
از درج صدف ریخته شد سی گهر من	دردا و دریغا که چو در شست فتادم
همچون گلِ سرخ آن لب همچون شکر من ٢٠	دردا و دریغا که بصد درد فرو ریخت
تا شد چو گل زرد رخ چون قمر من	دردا و دریغا که مرا خوار نهادند
در خاک لحد ریخت همه برگ و بر من	دردا و دریغا که بیک باد جهانسوز
از دفتر عمر آیت عقل و بصر من	دردا و دریغا که ستردند بیک بار
بر خاک فرو ریخت همه خشک و تر من	دردا و دریغا که هم از خشک و تر ایام
تا کی نگرد در دل من دادگر من ٢٥	عطار دلی دارد و آن نیز بخون غرق
حقا که نیاید دو جهان در نظر من	گر حق بدلم یک نظر لطف رساند

MAWLAVÎ
مولوی

Mawlânâ Jalâluddîn Muhammad (1207–1273) was born to an ancient scholarly family in Balkh (modern Afghanistan). His father, Bahâ'uddîn Valad, fled with his family before the Mongol invasion, circa 1220, via Damascus to Konya in Anatolia (Rûm), hence Mawlavî's epithet, Rûmî, by which he is known in the West.

Rumi underwent a radical transformation of character after meeting a dervish named Shamsuddîn of Tabriz. So completely did he identify with Shamsuddîn, who vanished under mysterious circumstances in 1247, that the poet wrote his divan, the *Dîvân-i Shams*, in his beloved teacher's name. Dictated largely from enraptured trances, Rumi's lyric poetry is the most perfect example of the spontaneous outpouring of mystical love and visionary ecstasy in Persian—perhaps even in world literature.

صد بار ترا گفتم کم خور دو سه پیمانه   من مست و تو دیوانه. مارا که برد خانه؟

هر یك بتر از دیگر، شوریده و دیوانه   در شهر یکی کس را هشیار نمی‌بینم

جان را چه خوشی باشد بی‌صحبت جانانه؟   جانا، بخرابات آی تا لذت جان بینی

زآن ساقی سرمستی با ساغر شاهانه   هر گوشه یکی مستی، دستی زده بر دستی

٥   ای پیش چو تو مستی،¹ افسون من افسانه   ای لولی بربطزن، تو مستتری یا من؟

زین دخل بهشیاران مسپار یکی دانه   تو وقف خراباتی، خرجت می و دخلت می

در هر نظرش مضمر صد گلشن و کاشانه   از خانه برون رفتم، مستیم به پیش آمد²

وز حسرت آن، مرده صد عاقل فرزانه   چون کشتی بی‌لنگر کژ میشد و مژ³ میشد

نیمیم ز ترکستان، نیمیم ز فرغانه   گفتم «ز کجائی تو؟» تسخر⁴ زد و گفت «ای جان،

١٠   نیمیم لب دریا، باقی همه دُردانه»   نیمیم ز آب و گل، نیمیم ز جان و دل

گفتا که «بنشناسم من خویش ز بیگانه»   گفتم که «رفیقی کن با من که منت خویشم»

یک سینه سخن دارم، آن شرح دهم یا نه؟   من بی‌سر و دستارم، در خانه خمارم

✳

---

[1]*Chu tu mast-î*, "a drunk like you," is one syntactic unit and functions here as the complement of *pêsh-i*. In Persian it is possible, as here, to combine the entire construction *pêsh-i chu tu mast-î* with the vocative *ay*; in English the construction is too involved to incorporate the vocative too.

[2]*Mast-î'm ba pêsh âmad = mast-î ba pêsh-am âmad.*

[3]*Mazh* is a rhyming doublet with *kazh* and has no meaning on its own.

[4]For the meter, read *tas'khur* for *tasakhkhur*.

بنمای رخ که باغ و گلستانم آرزوست¹   بگشای لب که قند فراوانم آرزوست

ای آفتابِ حسن، برون آ دمی ز ابر   کآن چهرهٔ مشعشعِ تابانم آرزوست

بشنیدم از هوای تو آوازِ طبلِ باز   باز آمدم که ساعدِ سلطانم آرزوست

گفتی ز ناز «بیش مرنجان مرا، برو»   آن گفتنت که «بیش مرنجانم» آرزوست

وان دفع گفتنت که «برو، شه بخانه نیست»   وان نازِ وباز² و تندیِ دربانم آرزوست ۵

در دستِ هرکسیست ز خوبی قراضه‌ها   آن معدنِ ملاحت و آن کانم آرزوست

این نان و آبِ چرخ چو سیلست بیوفا   من ماهیَم، نهنگم، عمانم آرزوست

یعقوب‌وار وا اَسفاها همی‌زنم   دیدارِ خوبِ یوسفِ کنعانم آرزوست

والله که شهر بی‌تو مرا حبس می‌شود   آوارگی به کوه و بیابانم آرزوست

زین همرهانِ سست‌عناصر دلم گرفت   شیرِ خدا و رستمِ دستانم آرزوست ۱۰

جانم ملول گشت ز فرعون و ظلمِ او   آن نورِ رویِ موسیِ عمرانم آرزوست

زین خلقِ پرشکایتِ گریان شدم ملول   آن های وهویِ و نعرهٔ مستانم آرزوست

گویاترم ز بلبل، امّا ز رشکِ عام   مُهر است بر دهانم و افغانم آرزوست

دی شیخ با چراغ همی‌گشت گردِ شهر   کز دیو و دد ملولم و انسانم آرزوست

گفتند یافت می‌نشود، جُسته‌ایم ما   گفت آنک یافت می‌نشود آنم آرزوست ۱۵

هرچند مفلسم، نپذیرم عقیقِ خرد   کان عقیقِ نادرِ ارزانم آرزوست

پنهان ز دیده‌ها و همه دیده‌ها از اوست   آن آشکارصنعتِ پنهانم آرزوست

خودِ کارِ من گذشت ز هر آرزو و آز   از کون و از مکان پیِ ارکانم آرزوست

گوشم شنید قصهٔ ایمان و مست شد   کو قسمِ چشم؟ صورتِ ایمانم آرزوست

یک دست جامِ باده و یک دستِ جعدِ یار   رقصی چنین میانهٔ میدانم آرزوست ۲۰

باقیِ این غزل‌را، ای مطربِ ظریف،   زینسان همی‌شمار که زینسانم آرزوست

بنمای، شمسِ مفخرِ تبریز، رو ز شرق   من هدهدم،³ حضورِ سلیمانم آرزوست

✳

ای قوم بحجّ رفته، کجائید؟ کجائید؟   معشوق همینجاست. بیائید! بیائید!

معشوقِ تو همسایه و دیوار بدیوار   در بادیه سرگشته شما در چه هوائید؟

گر صورتِ بی‌صورتِ معشوق ببینید   هم خواجه و هم خانه و هم کعبه شمائید

ده بار ازان راه بدان خانه برفتید   یک بار ازین خانه برین بام برآئید

آن خانه لطیفست، نشانهاش بگفتید   از خواجهٔ آن خانه نشانی بنمائید

---

[1] *-am ârzû-st* "...is my desire."

[2] Here *bâz* is simply a rhyming doublet with *nâz*.

[3] *Hudhud*: the hoopoe was Solomon's scout, guide, and messenger.

یك دستهٔ گل کو اگر آن باغ بدیدید؟ یك گوهرِ جان کو اگر از بحر خدائید؟

با اینهمه آن رنجِ شما گنجِ شما باد افسوسَ که بر گنجِ شما پردَه شمائید

*

عقل آمد ، عاشقا ، خودرا بپوش وایِ ما ، ای وایِ ما از عقل و هوش

یا برو از جمعِ ما ، ای چشم و عقل یا شویم از ننگِ تو بی‌چشم و گوش

تو چو آیی ز آتشِ ما دور شو یا درآ در دیگِ ما ، با ما بجوش

گر نمی‌خواهی که خُردت بشکند مرده شو ، با موج و با دریا مکوش

گر بگوئی عاشقم هست امتحان سر مپیچ و رطلِ مردان‌را بنوش

میخروشم لیك از مستیِ عشق همچو چنگم بی‌خبر من از خروش

شمس تبریزی ، مرا کردی خراب هم تو ساقی ، هم تو می ، هم می‌فروش

If the almost 40,000-line divan were not enough to rank Mawlavî as the greatest overtly mystical poet in Persian, his voluminous *Masnavî-i ma'navî* (The Masnavi of Intrinsic Meaning), an encyclopedia of Sufism consisting of about 27,000 couplets, has been called "the Koran in the Pahlavi tongue." The opening canto of the *Masnavî* is given here. It is followed by a very short, amusing vignette.

بشنو از نی چون حکایت می‌کند از جدائیها شکایت می‌کند

کز نیستان تا مرا ببریده‌اند[1] از نفیرم مرد و زن نالیده‌اند

سینه خواهم شرحه شرحه از فراق تا بگویم شرحِ دردِ اشتیاق

هرکسی کو دور ماند از اصل خویش باز جوید روزگارِ وصل خویش

من بهرِ جمعیتی نالان شدم جفتِ بدحالان و خوشحالان شدم ۵

هرکسی از ظنِ خود شد یار من وز درونِ من نجُست اسرار من

سرِّ من از نالهٔ من دور نیست لیك چشم و گوش‌را آن نور نیست

تن ز جان و جان ز تن مستور نیست لیك کس‌را دیدِ جان دستور نیست

آتشست این بانگِ نای و نیست باد هرکه این آتش ندارد نیست باد[2]

آتشِ عشقست کاندر نی فتاد جوشش عشقست کاندر می فتاد ۱۰

---

[1]K'az = ki az; the conjunction ki introduces the words of the flute, which continue to the end. For the meter, read *bub'rîda* for *biburîda*.

[2]In the first hemistich *nîst bâd* is the verb *nîst* and the noun *bâd*; in the second, *bâd* is the verb, "may he be," and *nîst* is an adjective, "nonexistent."

پرده‌هایش پرده‌های۱ ما درید   نی حریفِ هرکه از یاری برید۲

همچو نی دمساز و مشتاقی که دید؟   همچو نی زهری و تریاقی که دید؟

قصه‌های عشق مجنون می‌کند   نی حدیثِ راه پرخون می‌کند

مر زبان‌را مشتری جز گوش نیست   محرم این هوش جز بیهوش نیست

۱۵   روزها با سوزها همراه شد   در غمِ ما روزها بیگاه شد

روزها گر رفت، گو «رو، باك نیست،» تو بمان، ای آنکه چون تو۳ پاك نیست

هرکه بی‌روزیست روزش دیر شد   هرکه جز ماهی ز آبش سیر شد۴

پس سخن کوتاه باید والسلام   در نیابد حالِ پخته هیچ خام

✳

بهرِ طاعت راکع و ساجد شدند   چار هندو در یکی مسجد شدند

در نماز آمد بمسکینی و درد   هر یکی بر نیّتی تکبیر کرد

«کای مؤذّن، بانگ کردی؟ وقت هست؟»   مؤذّن آمد. زان یکی لفظی بجَست

«هی، سخن گفتی و باطل شد نماز»   گفت آن هندوی دیگر از نیاز

چه زنی طعنه به او؟ خودرا بگو!»   آن سوم گفت آن دوم‌را «کای عمو،

درنیفتادم بچَه چون این سه تن»   آن چهارم گفت «حمدالله که من

عیب‌گویان بیشتر گم کرده راه   پس نمازِ هر چهاران شد تباه

هرکه عیبی گفت آن بر خود خرید   ای خنک‌جانی که عیبِ خویش دید،

✳

In the following selection from the *Masnaví*, a king has welcomed into his palace a "spiritual" physician, who he hopes will be able to cure his ailing favorite.

دست او بگرفت و برد اندر حرم   چون گذشت آن مجلس و خوان کرم

بعد ازان در پیشِ رنجورش نشاند   قصهٔ رنجور و رنجوری بخواند

هم علاماتش هم اسبابش شنید   رنگ و رو و نبض و قاروره بدید

آن عمارت نیست. ویران کرده‌اند   گفت «هر دارو که ایشان کرده‌اند

---

[1] The first *parda* means "musical note"; the second, "veil." See *parda-darídan* in the vocabulary.

[2] *Buríd* is intransitive here: "has been cut off."

[3] *Ay án ki chun tu* "O you, like whom..."

[4] "Everyone, except a fish, gets tired of water."

استعیذ الله مِمّا یفترون[1]   بی‌خبر بودند از حال درون

لیك پنهان کرد و با سلطان نگفت   دید رنج و کشف شد بر وی نهفت

بوی هر هیزم پدید آید ز دود   رنجش از سودا و از صفرا نبود

تن خوشست و او گرفتار دلست   دید از زاریش کو زار دلست

نیست بیماری چو بیماریِ دل   عاشقی پیداست از زاریِ دل

عشق اصطرلاب اسرارِ خداست   علت عاشق ز علت‌ها جداست

عاقبت مارا بدان سر رهبرست   عاشقی گر زین سر و گر زان سرست

چون بعشق آیم خجل باشم ازان   هرچ گویم عشق را شرح و بیان،

لیك عشق بی‌زبان روشنترست   گرچه تفسیر زبان روشنگرست

چون بعشق آمد قلم بر خود شکافت   چون قلم اندر نوشتن می‌شتافت

شرحِ عشق و عاشقی هم عشق گفت   عقل در شرحش چو خر در گل بخفت

گر دلیلت باید، از وی رو متاب   آفتاب آمد دلیل آفتاب

IRÂQÎ
عراقی

Fakhruddîn Ibrâhîm Irâqî of Hamadan (circa 1213–1289) studied with masters of Sufism from the Punjab to the Hejaz to Damascus, and his gnostic bent is clearly reflected in his verse. A student of Sadruddîn of Konya, who knew Mawlavî and was a disciple of the great theosophist of Murcia, Ibn al-Arabî, Irâqî combines the ecstatic outpourings of Rumi with the philosophical background of Ibn al-Arabi's essential monism. His *Lama'ât* (Lightning Flashes) is a profound and at the same time highly poetic investigation into the mystical love relationship.

The first ghazal given here shows the maturity the idiom of mysticism has reached by this time. The second is taken from his masnavi *Ushshâqnâma*, a simpler treatment of much the same material covered in the more obtuse *Lama'ât*.

ز چشمِ مستِ ساقی وام کردند   نخستین باده کاندر جام کردند

شراب بیخودی در جام کردند   چو با خود یافتند اهلِ طرب را

شراب عاشقانش نام کردند   لب میگون جانان جام درداد

ز بس دلها که بی‌آرام کردند   سرِ زلفِ بُتان آرام نگرفت

بجامی کارِ خاص و عام کردند   بمجلس نیك و بدرا جای دادند   ۵

---

[1] *Asta'îzu 'llâha mimmâ yaftarûn* (Ar.), "I seek refuge in God from what they falsely devise."

بیك جولانِ دو عالم رام كردند	چو گویِ حسن در میدان فكندند
مهیا شكَّر و بادام كردند	ز بهرِ نُقلِ مستان از لب و چشم
نصیبِ بیدلان دشنام كردند	ازآن لب كآرزویِ جمله دلهاست
سرِ زلفین خودرا دام كردند	دلیرا تا بدست آرند هردم
بدل ز ابرو دوصد پیغام كردند	بغمزه صد سخن گفتند با جان	۱۰
جهانیرا ازآن اعلام كردند	نهان با محرمی رازی بگفتند
بهم كردند و عشقش نام كردند	بعالم هركجا درد و غمی بود
عراقیرا چرا بدنام كردند؟	چو خود كردند رازِ خویشتن فاش

❋

هست روشن بنورِ الرحمان[1]	خانههایِ تن از دریچهٔ جان
پرتوِ نورِ اوست روحِ امین	هست او نورِ آسمان و زمین
مغزِ جانش برای آن نورست	هركرا در میانِ جان نورست
شامِ مشكوةرا بَدَل بصباح	كند اندر زجاجهٔ مصباح[2]
آهن از آتش آتشین باشد	جان چو با نور همنشین باشد	۵
نیك ازان روز گشت مارا كار	دوست تشبیه نور كرد بنار
بصرمرا بصیرت افزاید	چون كه معشوق رویِ بنماید
تا بنورِ خدای مینگرد	هیچكس زان نظر سبق نبرد
انَّهُ ناظرٌ بنورِ الله[3]	گر تو كردی بچشمِ خویش نگاه
چشم و گوش و زبان و مغزِ تو اوست[4]	چون تقرب كنی بطاعتِ دوست	۱۰
پیشِ هستیِ او تو نیست شوی	چون بدو گویی و بدو شنوی
چون نگردد ستاره ناپیدا؟	چون ز خورشید شد ضیا پیدا،
رویِ او هم بدو توانی دید	هیچ طالب بخود درو نرسید
جان مگر هم بجان كند ادراك	خاكرا نیست ره بعالمِ پاك
نیشِ اندیشه در دلش نوشت	در ثنایش كسی كه خاموشست	۱۵

---

[1]Nûru'r-rahmân (Ar.), "the light of the Merciful."

[2]Allusions to the Light Verse (Kor. 24:35): "The similitude of his light is as niche in a wall (mishkât), wherein a lamp (misbâh) is placed, and the lamp enclosed in a case of glass (zujâja); the glass appears as it were a shining star."

[3]Innahu nâzirun bi nûri'llâh (Ar.), "he sees through the light of God."

[4]A reference to the "hadîth of supererogation": "My servant continues to draw nigh unto Me through acts of supererogation until I love him, and when I love him I am the ear by which he hears, the eye by which he sees, and the tongue by which he speaks."

POETS OF THE MONGOL AND TIMURID PERIODS

SA'DÎ
سعدی

Shaykh Mushrifuddîn Sa'dî of Shiraz (ca. 1200–ca. 1292) travelled widely throughout the western Islamic world, studied at the Nizamiyya in Baghdad, was held prisoner by the Crusaders in Tripoli, preached in the major cities, and, in short, saw and heard much of the world. All this experience and the wisdom acquired thereby he compressed into two works universally acknowledged as masterpieces, the *Bûstân* and the *Gulistân*. The *Bûstân* "contains within its ten sections of facile and often beautiful verse, dissertations on justice, good government, beneficence, earthly and mystic love, humility, submissiveness, contentment, and other excellences." The *Gulistân* contains eight divisions, "each with its own cluster of gay and sombre stories, in that seductive inter-mixture of rhymed prose and verse which had...come to be regarded as the prerequisite of elegant composition." It is probably safe to say that, with the exceptions of Rumi's *Masnavî* and Firdawsî's *Shâhnâma*, no book holds a place of importance equal to these; and, inasmuch as the *Gulistân* was used for centuries as a primer for the schoolchildren of greater Iran, India, and Turkey, it has certainly been read more widely than any other book in the entire Muslim world, save of course the Koran.

However, it is in the realm of the lyric, the ghazal, that Sa'dî's major contribution to Persian poetry lies, for he was the first to popularize the ghazal as a vehicle for the treatment of human passion and to effect the transition away from the formal qasida. His ghazals are characterized by technical control, fluency of diction and a pleasing formality; and in the lyric ghazal he is judged to be excelled only by Hâfiz.

The first selection, a masnavi, is taken from the *Bûstân* and elaborates allegorically the self-sacrifice of the lover. The following ghazals are from several of the "books" into which Sa'dî divided his divan.

شنيدم كه پروانه با شمع گفت   شبی ياد دارم كه چشمم نخفت

كه "من عاشقم. گر بسوزم رواست.   ترا گريه و سوز باری چراست؟"

برفت انگبين يارِ شيرينِ من   بگفت "ای هوادار مسكين من،

47

چو شیرینی از من بدر می‌رود   چو فرهادم آتش بسر¹ می‌رود»

همی‌گفت و هر لحظه سیلاب درد   فرو می‌دویدش برخسار زرد   ۵

که «ای مدعی، عشق کار تو نیست که نه صبر داری، نه یارای ایست

تو بگریزی از پیش یك شعله خام   من استاده‌ام تا بسوزم تمام

ترا آتش عشق اگر پر بسوخت   مرا بین که از پای تا سر بسوخت»

همه شب در این گفتگو بود شمع   بدیدار او وقت اصحاب جمع

نرفته ز شب همچنان بهرهٔ   که ناگه بکشتش پریچهرهٔ   ۱۰

همی‌گفت و می‌رفت دودش بسر   که اینست پایان عشق، ای پسر

اگر عاشقی خواهی آموختن   بکشتن فرج یابی از سوختن

مکن گریه بر گور مقتول دوست   برو، خرمی کن که مقبول اوست

اگر عاشقی سر مشوی از مرض   چو سعدی فرو شوی دست از غرض

فدائی نداند ز مقصود جنگ   وگر بر سرش تیر بارند و سنگ   ۱۵

بدریا مرو، گفتمت زینهار   وگر می‌روی، تن بطوفان سپار

❋

بخت آئینه ندارم که درو می‌نگری   خاك بازار نیرزم که برو می‌گذری

من چنان عاشق رویت که ز خود بیخبرم   تو چنان فتنه خویشی که ز ما بیخبری

بچه مانند کنم در همه آفاق ترا؟   کآنچه در وهم من آید تو از‌آن خوبتری

برقع از پیش چنین روی نشاید برداشت   که بهر گوشه چشمی دل خلقی ببری

دیدهٔ‌را که بدیدار تو دل می‌نرود   هیچ علت نتوان گفت بجز بی‌بصری

گفتم از دست غمت سر بجهان در بنهم   چون توانم؟ که بهرجا بروم، در نظری

بفلك می‌رود آه سحر از سینهٔ ما   تو همی برنکنی دیده ز خواب سحری

خفتگان‌را خبر از محنت بیداران نیست   تا غمت پیش نیاید، غم مردم نخوری

هرچه در وصف تو گویند بزیبائی هست   عیبت آنست که هر روز بطبعی دگری

گر تو از پرده برون آئی و رخ بنمائی   پرده بر کار همه پرده‌نشینان بدری

عذر سعدی ننهد هرکه ترا نشناسد   حال دیوانه نداند که ندیدست پری

❋

یك روز بشیدائی در زلف تو آویزم   زان دو لب شیرینت صد شور بر انگیزم

گر قصد جفا داری، اینك من اینك سر   ور راه وفا داری، جان در قدمت ریزم

بس توبه و پرهیزم کز عشق تو باطل شد   من بعد بدان شرطم کز توبه بپرهیزم

---

¹Chu Farhâd-am âtash ba sar = chu Farhâd, âtash ba sar-am.

خاك سر هر كوبى بيفايده مى‌بيزم   سيم دل مسكينم در خاك درت گم شد

تا بر دف عشق آمد تير نظر تيزم   در شهر برسوانى دشمن بدفم برزد

فرهادِ لبِ شيرين چون خسروِ پرويزم   مجنونِ رخِ ليلى چون قيس بنى‌عامر

فرمان‌برمت، جانا، بنشين و برخيزم   گفتى «بغمم بنشين يا از سرِ جان برخيز»

ور با تو بود دوزخ، در سلسله آويزم   گر بى‌تو بُوَد جنت، بر كنگره ننشينم

چون دوست يگانه شد، با غير نيآميزم   با ياد تو گر سعدى در شعر نميگنجد

٭

اى ساربان، آهسته ران كآرام جانم ميرود

وان دل كه با خود داشتم با دلستانم ميرود

من مانده‌ام مهجور ازو، بيچاره و رنجور ازو

گويى كه نيشى دور ازو در استخوانم ميرود

گفتم بنيرنگ و فسون پنهان كنم ريش درون

پنهان نمى‌ماند كه خون بر آستانم ميرود

محمل بدار، اى ساروان، تندى مكن با كاروان

كز عشقِ آن سرو روان گويى روانم ميرود

او ميرود دامن‌كشان، من زهرِ تنهائى چشان

ديگر مپرس از من كز نشان كز دل نشانم ميرود

برگشت يارِ سركشم بگذاشت عيش ناخوشم

چون مجمرى پرآتشم كز سر دخانم ميرود

با آنهمه بيداد او وين عهد بى‌بنيادِ او

در سينه دارم يادِ او يا بر زبانم ميرود؟

بازآى و بر چشمم نشين، اى دلستانِ نازنين

كآشوب و فرياد از زمين بر آسمانم ميرود

شب تا سحر مى‌نغنوم و اندرز كس مى‌نشنوم

وين ره نه قاصد ميروم كز كفِ عنانم ميرود

گفتم «بگريم تا ابل چون خر فروماند بگل

وين نيز نتوانم كه دل با كاروانم ميرود

صبر از وصالِ يارِ من برگشتن از دلدارِ من

گرچه نباشد كارِ من هم كار ازانم ميرود

در رفتن جان از بدن گويند هر نوعى سخن

من خود بچشم خويشتن ديدم كه جانم ميرود

سعدی فغان از دست ما لایق نبود ، ای بیوفا
طاقت نمیآرم جفا ، کار از فغانم میرود

*

کاروانی شکر از مصر به شیراز آید　　اگر آن یار سفر کردهٔ ما باز آید
گو تو باز آی که گر خون منت درخوردست　　پیشت آیم چو کبوتر که به پرواز آید
نام و ننگ و دل و دین گو برود ، این مقدار　　چیست تا در نظر عاشق جانباز آید؟
من خود این سنگ بجان میطلبیدم همه عمر　　کاین قفس بشکند و مرغ به پرواز آید
اگر این داغ جگرسوز که بر جان منست　　بر دل کوه نهی سنگ بآواز آید
من همانروز که روی تو بدیدم گفتم　　هیچ شك نیست که از روی چنین ناز آید
هرچه در صورت عقل آید و در وهم و قیاس　　آنکه محبوب منست از همه ممتاز آید
گر تو باز آیی و بر ناظر سعدی بروی　　هیچ غم نیست که منظور باعزاز آید

KHUSRAW
خسرو

The "parrot of India," Abu'l-Hasan Yamînuddîn Amîr Khusraw of
Delhi (1253–1325) was born in Patyali to a Turkish military nobleman
in the service of the Delhi princes and an Indian mother, and through-
out his life the poet was attached to numerous, short-reigned rulers of
the Delhi Sultanate. Initiator of the literary "remake," Khusraw was the
first of many to attempt to emulate Nizâmî's *Khamsa*. No slavish recre-
ations, however, these "remakes" display each a remarkably different at-
titude toward and conceptualization of the characters and events origi-
nally versified by Nizâmî. Khusraw also compiled five divans from 1273
on, each named for the period of life during which it was written, thus
giving a rare chronological ordering to his lyrics.

For all his versatility in romances and historical epics, it is Khusraw's
ghazals that have assured him lasting fame; and few, if any, have ever
succeeded in rivaling the light, sometimes flippant, nonchalant ease with
which Khusraw can "toss off" an exquisite lyric. A superb musician in
his own right and credited with the invention of several musical instru-
ments and with having laid the theoretical basis for much of Indo-
Muslim music, Khusraw imparted to his ghazals a lilt and melody that
have assured their inclusion in musical programs in India to the present
day. His poetry was especially admired by the Timurids of Herat and
the Mughals, who decorated his collected works with lavish miniatures.

The first ghazal given here shows the outrageously dégagé Khusraw, while the second exhibits his lyric side at its loveliest, and the third fairly demands to be sung. The fourth ghazal, after the manner of Sa'dî, whom Khusraw admired greatly, is a panegyric on Nizâmuddîn Awliyâ, the Saint of Delhi, and is filled with the type of word play of which Khusraw was so fond.

چو ترکِ مستِ من هر لحظهٔ سوی دگر غلطد
شود نظّارگی دیوانه و زو مست‌تر غلطد

بچوگان‌بازی آن ساعت که توسن را دهد جولان
بمیدان در خم چوگانش از هر سوی سر غلطد

نه گردآلود رویِ آن سوارِ من همی‌خواند
که افتد در زمین خورشید و اندر خاك درغلطد

شبش خوش باد، روز از دیدهٔ بیخواب پرخونم
چو او بر فرشِ عیشِ خویش مست و بیخبر غلطد

نغلطد کس چو من در شیوه‌های عاشقی در خون
مگر مجنون دگر زنده شود زینسان که درغلطد

بسی غلطید خسرو بهر خواب و نامدش اکنون
تو بنما چشمِ غلطانش که در خواب دگر غلطد

***

ابر می‌بارد و من می‌شوم از یار جدا   چون کنم دل بچنین روز ز دلدار جدا؟
ابر و باران و من و یار ستاده بوداع،   من جدا گریه‌کنان، ابر جدا، یار جدا
سبزه نوخیز و هوا خرم و بستان سرسبز   بلبل رویِ‌سیه مانده ز گلزار جدا
ای مرا در تهِ هر موی ز زلفت بندی   چه کنی بند ز بندم همه یكبار جدا؟
دیده از بهرِ تو خونبار شد، ای مردمِ چشم
مردمی کن، مشو از دیدهٔ خونبار جدا
نعمتِ دیده نخواهم که بماند پس ازین   مانده چون دیده ازان نعمتِ دیدار جدا
دیدهٔ صد رخنه شد از بهرِ تو، خاكی ز رهت زود برگیر و بكن رخنهٔ دیدار جدا
میدهم جان، مرو از من، وگرت باور نیست
بیش ازان خواهی بُستان و نگهدار جدا؟
حسنِ تو دیر نپاید چو ز خسرو رفتی   گل بسی دیر نماند چو شد از خار جدا

***

ای چهرهٔ زیبای تو، رشک بتان آذری

هرچند وصف میکنم در حسن ازان زیباتری

هرگز نیاید در نظر نقشی ز رویت خوبتر

حوری ندانم، ای پسر، فرزند آدم یا پری

آفاق را گردیدهام، مهر بتان ورزیدهام

بسیار خوبان دیدهام، اما تو چیز دیگری

ای راحت و آرام جان با قدّ چون سرو روان

زینسان مرو دامنکشان کآرام جانم میبری

عزم تماشا کرده، آهنگ صحرا کرده

جان و دل ما برده، اینست رسم دلبری

عالم همه یغمای تو، خلقی همه شیدای تو

آن نرگس رعنای تو آورده کیش کافری

خسرو غریبیست و گدا افتاده در شهر شما

باشد که از بهر خدا سوی غریبان بنگری؟

✳

ای پیر، خاک پای تو نور سعادست   مقراض توبهٔ تو چو لای[1] شهادتست

هستی تو آن نظام که نون خطاب تو[2]   محراب راست کرده برای عبادتست

دید آنکه طلعت تو و بیداریَش نبود   هست آن سگی که خفتن صبحش بعادتست

تو شمع صبح شعلهٔ شوقی که از تو خاست   زان هر یکی شراره چراغ هدایتست

علامهای که معرفت انبیاش هست   اورا به پیش تو محل استفادتست

در عهد تو قیام جهان از وجود تست   مانند صورتی که قیامش بمادتست

هر یک مرید تو چو هلالیست از رکوع   هر شب هلالوار از آن در زیادتست

بتوان مرید گفت ترا که اوست   آن مردمی[3] که فتنهٔ عین سعادتست

امّید کز تو واصل گردد چو خُرد و پیر   خسرو که بیوصال چو حرف ارادتست[4]

---

[1]*Lâ-yi shahâdat*: the *lâ* that begins the formula of faith, *lâ ilâh illâ 'llâ* (there is no god but God); the shape of the word *lâ* is likened to a pair of shears. The vow of repentance a disciple would take before Nizâmuddîn severed the connection to sin as if by shears.

[2]The first letter of Nizâmuddîn's name is *nûn*, which is likened to the *mihrâb* niche in a mosque.

[3]*Mardum*, both "man" and "pupil of the eye," to accord with *ayn-i sa'âdat*, both "happiness itself" and, literally, "the eye of happiness."

[4]In the word *irâdat* all the letters are disconnected (*bévisâl*).

HASAN

حسن

Amir Hasan Sijzî of Delhi (1255–1337), like his friend Amir Khusraw, was a disciple of Nizâmuddîn Awliyâ. In the ghazal style he followed Sa'dî and is known as the Sa'dî of Hindustan.

چندین چه ناز آموختی آن غمزهٔ غمازرا؟

دل بردی و جان سوختی. حدیست آخر نازرا

هرچند هندوی توام، چون دزدم از لعلت شکر

در هر کمین بنشانده‌ای ترکانِ تیراندازرا

هرگز نپرسد از کسی کعبه‌نشینان‌را نشان[1]

مستی[2] که او قبله کند، چون ما، بتی طنازرا

غالب نیاید عقل من بر عشق مهرویان، بلی

حدّ کبوتر کی بود کو صید گیرد بازرا؟

سبحه چه در دستم دهی؟ خرقه چه در پیشم نهی؟

با زاهدان نسبت مکن این پیرِ شاهدبازرا

سازی که بود، ای مدعی، کردی ازین مجلس برون

با تو بهم آتش زنم این مجلس بی‌سازرا

هان، ای حسن، تا زنده‌ای، دل نه بزندانِ غمش

چاره نباشد از قفس مرغانِ خوش‌آوازرا

*

با من نمی‌سازی دمی، ای یادِ تو دمسازِ من

امشب که همرازِ تو ام چون صبح بگشا رازِ من

گه‌گه سری می‌باختم، در کویِ تو می‌تاختم

با ناله خوش می‌ساختم، برهم شکستی سازِ من

زابرو کمانی ساختی، بر ما خدنگ انداختی

از خویش دورم ساختی، ای ترکِ دورانداز من

در سینه دارم تب ز تو، حلقی پر از یارب ز تو

ای مردنم امشب ز تو، یاد آیدت فردا ز من؟

---

[1] Ka'banishînân-râ nishân = nishân-i ka'banishînân.

[2] Mast-î is the subject of napursad.

گفتم حسن از تست و بس ، هرگز نگفتی یك نفس

کاینك گرفتارِ قفس مرغِ سخن پردازِ من

UBAYD
عبید

Khwâja Nizâmuddîn Ubaydullâh Zâkânî of Qazwin (d. 1371), who has
been called Persia's Voltaire, is the greatest satirist of classical Persian lit-
erature. Born in Qazvin but a resident of Shiraz during the reign of
Shaykh Abu-Ishâq Injû, Ubayd Zâkânî dedicated most of his consider-
able poetic talents to ribaldry and biting satire. His *Akhlâqu'l-ashrâf*
(Ethics of the Nobles, 1340) mocks the decline of morality and virtue,
and in his *Ta'rîfât* (Definitions) the poet ridicules all manner of corrup-
tion and weakness with a pithy definition of each class of men. His
Risâla-i Dilgushâ (Delightful Treatise) contains amusing and delightfully
indecent anecdotes in Arabic and Persian; and while his *'Ushshâqnâma*
(Book of Lovers) has the same title and format as that of Irâqî, it is dedi-
cated to a treatment of much more profane love.

    Ubayd's *Mûsh u Gurba* (The Mouse and the Cat), replete with polit-
ically satirical overtones, is given here in full. By form it is a qasida, a
very unusual form for a narrative.

بیا بشنو حدیث گربه و موش   اگر داری تو عقل و دانش و هوش

که در معنای آن حیران بمانی   بخوانم از برایت داستانی

قصهٔ موش و گربه برخوانا[1]   ای خردمند عاقل و دانا

گوش کن همچو دُرِّ غلطانا   قصهٔ موش و گربهٔ منظوم

بود چون اژدها بکرمانا   از قضای فلك ، یکی گربه   ٥

شیردم و پلنگ چنگانا   شکمش طبل و سینه‌اش چو سپر

شیر غرنده شد هراسانا   از غریوش بوقت غریدن

شیر از وی شدی گریزانا   سر هر سفره چون نهادی پای

از برای شکار موشانا   روزی اندر شرابخانه شدی

همچو دزدی که در بیابانا   در پسِ خم می‌نمود کمین   ١٠

جست بر خم می خروشانا   ناگهان موشکی ز دیواری

مست شد همچو شیر غرّانا   سر بخم برنهاد و مَی نوشید

---

[1] Almost every line in this qasida ends in a superfluous *alif*, technically called
alif-i ishbâ', a metrical device imported from Arabic.

گفت «کو گربه؟ تا سرش بکنم   پوستش پر کنم ز کاهانا

گربه در پیش من چو سگ باشد   که شود روبرو بمیدانا»

۱۵   گربه این‌را شنید و دم نزدی   چنگ و دندان زدی بسوهانا

ناگهان جست و موش‌را بگرفت   چون پلنگی شکار کوهانا

موش گفتا که «من غلام تو ام   عفو کن از من این گناهانا»

گربه گفتا «دروغ کمتر گوی   نخورم من فریب و مکرانا

می‌شنیدم هرآنچه می‌گفتی   آه از دین این مسلمانا»

۲۰   گربه آن موش‌را بکشت و بخورد   سوی مسجد شدی خرامانا

دست و رورا بشست و مسح کشید   ورد می‌خواند همچو ملانا

«بار الها که توبه کردم من   ندرم موش‌را بدندانا

بهر این خون ناحق، ای خلاق   من تصدق دهم دو من نانا»

آنقدر لابه کرد و زاری کرد   تا بحدی که گشت گریانا

۲۵   موشکی بود در پس منبر   زود برد این خبر این بموشانا

«مژدگانی که گربه تائب شد   زاهد و عابد و مسلمانا

بود در مسجد آن ستوده‌خصال   در نماز و نیاز و افغانا»

این خبر چون رسید بر موشان   همه گشتند شاد و خندانا

هفت موش گزیده برجستند   هر یکی کدخدا و دهقانا

۳۰   برگرفتند بهر گربه ز مهر   هر یکی تحفه‌های الوانا

آن یکی شیشهٔ شراب بکف   وان دگر بره‌های بریانا

آن یکی طشتکی پر از کشمش   وان دگر یک طبق ز خرمانا

آن یکی ظرفی از پنیر بدست   وان دگر ماست با کره نانا

آن یکی خوانچهٔ پلو بر سر   افشره آب لیموعمانا

۳۵   نزد گربه شدند آن موشان   با سلام و درود و احسانا

عرض کردند با هزار ادب   «کای فدای رهت همه جانا

لایق خدمت تو پیشکشی   کرده‌ایم ما. قبول فرمانا»

گربه چون موشکان بدید بخواند   «رزقکم فی السماء حقانا»¹

من گرسنه بسی بسر بردم   رزقم امروز شد فراوانا

٤٠   روزه بودم بروزهای دگر   از برای رضای رحمانا

هرکه کار خدا کند بیقین   روزیش میشود فراوانا»

بعد ازان گفت «پیش فرمائید   قدمی چند، ای رفیقانا»

---

[1] *Rizqukum fi's-samâ'i haqqânâ* (Ar.), "your sustenance is truly in heaven."

موشکان جمله پیش میرفتند   تنشان همچو بید لرزانا

ناگهان گربه جست بر موشان   چون مبارز بروز میدانا

پنج موش گزیده‌را بگرفت   هر یکی کدخدا و ایلخانا ۴۵

دو بدین چنگ و دو بدان چنگال   یك بدندان چو شیر غرانا

آن دو موش دگر که جان بردند   زود بردند خبر بموشانا

که "چه بنشسته‌اید ای موشان   خاکتان بر سر، ای جوانانا

پنج موش رئیس‌را بدرید   گربه با چنگها و دندانا"

موشکان‌را از این مصیبت و غم   شد لباس همه سیاهانا ۵۰

خاک بر سر کنان همی‌گفتند   "ای دریغا رئیس موشانا"

بعد ازان متفق شدند که "ما   می‌رویم پای تخت سلطانا"

تا بشه عرضِ حال خویش کنیم   از ستمهای خیل گربانا"

شاه موشان نشسته بود بتخت   دید از دور خیل موشانا

همه یکبار کردندش تعظیم   "کای تو شاهنشاهی بدورانا ۵۵

گربه کردست ظلم بر ماها   ای شهنشه، اولوم بقربانا[1]

سالی یکدانه می‌گرفت از ما   حال حرصش شده فراوانا

این زمان پنج پنج می‌گیرد   چون شده تائب و مسلمانا"

درد دل چون بشاه خود گفتند   شاه فرمود "کای عزیزانا ۶۰

من تلافی بگربه خواهم کرد   که شود داستان بدورانا"

بعد یکهفته لشکری آراست   سیصد و سی هزار موشانا

همه با نیزه‌ها و تیر و کمان   همه با سیف‌های برانا

فوج‌های پیاده از یکسو   تیغ‌ها در میانه جولانا

چونکه جمع‌آوری لشکر شد   از خراسان و رشت و گیلانا ۶۵

یک موشی وزیر لشکر بود   هوشمند و دلیر و فطانا

گفت "باید یکی ز ما برود   نزد گربه بشهر کرمانا

یا بیا پای تخت در خدمت   یا که آماده باش جنگانا"

موشکی بود ایلچی ز قدیم   شد روانه بشهر کرمانا

نرم‌نرمك بگربه حالی کرد   که "منم ایلچی ز شاها ۷۰

خبر آورده‌ام برای شما   عزم جنگ کرده شاه موشانا

یا برو پای تخت در خدمت   یا که آماده باش جنگانا"

گربه گفتا که "موش گُگ خورده   من نیایم برون ز کرمانا"

لیکن اندر خفا تدارك کرد | لشکر معظمی ز گربانا

گربه‌های یراق شیرشکار | از صفاهان و یزد و کرمانا

لشکر گربه چون مهیا شد | داد فرمان بسوی میدانا ۷۵

لشکر موشها ز راه کویر | لشکر گربه از کهستانا

در بیابان فارس هر دو سپاه | رزم دادند چون دلیرانا

جنگ مغلوبه شد در آن وادی | هر طرف رستمانه جنگانا

آنقدر موش و گربه کشته شدند | که نیاید حساب آسانا

حمله سخت کرد گربه چو شیر | بعد ازان زد بقلب موشانا ۸۰

موشکی اسب گربه‌را پی کرد | گربه شد سرنگون ز زینانا

الله الله فتاد در موشان | که «بگیرید پهلوانانا»

موشکان طبل شادیانه زدند | بهر فتح و ظفر فراوانا

شاه موشان بشد بفیل سوار | لشکر از پیش و پس خروشانا

گربه‌را هر دو دست بسته بهم | با کلاف و طناب و ریسمانا ۸۵

شاه گفتا «بدار آویزند | این سگ روسیاه نادانا»

گربه چون دید شاه موشان‌را | غیرتش شد چو دیگ جوشانا

همچو شیری نشست بر زانو | کند آن ریسمان بدندانا

موشکان‌را گرفت و زد بزمین | که شدندی بخاك یکسانا

لشکر از یکطرف فراری شد | شاه از یك جهت گریزانا ۹۰

از میان رفت فیل و فیل‌سوار | مخزن و تاج و تخت و ایوانا

هست این قصه عجیب و غریب | یادگار عبید زاکانا

جان من، پند گیر ازین قصه | که شوی در زمانه شادانا

غرض از موش و گربه برخواندن | مدعا فهم کن، پسرجانا

AWHADÎ
اوحدی

Ruknuddîn Awhadî of Marâgha in Azerbaijan (circa 1270–1337) is one of the most famous Sufi poets of the fourteenth century. His masnavi *Jâm-i Jam*, a potpourri of mystical, social, and ethical topics, is very well known.

ای ساربان که رنج کشیدی ز راه دور | آمد شتر بمنزل لیلی. مکن عبور

اینجا نزول کن که ازین آب واین هوا | هم سینه یافت راحت وهم دیده یافت نور

اینست خارها که ازو چیده‌ایم گل | وین جای خیمه‌ها که درو دیده‌ایم حور

این لحظه آتشست بجائی که بود آب   وامروز ماتمست بجائی که بود سور

آن شب چه شد که بی‌رخِ لیلی نبود حیّ؟   وان روز کو که موقفِ دیدار بود طور؟

خون جگر بریخت دل من بیاد دوست   ای چشم اشکبار، چرائی چنین صبور؟

زین پیش بود نفرتم از دُور و از زمان   دُورم چنان گداخت که هستم زخود نفور

جز دستبوس دوست نباشد مرا مراد   روزی که سر ز خاک برآرم بنفخِ صور

ای اوحدی، چو روی کنی در نمازِ تو   بی‌روی او مکن که نمازست بی‌حضور

❋

دلخسته همی‌باشد زین شهر بهم رفته   خلقی همه سرگردان، دل مرده و دم رفته

یك بنده نمی‌یابم هنجارِ وفا دیده   یك خواجه نمی‌بینم بر صوبِ کرم رفته

راهی نه ز پیش و پس در شهرِ چنین بیکس   من خفته و همراهان با طبل و علم رفته

بر لوح جهان نقشی چون نیست بکام من   من نیز نهادم سر بر خطّ قلم رفته

از گفته و کردِ من وز محنت و دردِ من   شد چهرهٔ زردِ من در نیلِ نقم رفته

چون چرخ بسی گشتم من در پی کامِ دل

وین چرخ بکام من دردا که چه کم رفته

لافم نرسید ارچه این راه بسر رفتم   تا در چه رسد گوئی مرد بقدم رفته

با خلق ز هر جنسی مارا چه وفا بوده؟   وانگاه ز ناجنسان بر ما چه ستم رفته!

مشنو که براه آیند اینها بحدیثِ ما   کی رنگِ شفا گیرد جانِ بالم رفته؟

در سر مکن این سودا بسیار که خواهد بود

از کاسهٔ سر سودا وز کیسه درم رفته

آن روز شوی واقف زین حال که بینی تو   از چاه نژند تن این روحِ دژم رفته

گر چشم دلی داری از ماتم دلبندان   بس چشم ببینی تو در گریه و نم رفته

در پردهٔ این بازی بنگر که پیاپی شد   زن‌زاده، پسرمرده، خال‌آمده، عم رفته

خیل وحشم سلطان دیدی، پس ازین بنگر

زین مرحله سلطان را بی‌خیل وحشم رفته

در بیم بلا بوده یك چند و بصد حسرت   از بیم وجود آخر بر بام عدم رفته

KHWÂJÛ

خواجو

Abu'l-Atâ Kamâluddîn Mahmûd Khwâjû of Kirman (1281–1352) lived
in Kirman, Tabriz, and Shiraz. In addition to numerous masnavis, in-
cluding a *Khamsa*, the most famous section of which is *Humây and
Humâyûn*, his divan contains ghazals that follow Sa'di's style with a
heavier admixture of Sufism, a style that was to be perfected by Hâfiz.

شمع ما شمعیست کاو منظورِ هر پروانه نیست
گنج ما گنجیست کاو در کنجِ هر ویرانه نیست

هرکرا سودای لیلی نیست مجنون آنکس است
ورنه مجنون‌را چو نیکو بنگری دیوانه نیست

چشم صورت‌بین نبیند روی معنی‌را بخواب
زانکه در هر کان دُر و در هر صدف دُردانه نیست

حاجیان‌را کعبه بتخانه است¹ و ایشان بت‌پرست
ور ببینی در حقیقت کعبه جز بتخانه نیست

مرغِ وحشی گر ببوی دانه در دام اوفتد
تا چه مرغم؟ زانک دامی در رهم جز دانه نیست

هرکرا بینی درینجا مسکن و کاشانه است
جای ما جاییست کانجا مسکن و کاشانه نیست

گر سرِ شه‌مات داری، پیش اسبش رخ بنه
کانکه پیشِ شه دم از فرزین زند فرزانه نیست

گفتمش "پروای درویشان نمی‌باشد ترا"
گفت "ازین بگذر که اینها هیچ درویشانه نیست"

گرچه باشد در رهِ جانانه جسم و جان حجاب
جانِ خواجو جز حریمِ حضرتِ جانانه نیست

٭

ز چشمِ مستِ تو آنها که آگهی دارند   مدام معتکف آستانِ خمّارند
ازان بخاکِ درت مست می‌سپارم جان   که³ هم بکویِ تو مستم² بخاک بسپارند

---

¹For the meter, read *butkhâna 'st*.
²The enclitic *-am* here is the direct object of the verb *bis'pârand*.
³*Azân...ki = az ân-ki* "because."

که ملك روی زمین را بهیچ نشمارند   چرا بهیچ شمارند می‌پرستان را؟

غریب نبود[1] اگر خاطرش بدست آرند   هر آن غریب که خاطر بخوبرویان داد

روا مدار جدائی که خود ترا دارند   ز بیدلان که ندارند بی‌تو صبر و قرار

اگر بفرق نپویند نقش دیوارند   چو سایه راه‌نشینان به پای دیوارت

دران زمان که مرا خاك بر سر انبارند   ز سر برون نکنم آرزوی خاك درت

چو بلبلان چمن در هوای گلزارند   بکنج صومعه آنها که ساکنند امروز

ز خانه خیمه برون زن که اهل دل، خواجو،

شراب و دامنِ صحرا ز دست نگذارند

※

پیش صاحب‌نظران ملك سلیمان بادست

بلکه آنست سلیمان که ز ملك آزادست

آنکه گویند که بر آب نهادست جهان

مشنو، ای خواجه، که چون درنگری بر بادست

هر نفس مهر فلك بر دگری می‌افتد

چه توان کرد؟ چو این سفله چنین افتادست

دل درین پیرزن عشوه‌گر دهر مبند

کاین عروسیست که در عقد بسی دامادست

یاد دار این سخن از من که پس از من گوئی

یاد باد آنکه مرا این سخن از وی یادست

آنکه شدّاد در ایوان ز زر افکندی خشت

خشت ایوان شه اکنون ز سر شدّادست

خاك بغداد بمرگ خلفا می‌گرید

ورنه این شط روان چیست که در بغدادست

گر پُر از لالهٔ سیراب بود دامن کوه

مرو از راه که آن خون دل فرهادست

همچو نرگس بگشا چشم و ببین کاندر خاك

چند روی چو گل و قامت چون شمشادست

خیمهٔ انس مزن بر در این کهنه رباط

که اساسش همه بی‌موقع و بی‌بنیادست

---

[1]For the meter, read nab'vad.

حاصلی نیست بجز غم ز جهان خواجو را

شادیِ جانِ کسی کو ز جهانِ آزادست

IMÂD
عماد

The *Mahabbatnâma* of Imâduddîn Faqîh of Kirman (d. 1371), from which the first selection is taken, was dedicated to the Ilkhanid Sultan Abu-Sa'îd Khan (r. 1317–35). The masnavi gives dialogues between the topical lover–beloved pairs in Persian poetry, nightingale and rose, moth and candle, the dust-mote and the sun, &c. The second selection is representative of his divan, almost all the poems in which are tinged with mysticism.

شنیدم از ملکخویی پریچهر   حدیث ماجرای ذره و مهر

که ذره گفت با خورشید انور   که «ای روشن‌دل پاکیزه‌گوهر

توئی شمع شبستان زمانه   گل خوشرنگِ بُستان زمانه

زوایای ملایک روشن از تست   خراب‌آباد عالم گلشن از تست

توئی قندیلِ گردون معلّق   چراغِ هفت مشکات مطبّق   ۵

منوّر طلعتت مشهورِ آفاق   لوای صبحِ تو منصورِ آفاق

من آن گردم که از راه تو برخاست   بنور رویِ زیبای تو پیداست

دل سرگشته در مهر تو بستم   خیالی شد وجود نیست و هستم

چو با مهرم بُوَد پیوند جانی   سزد گر دم زنم از مهربانی

نه آن شخصم که در چشم کس آیم   که در کوی حقارت گشت جایم   ۱۰

سروپایی ندارم. چون توان کرد؟   دل و رایی ندارم. چون توان کرد؟

دل سرگشته باشد در هوایت   بامیّد و تمنّای لقایت

ز خاکم جذبۀ مهر تو برداشت   بحمدالله مرا محروم نگذاشت

منم رقاص بزم چون جنانت   معلّق باز زرّین ریسمانت

گهی گیرد صبا تنگم در آغوش   که «این از بادۀ مهرست مدهوش   ۱۵

گهم گوهر فشاند ابر بر سر   که هست از عاشقان طلعت خور

مرا در مهر تو کامی برآمد   که با نام توام نامی برآمد

تو یار سست‌مهر بی‌وفائی   که هر شب می‌کنی از من جدائی

ندانم شب در آغوش که خفتی   کجا باشی و در دستِ که افتی

خوشا آنکس که مهمانش تو باشی   برُخ شمع شبستانش تو باشی»   ۲۰

چو بشنید این سخن خورشید رخشان   رخش شد سرخ چون لعل بدخشان

ز کینش گرم گشت و گفت «کاین کیست که با مهرش میسر شد چنین زیست؟

من آن شاهم که از تیغم چکد خون نهاده زین برین یکران شبگون

نهفته در نقاب آسمانی عذار لاله‌رنگ ارغوانی

وطن در عالم علوی گزیده امید از خطهٔ سفلی بریده ۲۵

کسی در من نیارد دیدن از دور که دارم دورباشی روشن از نور

کسم هرگز بشب جایی ندیدست فلک چون من هم‌آوایی ندیدست

هنوز، ای ذره، از طعنه نجستم ز تعنیف بداندیشان نرستم

ترا در حق من چون این گمانست، ز مهر ار دم زنی لاف زیانست»

*

ما بصیت کرمت از ره دور آمده‌ایم از در فاقه، نه از کوی غرور آمده‌ایم

کعبهٔ اهل کمالست مقام تو و ما بسته احرام ز نزدیك و ز دور آمده‌ایم

شمع رخسار تو آورد بدین مجلس نور همه پروانه‌صفت از پی نور آمده‌ایم

گر بیابیم اثر نور تجلی، چه عجب؟ که ز وادیِ مقدس¹ سوی طور آمده‌ایم

گر بزودی نشود کام دل ما حاصل بر نگردیم ازین در که صبور آمده‌ایم

با کسی در دو جهان انس نگیرد دل ما تا بدانی که ز غیر تو نفور آمده‌ایم

نه غم فرقت خلق و نه سر وصلت کس فارغ از ماتم و آسوده ز سور آمده‌ایم

نرویم از پی شادی نفسی همچو عماد نه درین کلبهٔ احزان² بسرور آمده‌ایم

فارغیم از همه خوبان سیه‌چشم جهان نه درین روضه بنظارهٔ حور آمده‌ایم

SALMÂN
سلمان

Jamâluddîn Salmân Sâvajî (circa 1300–1376) was attached to the Jalayirid
court in Baghdad. In addition to his superb ghazals, many of which are
so close in style to Hâfiz's ghazals that some have been mistakenly at-
tributed to Hâfiz, he has two well-known masnavis, *Jamshêd u Khur-
shêd* and *Firâqnâma*.

صحبتی خوش درگرفت امشب میان شمع و من

ماهرویی دیدمش چشم و چراغ انجمن

---

¹*Vâdî-i muqaddas*: Moses went to Sinai from the "sacred valley" of Tuwâ (see
Kor. 20:12).

²*Kulba-i ahzân*: when Joseph's brothers sold him into slavery, Joseph's father,
Jacob, built in Canaan a "hut of sorrows," in which he sat and cried his eyes blind
over his beloved son.

دلبری عذرا عذار و شاهدی شیرین‌نژاد

آیتی در شانِ او مُنزل ز لطفِ ذوالمنن

ماه‌رخساری معنبر زلف را ماند که او

سر برآرد هر شبی از جیبِ شمعی پیرهن

رشتهٔ جان من و او و هر دو در تابست و تب

لیك او سررشتهٔ دارد بکف بر عکس من

با زبانی پر بخار و با لبی پر آبله

از چه سوزد گر تب محرق ندارد در بدن؟

تب بتار رشته[1] می‌بندند مردم، لیك او

هر شبی بندد بتار رشته تب بر خویشتن

آنکه بخشیدش کلاه و بر سرش مقراض راند

گر سرش برّد نشاید سر ز حکمش تافتن

گر نه ضحاکست چون بر کرد سر مارش ز دوش

ورنه ذوالقرنین[2] چون بر ظلمت آرد تاختن؟

می‌کند پروانه‌ها پرّان بهر جانب ولی

پادشاهست و فراز تختِ زر دارد وطن

روز تا شب مرده است، و زنده باشد تا بروز

نیست این زردیِ رنگِ رویش الّا از وسن

✳

در ازل عکس می لعل تو در جام افتاد   عاشق سوخته‌دل در طمع خام افتاد

جام را از شکر لعل لبت نُقلی کرد   راز سربستهٔ خُم در دهن عام افتاد

خالِ مشکین تو در عارض گندمگون دید   آدم آمد ز پی دانه[3] و در دام افتاد

باد زُنّار سر زلف تو از هم بگشود   صد شکست از طرف کفر بر اسلام افتاد

عشق بر کشتنِ عشاق تفاؤل میکرد   اولین قرعه که زد بر من بدنام افتاد

عشقم از روی طمع پردهٔ تقوی برداشت   طبل پنهان چه زنم؟ طشت من از بام افتاد[4]

---

[1] A reference to the practice of binding the heads of the sick with bandages.

[2] Alexander (Zu'l-Qarnayn) went into the realm of darkness searching for the fountain of eternal youth. He never found it, but his cook, Andreas, known in Islamic legend as Khizr, fell into the fountain by accident and became immortal.

[3] *Dâna*: in the Islamic version of the Adam and Eve story, Eve tempted Adam with a grain of wheat, not an apple.

[4] *Tasht az bâm uftâd*: a proverbial expression equivalent to "having one's dirty laundry exposed in public."

دوش سلمان بقلم شرح غم دل میداد   آتش اندر ورق و دود در اقلام افتاد

HÂFIZ
حافظ

During the tumultuous years leading to Amir Temür (Tamerlane)'s campaigns into and through Iran, Khwâja Shamsuddîn Muhammad Hâfiz (1326–1389) was a lifelong resident of the relatively tranquil Shiraz and enjoyed the patronage of several viziers and rulers of the Inju and Muzaffarid dynasties.

If Sa'dî's *Gulistân* has been read by more people, and Mawlavî's *Masnavî* has been called the Koran in Persian, no book has been so reverenced, no poet so celebrated, and no verse so cherished as Hâfiz's ghazals. Auguries from his divan have decided the fates of individuals and empires, rebels and heretics as well as the pious have died with lines by Hâfiz on their lips, and religious and philosophic arguments have been won by apt quotation of a hemistich.

Hâfiz sang a rare blend of human and mystic love so balanced, proportioned, and contrived with artful ease that it is impossible to separate the one from the other; and rhetorical artifice is so delicately woven into the fabric of wisdom and mysticism that it imparts a vivacity and freshness to ideas that, in and of themselves, may not have been new or original with Hâfiz.

اگر آن ترک شیرازی بدست آرد دل مارا

بخال هندویش بخشم سمرقند و بخارارا

بده ساقی می باقی که در جنت نخواهی یافت

کنار آب رکناباد و گلگشت مصلارا

فغان کاین لولیان شوخ شیرین‌کار شهرآشوب

چنان بردند صبر از دل که ترکان خوان یغمارا

من از آن حسنِ روزافزون که یوسف داشت دانستم

که عشق از پردهٔ عصمت برون آرد زلیخارا[1]

ز عشق ناتمام ما جمال یار مستغنیست

بآب و رنگ و خال و خط چه حاجت روی زیبارا؟

بدم گفتی و خرسندم، عفاك الله نکو گفتی

جواب تلخ می‌زیبد لبِ لعلِ شکرخارا

---

[1]Zulaykha, the wife of the biblical Potiphar, was so smitten by Joseph's beauty that she disgraced herself by trying to seduce him.

نصیحت گوش کن ، جانا ، که از جان دوستتر دارند

جوانان سعادتمند پند پیر دانارا

حدیث از مطرب و می گوی و راز دهر کمتر جو

که کس نگشود و نگشاید بحکمت این معمارا

غزل گفتی و دُر سفتی. بیا و خوش بخوان ، حافظ

که بر نظم تو افشاند فلک عقد ثریارا

*

دوش دیدم که ملایک در میخانه زدند   گل آدم بسرشتند و به پیمانه زدند[1]

ساکنان حرم و ستر و عفاف ملکوت   با من راه‌نشین بادهٔ مستانه زدند

شکر ایزد که میان من و او صلح افتاد   قدسیان رقص‌کنان ساغر شکرانه زدند

جنگ هفتاد و دو ملت[3] همه‌را عذر بنه   چون ندیدند حقیقت، ره افسانه زدند[2]

آسمان بار امانت[4] نتوانست کشید   قرعهٔ فال بنام منِ دیوانه زدند

ما بصد خرمنِ پندار ز ره چون نرویم،   چون[6] رهِ آدمِ خاکی بیکی دانه[5] زدند؟

آتش آن نیست که بر شعلهٔ او خندد شمع   آتش آنست که در خرمن پروانه زدند

کس چو حافظ نکشید از رخ اندیشه نقاب   تا سرِ زلف سخن‌را بقلم شانه زدند

*

یوسف گمگشته باز آید بکنعان ، غم مخور

کلبهٔ احزان[7] شود روزی گلستان ، غم مخور

ای دلِ غمدیده، حالت به شود ، دل بد مکن

وین سر شوریده باز آید بسامان ، غم مخور

---

[1]*Ba paymâna zadand,* the sense is to "throw" a pot as a potter throws, or shapes, a pot on a wheel.

[2]*Rah-i afsâna zadand: râh-zadan* is to engage in highway robbery, i.e., they waylayed legend and stripped it of its goods.

[3]A reference to the quotation attributed to the Prophet Muhammad: "The Jews split into seventy-one sects; the Christian split into seventy-two sects; my community will split into seventy-three sects, all but one of which will go to Hell."

[4]*Amânat:* the "covenant" or "trust" that was offered to the heavens, the earth, and the mountains. They all refused to bear the burden, but mankind accepted it: "he was unjust to himself, and foolish" (Kor. 33:72).

[5]*Dâna:* see p. 63, note 3.

[6]*Chun* in the first hemistich is the subordinating conjunction "since," or "if"; the *chun* in the second hemistich is the interrogative "how."

[7]*Kulba-i ahzân:* see p. 62, note 2.

دورِ گردون گر دو روزی بر مرادِ ما نگشت

دائماً یکسان نماند حالِ دوران ، غم مخور

گر بهار عمر باشد باز بر طرفِ چمن

چترِ گل بر سر کَشی ، ای مرغِ خوشخوان ، غم مخور

هان مشو نومید چون واقف نه‌ای از سرِّ غیب

باشد اندر پرده بازی‌های پنهان ، غم مخور ۵

در بیابان گر بشوق کعبه خواهی زد قدم

سرزنش‌ها گر کند خارِ مغیلان ، غم مخور

حالِ ما در فرقتِ جانان و ابرامِ رقیب

جمله می‌داند خدای حال‌گردان ، غم مخور

ای دل ، ار سیلِ فنا بنیادِ هستی بر کند

چون ترا نوحست کشتیبان ، ز طوفان غم مخور

گرچه منزل بس خطرناکست و مقصد ناپدید

هیچ راهی نیست کآن‌را نیست پایان ، غم مخور

حافظا ، در کنجِ فقر و خلوتِ شبهای تار

تا بود وردت دعا و درسِ قرآن ، غم مخور ۱۰

٭

زلفْ آشفته و خوی‌کرده و خندان‌لب و مست

پیرهن‌چاک و غزل‌خوان و صراحی در دست

نرگسش عربده‌جوی و لبش افسوس‌کنان

نیم‌شب دوش ببالین من آمد ، بنشست

سر فراگوشِ من آورد و بآوازِ حزین

گفت «ای عاشقِ دیرینهٔ من ، خوابت هست؟»

عاشقی‌را که چنین بادهٔ شبگیر دهند

کافرِ عشق بود گر نشود باده‌پرست

برو ، ای زاهد ، و بر دُردکشان خرده مگیر

که ندادند جزین تحفه بما روزِ الست[1]

خندهٔ جامِ می و زلفِ گره‌گیرِ نگار

---

[1] *Alast*, for *alastu bi-rabbikum* (Ar.) "am I not your Lord?", God's question of mankind, Kor. 7:172; *alast*, *bazm-i alast*, and *rôz-i alast* all refer to the time (day, banquet) in eternity when humanity acknowledged God's lordship and thereby accepted the burden of responsibility.

ای بسا توبه که چون توبهٔ حافظ بشکست

٭

وانچه خود داشت ز بیگانه تمنا میکرد   سالها دل طلب جام جم[1] از ما میکرد

طلب از گمشدگان لب دریا میکرد   گوهری کز صدف کون و مکان بیرونست

کو بتأیید نظر حلّ معمّا میکرد   مشکل خویش بر پیر مغان بردم دوش

واندران آینه صد گونه تماشا میکرد   دیدمش خرم و خندان، قدح باده بدست

گفت آن روز که این گنبد مینا میکرد ٥   گفتم این جام جهان‌بین بتو کی داد حکیم؟

او نمیدیدش و از دور خدارا میکرد   بیدلی[2] در همه احوال خدا با او بود

سامری[3] پیش عصا و ید بیضا میکرد   اینهمه شعبدهٔ خویش که میکرد اینجا

جرمش این بود که اسرار هویدا میکرد   گفت آن یار کزو گشت سر دار بلند

دیگران هم بکنند آنچه مسیحا میکرد   فیض روح‌القُدُس ار باز مدد فرماید

گفت حافظ گلهٔ از دل شیدا میکرد ١٠   گفتمش سلسلهٔ زلف بتان از پی چیست؟

٭

بیار باده که بنیاد عمر بر بادست   بیا که قصر امل سخت سست‌بنیادست

ز هرچه رنگ تعلق پذیرد آزادست[4]   غلام همت آنم که زیر چرخ کبود

که خاطر از همه غمها بمهر او شادست   مگر تعلق خاطر بماه‌رخساری

که این حدیث ز پیر طریقتم یادست   نصیحتی کنمت، یاد گیر و در عمل آر

که این عجوزه عروس هزار دامادست ٥   مجو درستی عهد از جهان سست‌نهاد

سروش عالم غیبم چه مژده‌ها دادست   چه گویمت که بمیخانه دوش مست وخراب

نشیمن تو نه این کنج محنت‌آبادست   که ای بلندنظر شاهباز سدره‌نشین،

ندانت که درین دامگه چه افتادست   ترا ز کنگرهٔ عرش میزنند صفیر

که این لطیفهٔ نغزم ز رهروی یادست   غم جهان مخور و پند من مبر از یاد

---

[1]Jamshed's goblet revealed to the looker everything in the world.

[2]The *bêdil* is an allusion to Hallâj (d. 922), the martyr-mystic who in the later Sufi tradition was blamed for making public his famous dictum, *ana'l-haqq* "I am God." His sleight-of-hand tricks, which were tauted as miracles, are referred to in the next line. In line 8 is a reference to the gibbet (*dâr*) on which Hallâj was executed.

[3]*Sâmirî*, the Samaritan, the sorcerer who was responsible for animating the golden calf the Israelites had brought out of Egypt. The staff (*asâ*) and the "white hand" (*yad-i bayzâ*, Kor. 20:22, 27:12, etc.) are allusions to Moses' prophetic miracles, the staff that was turned into a serpent, and the hand, which, when he withdrew it from his bosom in front of Pharaoh, was glistening white.

[4]This line runs on into the next.

که بر من و تو در اختیار نگشادست ۱۰   رضا بداده بده وز جبین گره بگشای

بنال، بلبل بیدل، که جای فریادست   نشان عهد و وفا نیست در تبسّم گل

قبول خاطر و لطف سخن خدادادست   حسد چه میبری ای سست‌نظم بر حافظ

NI'MATULLÂH VALÎ
نعمة‌الله ولی

Sayyid Nûruddîn Ni'matullâh Valî, born in Aleppo circa 1330, spent
most of his life in Samarkand, Herat, Yazd, and Mâhân in Kirman,
where he died in 1431, and where his tomb is venerated as a shrine to
this day. The eponymous founder of the Ni'matullâhî Order of
dervishes, he composed poetry of obviously mystical content.

مسکن اهل دلان گوشهٔ میخانه ماست   منزل جان جهان بر در جانانهٔ ماست

حرم قدس یکی گوشهٔ کاشانه ماست   خلوتی بر در میخانه گرفتیم ولی

نور شمع فلک از پرتو پروانهٔ ماست   تا ز شمع رخ او مجلس جان روشن شد

حاصل اشک جگرگوشهٔ جانانهٔ ماست   دیده‌ای لؤلؤ لالا که ز دریا آرند؟

زانکه گنجش ز ازل در دل ویرانهٔ ماست   تا ابد گنج غمش در دل ما خواهد بود

که مراد دو جهان یک لب پیمانهٔ ماست   ساقیا ساغر و پیمانه می سوی من آر

روز و شب همنفس و همدم میخانهٔ ماست   آنچه سیّد بدل و دیدهٔ جان میطلبد

❀

جان چه باشد گر نباشد عاشق جان‌پروری؟

دل چه ارزد گر نورزد مهر روی دلبری؟

من چه بازم گر نبازم عشق یار نازکی؟

باده‌نوشی، جان‌فزایی، دلبری، مه‌پیکری

دیده تا دیده جمالش در خیالش روز و شب

بی‌سر و پا سو بسو گردیده در هر کشوری

خسروِ شیرین خوبان جهان یار منست

فارغست از حالِ فرهادِ غریبی غم‌خوری

مهر رویش در دل ما همچو روحی در تنی

عشق او در جان ما چون آتشی در مجمری

دیدهٔ تردامنم تا میزند نقشی بر آب

در نظر دارد خیال عارض خوش‌منظری

QÂSIM
قاسم

Mu'înuddîn Alî of Tabriz (1356–1433), known as Qâsim-i-Anvâr, was the author of a popular masnavi entitled *Anîsu'l-'ârifîn* (Mystics' Companion), a explanation of Sufi terminology, and also of a divan of Sufi poetry. A well-known Sufi sheikh who had a large following in Herat, Qâsim-i-Anvâr was suspected of collaboration with an assailant who stabbed Shahrukh and was banished from Herat.

ره بیابانست و شب تاریك و پایم در گلست
عشق و بیماری و غربت مشکل اندر مُشكلست

اینچنین رهرا بدشواری توان رفتن ، مرا
همرهم عمرست و عمر نازنین مستعجلست

سخت حیرانست و سرگردان ، ولی دارد امید
دل بدان لطفی که ذرات جهان را شاملست

زاهدان گر قصه‌های عشق را منکر شوند
آشنا داند که مارا این سخن ناقابلست

صوفیِ خلوت نشین را کز محبت دل‌تهیست
گر بصورت می‌نماید حق ، بمعنی باطلست

ناصح از دردِ دل ما کی خبر دارد ؟ که ما
در میان موجِ دریائیم و او بر ساحلست

گفتمش "جان و دل و دین باختم در راه تو"
در تبسم گفت "قاسم ، صبر کن! کار دلست"

❊

ز چشمِ گوشه‌نشینان نشان سودا پرس   سوادِ زلفش از آشفتگان شیدا پرس
مرا که مست و خرابم ز جام و ساقی گوی   حدیث توبه و تقوی ز شیخ و مولا پرس
کمالِ ذوق ز مستان بی دل و دین جوی   نشانِ شوق ز رندان بی سر و پا پرس
در آن زمان که براندازد از جمال نقاب   بیا و از دلِ ما لذت تماشا پرس
علاجِ علقتِ دل را ز ارغنون بشنود   دوایِ دردِ کهن را ز جامِ صهبا پرس
کمالِ سحر مبین طرزِ غارتِ دل و دین.   ز چشمِ شیوه‌گرِ مستِ شیخِ شهلا پرس
طریقِ عشق و مودت ز جانِ قاسم جوی   نشانِ دُرِّ ثمین از درونِ دریا پرس

SHÂHÎ
شاهی

Amîr Âq-Malik Shâhî (d. 1453) was descended from the Sarbadâr
rulers of Sabzavar, and his melodious poetry has been enjoyed for cen-
turies.

گر نمی‌سوزد دلم ، این آه دردآلود چیست؟
آتشی گر نیست ، در کاشانه چندین دود چیست؟

عاقبت چون روی در نابود دارد بود ما
این همه اندیشهٔ بود و غم نابود چیست؟

ناوکِ آن غمزه هرکس‌راست ، مارا هم رسد
چون مقرر گشته روزی ، فکر دیر و زود چیست؟

یکدم ، ای آرامِ جان ، زان زلف سرکش باز پرس
کز پریشانیِ دلها آخرت مقصود چیست؟

محنت شاهی و تعظیم رقیبان تا بچند؟
بندگانیم ، آن یکی مقبول و این مردود چیست؟

*

بیک کرشمه که بر جان زدی ز دست شدم دگر شراب مده ساقیا که مست شدم
سرم بحلقهٔ روحانیان فرو نامد   کمند زلف تو دیدم که پای‌بست شدم
میان مردم از آن رو بلند شد نامم   که زیر پای سگانت چو خاک پست شدم
رو ، صلاح ، چه پویم چو عشق ورزیدم؟   بقبله روی چه آرم چو بت‌پرست شدم
شکسته‌بسته بُوَد گفت‌وگوی من ، شاهی   چنان که بستهٔ آن زلف پرشکست شدم

IBN-I-HUSÂM
ابن حسام

Muhammad ibn-i Husâmuddîn of Khûsf in Quhistan (d. 1470) is the
author of the *Khâvarânnâma*, an account of the legendary exploits of
Alî ibn Abî-Tâlib that was very popular in its day.

هر صبحدم مصوّرِ این چرخ اخضری   از کان لاجورد دهد زرِّ جعفری
مخفی کند مشاعلِ ایوان نیل‌فام   از عکسِ نورِ شعشعهٔ شمعِ خاوری
استبرقِ مرصّعِ گلگون بگسترد   بر چار طاقِ رفرفِ خضرا و عبقری
تزیین دهد بحسنِ زلیخای روزرا   همچون جمالِ یوسفِ کنعان بدلبری

از هر کنار دامنِ کافورگون حریر   بندد بر آستین و گریبانِ عنبری ٥

خاتونِ چار بالشِ قصرِ رفیع را¹   تزیین دهد بکسوتِ زریفتِ اصفری

بیرون دهد ز کانِ زبرجد عقیقِ ناب   چون بر بسیطِ ارضِ خضر لالهٔ طری

بر خاتمِ زبرجدِ مینا زند نگین   هنگام صنعِ قدرتش از لعلِ گوهری

این نُه طبقِ لآلی عقدِ خوشاب را   سازد نثارِ افسرِ خورشید یکسری ١٠

زرکش کند کتابهٔ ایوان و بام را   نه جدول و نه مسطر و نه زر، نه زرگری

بر اوجِ بامِ گلشنِ مینا ز عکسِ روز   مینوصفت کند چمن باغِ اغبری

بر خوانِ نقرهگون نهد آن قرصِ سیمِ خام   هر روز بارگاهِ فلک را مقرری

بر رویِ آبِ زورقِ زرّین روان کند   بیحرکت² و سکونتِ بادی و لنگری ١٥

بر سبز خنگِ عالمِ خضرا بجای عقد   چنبر کند قلادهٔ این طوقِ چنبری

تیغ و سپر ز مطلعِ فجر آورد برون   تیر و کمانِ چرخ بدان گردد اسپری

JÂMÎ

جامی

Born in the Jâm district of Khurasan and educated in Herat and Samarkand in the religious, literary, and Sufi tradition, Nûruddîn Abdul-Rahmân Jâmî (1414–1492), in collaboration with Sultan-Husayn Mirza (r. 1470–1506) and Mir Ali-Sher Navâ'î, established Herat as the literary capital of the age.

A prolific author, Jâmî composed, in addition to numerous prose and mixed prose-poetry works, a voluminous tripartite divan and a set of seven masnavis known collectively as the *Haft awrang* (The Seven Thrones). The seven are *Silsilatu'z-zahab* (Chain of Gold), a Naqshbandi doxology; *Salâmân u Absâl*, a philosophical allegory; *Tuhfatu'l-ahrâr* (Gift of the Free) in imitation of Nizâmî's *Makhzanu'l-asrâr*; *Subhatu'l-abrâr* (Rosary of the Pious), a theologico-mystico-ethical treatise after Amir Khusraw's *Nuh sipihr*; *Yûsuf u Zulaykhâ*, the allegorical romance between Joseph and Zulaykha, Potiphar's wife; *Laylî u Majnûn*, and *Khiradnâma-i Iskandarî*, both in imitation of Nizâmî.

Jâmî scarcely wrote a line of poetry that does not reverberate with mystical overtones; and in him and the Herat school of poets, many of whom migrated to the Indian subcontinent after the fall of Herat to the Uzbeks and then to the Safavids shortly after Jâmî's death, the subtle twists of meaning and calculated use of mystically ambiguous vocabulary that is normally said to characterize the "Indian" style of Persian

---

[1] The sun occupies the fourth celestial sphere. See p. 27, note 7.
[2] For the meter, read *har'kat*.

poetry surface from the accumulated stock of topoi and tropes inherent to the poetic idiom. With Hâfiz, the reader is never quite certain which meaning is intended to predominate; from Jâmî's time on, one may be certain that all possible meanings are intended, but especially the "sufistic."

The first selection, an animal fable in masnavi, is taken from the *Khiradnâma-i Iskandarî*. The second is from *Subhatu'l-abrâr*. The last three poems are ghazals from Jami's divan.

فرو ماند از ضعفِ پیری ز کار	یکی خاد ، مرغ هوائی‌شکار١
بصید غرض چنگش از ساز رفت	ز بال و پرشِ زورِ پرواز رفت
وطن ساخت گرد یکی آبگیر	ز بیقوتیَش خاست از جان نفیر
در افتاد غوکیش٢ ناگه بچنگ	پس از مدتی کرد آنجا درنگ
که "ای سورم از دست تو گشته سوك٣ ٥	برآورد فریاد بیچاره غوک
زمام شتاب از هلاكم بتاب	مکن یك زمان در هلاكم شتاب
نه در كام نیكم، نه در معده خوب	نیم من بجز طعمهٔ طبع‌كوب
بآن كی قناعت كند گوشت‌خوار؟	تنم نیست جز پوستی ناگوار
فرستی بدل مژدهٔ شادیَم	اگر لب گشائی بآزادیَم
بتو ماهیی‌را شوم رهنمون ١٠	بهر لحظه ز آئین سحر و فسون
ز الوان نعمت خورش‌یافته	در آب روان پرورش‌یافته
ازو پوست دور، استخوان نیز كم	تن او همه گوشت سر تا بدُم
بچشمان چو عكس كواكب در آب	به پشت آبگون وز شكم سیم ناب
همه پشت و پهلوی او پردرم	چو در شب سپهر از نثار كرم
یكی لقمه از وی به از صد چو من ١٥	نه در طبع اهلِ خرد رد چو من
بتلقین سوگندهای عظیم"	گشا لب گرت هست ازین وعده بیم
تهیِ‌معدگی‌را فراموش كرد	چو خاد این سخن‌را ز وی گوش كرد
ز منقار او غوك بیرون فتاد	بتلقین سوگند لب‌ها گشاد
بحرمان دگر باره شد خاد اسیر	بیك جستن افتاد در آبگیر
نه غوكش بپنجه، نه ماهی بشست ٢٠	گرسنه بخاك تباهی نشست
ره خرّمی بر دل و جان زده	منم، همچو آن خاد ، حرمان‌زده
ز نقصانِ فكرم سخن پرقصور	ز فكر سخن رفته از دل حضور

---

[1] *Murgh-i-havâî-shikâr*, "a hunter of birds of the air."
[2] *Ghôk-î'sh*: the enclitic *-ash* goes with *chang*.
[3] Read here *sôk* for *sôg*, to rhyme with *ghôk*.

نه جمعیتِ دل، نه لطفِ سخن   بدستم ز محرومیِ بخت من

فلک‌وار دورِ پیاپی بیار   بیا ساقیا، ساغر می بیار

خلاصی ز آلایشِ گل دهد ۲۵   ازان می که آسایشِ دل دهد

بیک گوشمال آورش در خروش   بیا، مطربا، عود بنهاده گوش

بدانا پیامِ سروش آورد   خروشی که دل‌را بهوش آورد

٭

پا بمیدانِ توکل می‌سود   صوفیی راهِ یقین می‌پیمود

یک شبی زندهٔ از حیِّ عرب[1]   روز در بادیه می‌برد بشب.

ساختش شمعِ سیه‌خانه خویش[2]   آمدش در ره آن بادیه پیش

دید شبرنگ غلامی چون ماه   کرد در ساحت آن خیمه نگاه

قدرتش نی که بجنبد از جای ۵   در غل و بند ز گردن تا پای

پیش مهمان بتضرع نالید   بر زمین روی تواضع مالید

نزند جز به ره لطف قدم   که «بُوَد خواجهٔ من اهلِ کرم

نکند ردِّ سخن مهمان‌را   نشود سدِّ روش احسان‌را

رحم بر عجز و گرفتاریِ من»   خواه ازو عفوِ گنهکاریِ من

وز پی طعمهٔ او خوان آورد ۱۰   خواجه چون رویِ بمهمان آورد

تا نبخشی گنه این سیهم»   گفت «انگشت بخوانت ننهم

لیک بشنو که چه از وی دیدم   خواجه گفتا «گنهش بخشیدم

در هنر نادر و در شکل عجیب   شتران بود مرا، جمله نجیب

پشته‌پشتان همه و صحراگرد   کوه‌کوهان همه و دشت‌نورد

پیل‌کردار تنومند و بلند ۱۵   کرگدن‌وار بسی نیرومند

چون ارم پیکرشان ذاتِ عماد   سخت‌رفتارتر از صرصرِ عاد[3]

وز جرس نوبتِ فیروزیِ من   از سفر واسطهٔ روزیِ من

کردشان بارِ گرانِ مستعجل   دو سه روزه ره این سرمنزل

تا به یک روز بدین جای رسید   وز حدی صوتِ طربزای کشید

برگرفتند همه راهِ عدم ۲۰   بارشان چون بگشادند زهم

جز بصحرای عدم یک شترم»   نیست اکنون که دل از غصه پرم

---

[1] A run-on line. Hayy, which means "tribe," also means "alive," a play on zinda.

[2] Âmad-ash…pêsh = âmad pêsh-ash. To make someone the "candle of the house" is to receive him as an honored guest.

[3] Sarsar-i Âd: Âd was a pre-Islamic Arabian tribe who were destroyed by a fierce cold wind (sarsar) for their disobedience.

گفت صوفی بخداوند غلام　　　　«کای بدلجوئیِ من کرده قیام

هستم از وصف خوش‌آوازیِ او　　　آرزومند حدی‌سازیِ او»

خواجه گفتش که «حدی کُن آغاز»　　داد قانونِ حدی‌سازی ساز

بود صوفی به ادب بنشسته　　　　شتری در نظرِ او بسته　　۲۵

صوفی از ذوق گریبان زد چاک　　　وز جهان بیخبر افتاد بخاک

وان شتر کرد رسن‌را پاره　　　　روی در بادیه گشت آواره

❊

خاست هر سو فتنه، گوئی فتنه‌جوی من رسید

بر سمند ناز، تُرکِ تندخوی من رسید

بادِ عنبربو چرا شد؟ گردِ مشکین بهرِ چیست؟

گرنه از صحرا غزالِ مشکبوی من رسید

اشکِ خونین بر رخِ زردم نشانی بیش نیست

زانچه در شبهای تنهائی بروی من رسید

تیغِ اورا داده‌اند آب از زلالِ زندگی

جان دیگر یافتم چون بر گلوی من رسید

ز آسمان هر سنگِ بیدادی که آمد بر زمین

کرد بختِ بد مدد کآن بر سبوی من رسید

ای خوش آن ساعت که گفتی چون شدم پیدا ز دور

«اینک آن دیوانهٔ ژولیده‌موی من رسید»

همچو جامی سرمهٔ چشمِ جهان‌بین ساختم

هر غباری کز سمِ اسبِ تو سوی من رسید

❊

پرتوِ شمعِ رُخت عکس بر افلاک انداخت

قرصِ خورشید شد[1] و سایه برین خاک انداخت

برقی از شعشعهٔ طلعتِ رخشانِ تو جست

شعله در خرمنِ مُشتی خس و خاشاک[2] انداخت

---

[1] *Shud* here means "went away."

[2] The world is often referred to as a "handful of flotsom and jetsam." The image of lightning striking a haystack *(kharman)* and reducing it to nothing is very common.

خوش بران رَخش که عشقت فلك سرکش را
طوق در گردن از آن حلقهٔ فتراك انداخت[1]

میخرامیدی و ارواح قُدس میگفتند
ای خوش آن خاك که سر در رهِ این پاك انداخت

ذوقِ مستانِ صبوحی زدهٔ بزمِ تو دید
صبح در اطلسِ فیروزهٔ خود چاك انداخت[2]

طوطیِ ناطقه را سرِ خط و عارضِ تو
زنگِ تشویر در آئینهٔ ادراك انداخت[3]

جامی اهلیتِ اندیشهٔ عشق تو نداشت
همّتش رخت درین موجِ خطرناك انداخت

✳

ریزم ز مژه کوکب بی ماه رخت شبها   تاریك شبی دارم با این همه کوکبها
چون از دلِ گرم من بگذشت خدنگِ تو   از بوسهٔ پیکانش شد آبله ام لبها
از بسکه گرفتاران مُردند بکوی تو   بادش همه جان باشد ، خاكش همه قالبها
از تاب و تبِ هجران گفتم سخن وصلت   بود این هذیان آری خاصیت آن تبها
تا دست برآوردی زآن غمزه بخونریزی   بر چرخ رود هر دم از دست تو یاربها

HILÂLÎ
هلالی

Nûruddîn "Hilâlî," known as Chaghatâyî, of Astarabad served at the court of Sultan-Husayn Mirza in Herat, and after the Uzbek invasion of Khurasan, Hilâlî was executed in 1529. He wrote two well-known mas-navis, *Shâh u darvêsh* (King and Dervish) and *Sifâtu'l-'âshiqîn* (Qualities of Lovers).

---

[1]The image here involves love's putting a collar (*tawq*) around the neck of the refractory celestial sphere, pictured as a horse with its neck through the ring of the saddle-strap (*halqa-i fitrâk*).

[2]*Subh* is the subject of both verbs, *dîd* and *andâkht*.

[3]The mystery of the down on the beloved's lip and cheek has cast the "rust of confusion" into the "speaking" (i.e., rational) parrot's mirror of comprehension. Parrots are pictured as speaking to themselves before a mirror. The dark color of the down on the lip is equivalent to the rust of confusion in the mirror. The speaking parrot is a metaphor for the rational soul (see p. 21, note 2), whose ability to understand has been destroyed by the "rust of confusion" caused by the down on the beloved's cheek.

گل سراسر آتشست اما نسوزد خاررا   یار ما هرگز نیآزارد دل اغیاررا

چند پوشم سینهٔ ریش و دل افگاررا؟   دیگر از بیطاقتی خواهم گریبان چاک زد

مرهمی نه کز دلم بیرون برد آزاررا   بر منِ آزرده رحمی کن، خدارا ای طبیب

چشم من آب دگر داد آن گل رخساررا   باغ حسنت تازه شد از دیدهٔ گریان من

آرزوی صحت از دل کی رود بیماررا؟   روز هجر از خاطرم اندیشهٔ وصلت نرفت

صبر اندکرا بگویم یا غم بسیاررا؟   حال خود گفتی، بگو بسیار واندک هرچه هست

از خدا خواهد هلالی دولت دیداررا   دیدن دیدار جانان دولتی باشد عظیم

٭

شیشهٔ می دور از آن لبهای میگون میگریست
تا دل خودرا دمی خالی کند خون میگریست

دوش بر سوز دل من گریهها میکرد شمع
چشم من آن گریهرا میدید و افزون میگریست

آن نه شبنم بود در ایام لیلی هر صباح
آسمان شب تا سحر بر حال مجنون میگریست

سیل در هامون، صدا در کوه، میدانی چه بود؟
از غم من کوه مینالید و هامون میگریست

چیست دامان سپهر امروز پرخون از شفق؟
غالبا امشب ز درد عشق گردون میگریست

بر رخ زردم ببین خطهای اشک سرخرا
این نشانیهاست کامشب چشم من خون میگریست

شب که میخواندی هلالیرا و میراندی بناز
در درون پیش تو میخندید و بیرون میگریست

POETS OF THE SAFAVID AND MUGHAL PERIODS

AHLÎ
اهلی

"Ahlî" of Shiraz (d. 1535), a contemporary of the Safavid Shah Isma'il I (r. 1501–24), is known for his use of rhetorical devices in poetry. He wrote a number of masnavis, of which *Sihr-i halâl* (Licit Magic) and *Sham' u parvâna* (The Candle and the Moth) are the best known.

اکنون که تنها دیدمت، لطف ارنه آزاری بکن
سنگی بزن، تلخی بگو، تیغی بکش، کاری بکن

گیرم نداری میل من، ای مردم چشم کسی
از گوشهٔ چشمی بما نظاره‌یی باری بکن

ای یوسف جان، میخرد خلقی بجان وصل ترا
رسم گرانجانی بهل، میل خریداری بکن

مُردیم دور از روی تو. در خانه مانی تا بکی؟
بیرون خرام آخر، گهی گلگشت بازاری بکن

تا کی طبیب عاشقان غافل ز حالت بگذرد؟
اهلی، بکش آهی ز دل یا نالهٔ زاری بکن

※

آن شمع گلرخان که رخش لاله‌زار ماست   طوفان آتشیست که در روزگار ماست
ما خوشه‌چین خرمن صاحبدلان شدیم   تخم محبت همه در کشت و کار ماست
زین آتش نهفته که در خاک می‌بریم   تا حشر لاله‌ای که دمد داغدار ماست
در دام عشق ما ز سر شوق می‌رویم   کآنکس‌که صید ما کند اول شکار ماست
ما تشنه‌لب بمسجد و ساقی بمیکده   بر کف شراب کوثر و در انتظار ماست
اهلی بمال چهرهٔ زردی که زر شوی   زان کیمیای عشق که خاک مزار ماست

VAHSHÎ

وحشی

For most of his career, Kamâluddîn Vahshî (d. 1582) of Bâfq, near Kirman, was a panegyrist for Shâh Tahmâsp the Safavid (r. 1524–76) and Ghiyâsuddîn Mîr-Mîrân, the governor of Yazd.

Vahshî's masnavis include *Khuld-i barîn* (Eternity Sublime), *Nâzir u Manzûr* (Beholder and Beheld), and *Farhâd u Shîrîn*, all in imitation of Nizâmî's masnavis. His chief importance lies, however, in his *tarkîb-bands*, a form that is found in the divans of most poets but was less cultivated than the ghazal, masnavi, and qasida.

To perhaps a greater extent than most other Persian poets, Vahshî allows a glimpse into the depth of his emotional states. He possesses a rare, candid idiom, which, while couched in traditional topoi and customary metaphor, seems to impart something more of the poet himself, his longings and his frustrations, than is normally expected from a conventional idiom.

دوستان، شرح پریشانی من گوش کنید   داستان غم پنهانی من گوش کنید

قصهٔ بی‌سروسامانی من گوش کنید   گفتگوی من و حیرانی من گوش کنید

شرح این آتش جانسوز نهفتن تا کی؟

سوختم، سوختم، این سوز نهفتن تا کی؟

روزگاری من و دل ساکن کوئی بودیم   ساکن کوی بت عربده‌جوئی بودیم

عقل و دین باخته، دیوانه روئی بودیم   بستهٔ سلسلهٔ سلسله‌موئی بودیم

کس در آن سلسله غیر از من دلبند نبود

یک گرفتار ازین جمله که هستند نبود

نرگس غمزه‌زنش اینهمه بیمار نداشت   سنبل پرشکنش هیچ گرفتار نداشت

اینهمه مشتری و گرمی بازار نداشت   یوسفی بود ولی هیچ خریدار نداشت

اول آنکس که خریدار شدش من بودم

باعث گرمی بازار شدش[1] من بودم

عشق من شد سبب خوبی و رعنائی او   داد رسوائی من شهرت زیبائی او

بسکه دادم همه جا شرح دلآرائی او   شهر پر گشت ز غوغای تماشائی او

این زمان عاشق سرگشته فراوان دارد

کی سر برگ من بی‌سروسامان دارد؟

پیش او یار نو و یار کهن هردو یکیست   حرمت مدعی وحرمت من هردو یکیست

---

[1]Interpolate from the first hemistich: *avval ânkas ki bâ'is-i…shud-ash.*

قول زاغ و غزل مرغ چمن هر دو یکیست   نغمهٔ بلبل و فریاد زغن هردو یکیست

این ندانست که قدر همه یکسان نبود

زاغ را مرتبهٔ مرغ خوش‌الحان نبود

چون چنینست پی کار دگر باشم به   چند روزی پی دلدار دگر باشم به

عندلیب گل رخسار دگر باشم به   مرغ خوش نغمهٔ گلزار دگر باشم به

تو گلی کو که شوم بلبل دستان سازش؟

سازم از تازه‌نهالان چمن ممتازش

گرچه از خاطر وحشی هوس روی تو رفت   وز دلش آرزوی قامت دلجوی تو رفت

شد دل آزرده و آزرده‌دل از کوی تو رفت   با لب پرگله از ناخوشی خوی تو رفت

حاش لله که وفای تو فراموش کند

سخن مصلحت‌آمیز کسان گوش کند

MUHTASHAM

محتشم

A good poet in qasida, ghazal, and qit'a, Shamsu'sh-shu'arâ Muhtasham
of Kashan (d. 1587) was especially renowned in his time for his qasidas.
A panegyrist of Shâh Tahmâsp (r. 1524–76), he is credited with several
divans. His most famous work, and by far the most famous example of
the genre, is his *marsiya* (elegy) on Husayn ibn Ali, grandson of the
Prophet Muhammad and Third Imam of the Shia. Refusing to ac-
knowledge the legitimacy of succession of the Umayyad caliph Yazîd ibn
Mu'âwiya (680–83), Husayn and his family were cut down on the
battlefield of Kerbela (Iraq) on *âshûrâ*, the tenth of Muharram, A.H. 61
(October 10, 680). Âshûrâ has since been commemorated by Shiites as a
day of lamentation over Husayn's suffering and martyrdom. The mar-
siya was particularly cultivated by the Safavids, who established Twelver
Shiism as the state religion of their empire and patronized all manner of
literature that was supportive of Shiism.

Muhtasham's elegy, too long to be given here in full, remains to this
day, along with Mullâ Husayn Vâ'iz Kâshifî's *Rawzatu'sh-shuhadâ*
(Garden of the Martyrs), as standard fare in the commemorative ses-
sions held in the Shiite world during the first ten days of Muharram.

باز این چه شورشست که در خلق عالمست؟

باز این چه نوحه و چه عزا و چه ماتمست؟

باز این چه رستخیز عظیمست کز زمین   بی‌نفخ صور خاسته تا عرش اعظمست؟

این صبح تیره باز دمید از کجا؟ کزو   کار جهان و خلق جهان جمله درهمست

کآشوب در تمامیِ ذراتِ عالمست   گویا طلوع میکند از مغرب آفتاب

این رستخیزِ عام که نامش مَحرَمست   گر خوانمش قیامتِ دنیا ، بعید نیست

سرهای قدسیان همه بر زانویِ غمست   در بارگاهِ قدس که جای ملال نیست

گویا عزای اشرفِ اولادِ آدمست   جن و ملک بر آدمیان نوحه میکنند

خورشیدِ آسمان و زمین ، نورِ مشرقین

پروردهٔ کنارِ رسولِ خدا ، حسین

در خاک و خون فتاده بمیدان کربلا   کشتیِ شکست خوردهٔ طوفانِ کربلا

خون میگذشت از سرِ ایوان کربلا   گر چشمِ روزگار برو فاش میگریست

زان گل که شد شکفته ببستان کربلا   نگرفت دستِ دهر گلابی بغیرِ اشك

خوش داشتند حرمتِ مهمان کربلا   از آب هم مضایقه کردند کوفیان¹

خاتم ز قحطِ آبِ سلیمان کربلا   بودند دیو و دد همه سیراب و میمكید

فریادِ «العَطَش»² ز بیابان کربلا   زان تشنگان هنوز بعیوق میرسد

کردند رو بخیمهٔ سلطان کربلا   آه از دمی که لشکرِ اعدا نکرده شرم

آندم فلک بر آتشِ غیرت شپند شد

کز خوفِ خصم در حرم افغان بلند شد

اول صَلا بسلسلهٔ انبیا زدند   بر خوانِ غم چو عالمیان را صَلا زدند

زان ضربتی که بر سرِ شیرِ خدا³ زدند   نوبت به اولیا چو رسید ، آسمان طپید

افروختند و بر حسنِ مجتبی⁴ زدند   بس آتشی ز اخگرِ الماس ریزه‌ها

کندند از مدینه و در کربلا زدند   پس آن سرادقی که مَلک محرمش نبود

بس نخلها ز گلشنِ آلِ عبا⁵ زدند   وز تیشهٔ ستیزه دران دشت ، کوفیان

بر حلقِ تشنهٔ خلفِ مرتضا زدند   پس ضربتی کزان جگرِ مصطفی درید

فریاد بر درِ حرمِ کبریا زدند   اهلِ حرم ، دریده‌گریبان ، گشاده‌موی ،

روح‌الامین نهاده بزانو سرِ حجاب

تاریک شد ز دیدنِ او چشمِ آفتاب

خورشید سربرهنه برآمد ز کوهسار   روزی که شد بنیزه سرِ آن بزرگوار

---

[1]The people of Kufah refused to give water to Husayn's band.

[2]al-atash (Ar.), "thirst."

[3]Shér-i khudá, the Lion of God, Ali b. Abi-Talib, the First Imam of the Shia, was assassinated.

[4]Hasan-i Mujtabá, Hasan the Chosen, Second Imam of the Shia, was killed by diamond dust in his food.

[5]Ál-i abá, the "people of the cloak," the Prophet, his daughter Fatima, her husband Ali, and their sons Hasan and Husayn, all five of whom could fit under the Prophet's cloak.

موجی بجنبش آمد و برخاست کوه کوه   ابری بِبارش آمد و بگریست زار زار

گفتی تمام زلزله شد خاکِ مطمئن   گفتی فتاده از حرکت چرخِ بیقرار

عرش آنچنان بلرزه درآمد که چرخِ پیر   افتاد در گمان که قیامت شد آشکار

آن خیمه که گیسویِ حورش طناب بود   شد سرنگون ز بادِ مخالف حباب‌وار

جمعی که پاسِ محملشان داشت جبرئیل   گشتندی بی‌عماری و محمل ، شترسوار

با آنکه سر زد این عمل از امتِ نبی   روح‌الامین ز رویِ نبی گشت شرمسار

وانگه ز کوفه خیلِ حرم رو بشام کرد

نوعی که عقل گفت قیامت قیام کرد

بر حربگاه چون رهِ آن کاروان فتاد   شورِ نشور در همه کون و مکان فتاد

هم بانگِ نوحه غلغله در شش جهت فکند   هم گریه بر ملایک هفت آسمان فتاد

هرجا که بود آهوئی از دشت پا کشید   هرجا که بود طایری از آشیان فتاد

شد وحشتی که شورِ قیامت بگرد رفت   چون چشمِ اهلِ بیت بران کشتگان فتاد

هرچند بر تنِ شهدا چشم کار کرد   بر زخمهایِ کاریِ تیغ و سنان فتاد

ناگاه چشمِ دخترِ زهرا دران میان   بر پیکرِ شریفِ امامِ زمان فتاد

بی‌اختیار نعرهٔ «هٰذا حسین»[1] ازو   سر زد چنانکه آتش ازو در جهان فتاد

پس با زبان پرگله آن بضعةالبتول[2]

رو در مدینه کرد که «یا ایها الرسول[3]

این کشتهٔ فتادهٔ بهامون حسین تست   وین صید دست‌وپازده در خون حسین تست

این نخلِ تر کز آتشِ جانسوزِ تشنگی   دور از زمین رسانده بگردون حسین تست

این ماهی فتاده بدریایِ خون که هست   زخم از ستاره بر تنش افزون حسین تست

این غرقهٔ محیطِ شهادت که رویِ دشت   از موجِ خونِ او شده گلگون حسین تست

این خشکلب فتاده و ممنوع از فرات   کز خونِ او زمین شده جیحون حسین تست

این شاه کم‌سپاه که با خیلِ اشک و آه   خرگاه ازین جهان زده بیرون حسین تست

این قالبِ طپان که چنین مانده بر زمین   شاه شهید ناشده مدفون حسین تست

پس رویِ در بقیع بزهرا خطاب کرد

مرغِ هوا و ماهیِ دریا کباب کرد

کای مونسِ شکسته‌دلان ، حالِ ما ببین   مارا غریب و بیکس و بی‌آشنا ببین

اولادِ خویش‌را که شفیعانِ محشرند   در ورطهٔ عقوبتِ اهلِ جفا ببین

در خلد بر حجابِ دو کون آستین‌فشان   کاندر جهان مصیبتِ مارا بیا ببین

---

[1]Hâzâ Husayn (Ar.), "this is Husayn."

[2]Biz'atu'l-batûl (Ar.), "offspring of the virgin (epithet of Fatima)," i.e., Fatima's daughter Zaynab.

[3]Yâ ayyuha'r-rasûl (Ar.), "O Apostle."

نی نی درآ ، چو ابر خروشان بکربلا   طغیانِ سیلِ فتنه و موجِ بلا ببین

تنهای کشتگان همه در خاک و خون نگر   سرهای سروران همه بر نیزه‌ها ببین

آن سر که بود بر سرِ دوشِ نبی مدام   یک نیزه‌اش ز دوشِ مخالف جدا ببین

آن تن که بود پرورشش در کنارِ تو   غلطان بخاکِ معرکهٔ کربلا ببین

یا بضعةَالرسول ، [2] ز ابنِ زیاد [1] داد!

کو خاکِ اهلِ بیتِ رسالت ببادِ داد!»

خاموش محتشم ، که دلِ سنگ آب شد   بنیادِ صبر و خانهٔ طاقت خراب شد

خاموش محتشم ، که ازین حرف سوزناک   اشک دو چشمِ مستمعان دُرِّ ناب شد

خاموش محتشم ، که ازین حرف خونچکان   مرغِ هوا و ماهیِ دریا کباب شد

خاموش محتشم ، که ازین شعر گریه‌خیز روی زمین ز اشکِ جگر خونخضاب شد

خاموش محتشم ، که ز شورِ تو آفتاب   از گردِ راهِ ماتمیان ماهتاب شد

خاموش محتشم ، که فلک بسکه خون گریست   دریا هزار مرتبه گلگون حباب شد

خاموش محتشم ، که ز گردِ غمِ حسین   جبریل را ز رویِ پیمبر حجاب شد

تا چرخِ سفله بود ، خطائی چنین نکرد

با هیچ آفریده جفائی چنین نکرد

FAYZÎ

فیضی

Born in Akbarabad (Agra), Abu'l-Fayz Fayzî Fayyâzî (1547–1595) was
Akbar Shah (r. 1556–1605)'s poet-laureate. In addition to many fine
ghazals and qasidas, he composed masnavis on Solomon and the Queen
of Sheba (Sulaymân u Bilqîs), the Indian story of Nala and Damayanti
(Nal u Daman) from the Mahabharata, and tales from the Bhagavad
Gita.

فلک ، زین کجروی‌هایت نمی‌گریم که برگردی

شبِ وصلست. خواهم اندکی آهسته‌تر گردی

ز مهتابِ رُخش ویرانهٔ من روشنست امشب

اگر وقتِ طلوعت آید ، ای خورشید ، برگردی

پس از عمریست امشب کوکبِ اقبالِ من طالع

ترا ، ای شب ، نمی‌خواهم بوقتِ خود سحر گردی

عجب نبود که جز روزِ قیامت پرده نگشائی

---

[1] Ubaydullâh ibn Ziyâd was the Umayyad governor of Iraq.

[2] Yâ biz'ata'r-rasûl (Ar.), "O offspring of the Apostle."

که، ای صبح سعادت، از شبِ من باخبر گردی

تو، ای اخترشناس، امشب توانی گفت گردونْ را

که بهر خاطرم بر عکس شبهای دگر گردی

مها، امشب بجانان درد دل دارم. میا بیرون!

که می‌ترسم خدنگِ آهِ فیضی را سپر گردی

URFÎ
عرفی

Born in Shiraz, Jamâluddîn Muhammad Urfî (1556–1591) went early in
life to Fatehpur-Sikri, then for a short time the capital of the Mughal
Empire, where he was patronized first by the poet Abu'l-Fayz Fayzî of
Akbarabad and then by the court physician Hakîm Abu'l-Fath Gîlânî,
who introduced him to the grand literary patron of the age, Abdul-
Rahîm Khânkhânân. After his fame had spread, Urfî was enlisted in the
emperor Akbar's retinue.

Although disfigured by the pox and personally unattractive and un-
popular, Urfî's poetry in all genres was much admired during his life-
time, as was his prose style. When he died at the age of thirty-six, he
was working on imitations of Nizâmî's *Makhzanu'l-asrâr* and *Khus-
raw u Shîrîn*. After his death his divan was turned over the the Khan-
khanan's munshees for final arrangement.

Urfî's fame rests mainly on his ornate qasidas composed in praise of
his various patrons. In these odes he displays his mastery over the
Persian idiom as well as his familiarity with recherché words and con-
structions. In his poetry the penchant for the bizarre comparison and
the purely cerebral metaphor, culminating in the poets of the next gen-
eration like Kalîm and Sâ'ib, can be clearly seen.

The first selection is taken from a long qasida of almost 200 lines en-
titled *Tarjumatu'sh-shawq* (Biography of Yearning) in praise of the
Imam Ali ibn Abi-Talib, a genre, called *manqibat*, cultivated particularly
in Mughal India, where, although the ruling dynasty was Sunni, a great
many nobles, especially the Iranians, were Shiite. The second specimen
is a ghazal in which the development of this genre as a catch-all for the
well-turned phrase, pseudo-philosophizing, and sufistic jargon, de-
signed to be a "hit" at any *majlis*, is evident.

جهان بگشتم و دردا بهیچ شهر و دیار   نیافتم که فروشند بخت در بازار

کفن بیاور و تابوت و جامه نیلی کن   که روزگار طبیب است و عافیت بیمار

زمانه مرد مصافست و من ز ساده‌دلی   کنم بجوشنِ تدبیر وهم دفعِ مضار

ز منجنیق فلک سنگِ فتنه می‌بارد   من ابلهانه گریزم در آبگینه حصار

چنین که ناله ز دل جوشد و نفس نزنم   عجب مدار گر آتش برآورم چو چنار

اگر کرشمهٔ وصلم کُشد وگر غم هجر   نه آفرین ز لبم بشنوند و نه زنهار

دل ز دردِ گرانمایه چون جگر ز فغان   دماغم از گله خالی چو خاطرم ز غبار

گلِ حیاتِ من از بسکه هست پژمرده   اجل نمی‌زند از ننگ بر سر دستار

ز دوستانِ منافق چنان رمیده دلم   که پیش رویِ ز الماس می‌کنم دیوار

برونِ صورتِ دیبایِ بالشم کس نیست   کز آستین نم اشکم بچیند از رخسار

کدام فتنه بشب سر نهاده بر بالین   که صبحدم نشد از خواب رو بمن بیدار؟

٭

خیز و شرابِ حیرتم زان قد جلوه‌ساز ده

رویِ بروی عشوه کن، دستِ بدستِ ناز ده

ای دل ساده، گفتمت نام وفا مبر کنون

مرهمِ داغِ خویش‌را از نمک امتیاز ده

توسنِ ناز کرده زین، ای دلِ عافیت‌گزین

مویِ بمویِ خویش‌را مژدهٔ ترکتاز ده

کی دو عروس‌را بهم تاب مشارکت بود؟

یا درِ مردمی مزن، یا سه طلاقِ آز ده

شیوهٔ سامری بُوَد ننگِ کرشمه‌های تو[1]

ما بفدای عشوه‌ات، پا برکابِ ناز ده

یا رب، ازان کرشمه‌ام کاوش دل نصیب کن

سینهٔ کبک داده‌ای، ناخنِ شاهباز ده

دم زده عرفی از وفا. باز دهش بامتحان

دشنهٔ زهرداده‌اش زان مژهٔ دراز ده

<h2 align="center">TÂLIB
طالب</h2>

Maliku'sh-shu'arâ Muhammad-Tâlib of Âmul (d. 1626) on the Caspian coast migrated to India during the reign of Jahângîr (r. 1605–27), who appointed him poet-laureate in 1618.

---

[1]*Shéva-i Sâmirî* is equivalent to sorcery: for Sâmirî, see p. 67, note 3. I.e., it would be beneath your blandishments to engage in mere sorcery.

همانا ترک مستی سوی این ویرانه می‌آید
که بوی خونی از زنجیر این دیوانه می‌آید

بتن گو هر سر مو تازه شو آمادهٔ زخمی
که باز آن فتنه‌جو می‌آید و مستانه می‌آید

چراغان گلی امشب به پای شمع می‌بینم
مگر بلبل بطرف مشهد پروانه می‌آید

کدامین گل چراغ خانهٔ خمّار شد کامشب
نسیمی کز چمن می‌آمد از خمخانه می‌آید

حدیث هجر تا کی؟ همنشین، نقل دگر سر کن
که بوی خواب مرگ از طرز آن افسانه می‌آید

در فیضست اینجا حاجبی و پرده‌داری نیست
بدین در آشنا می‌آید و بیگانه می‌آید

بدل نقش صنم، چون می‌روم زین خاکدان بیرون
باستقبال هر مویم صد آتشخانه می‌آید

دوای درد عشق از دردمند عشق جو، طالب
که زخم شعله‌را جراحی از پروانه می‌آید

KALÎM
کلیم

Mîrzâ Abû-Tâlib Kalîm (1582–1651) was born in Kashan and raised in Hamadan. Following the fashion of the age, he set out for Hindustan and, arriving in the Deccan state of Bijapur, was a protégé of the Shah-navaz Khan Shirazi, minister to Ibrahim Adilshah, until he went back to Iran in 1619. Returning to India in 1621, Kalîm remained under the patronage of the Mîr Jumla Shahrastânî until 1628, when he became attached to Shahjahan's court retinue and was the emperor's poet-laureate until his death in 1651. Disengaged from court intrigue, Kalîm withdrew to Kashmir before 1645, ostensibly to versify the history of Shahjahan's reign, and stayed there, an active participant in the literary circle of the governor, Zafar Khan, until his death.

پیری رسید و موسم طبع جوان گذشت ضعف تن از تحمّل رطل گران گذشت
باریک‌بینیت چو ز پهلوی عینکست باید ز فکر دلبر لاغرمیان گذشت
وضع زمانه قابل دیدن دوبار نیست رو پس نکرد هرک ازین خاکدان گذشت

در راه عشق گریه متاع اثر نداشت صد بار از کنار من ازین کاروان گذشت

از دستبرد حسن تو بر لشکر بهار یك نیزه خون گل ز سر ارغوان گذشت

حب‌الوطن نگر که ز گل چشم بسته‌ایم نتوان ولی ز مشت خس آشیان گذشت

طبعی بهم رسان که بسازی بعالمی یا همّتی که از سر عالم توان گذشت

در کیش ما تجرد عنقا تمام نیست در قید نام ماند اگر از نشان گذشت

مضمون سرنوشت دو عالم جز این نبود کآن سر که خاك راه شد از آسمان گذشت

بی دیده راه گر نتوان رفت، پس چرا چشم از جهان چو بستی ازو میتوان گذشت؟

بدنامی حیات دو روزی نبود بیش گویم، کلیم، با تو که آن‌هم چسان گذشت

یك روز صرف بستن دل شد باین وآن روز دگر بکندن دل از جهان گذشت

٭

دجلۀ اشك از بهار شوق طغیان کرده‌است

رازهای سینه‌را خاشاك طوفان کرده‌است

دل گمان دارد که پوشیدست راز عشق‌را

شمع‌را فانوس پندارد که پنهان کرده است

زاهد از حسن جهان‌آرای جانان میکند

آنقدَر ذوقی که دیوار گلستان کرده است

منّت باران بکِشت آرزویش می‌نهد

غمزه‌ات گر خسته‌ای‌را تیرباران کرده است

می‌شود اول ستمگر کشتۀ بیداد خویش

سیل دایم بر سر خود خانه ویران کرده است

در گلستان وفا بلبل بگل هرگز نکرد

آن نظربازی که چشمم با مغیلان کرده است

ربط سرها ماند با زانوی غم، دیگر سپهر

هرکجا دیدست پیوندی، پریشان کرده است

زلف هندوی ترا از دلبری خط توبه داد

کافری‌را کافر دیگر مسلمان کرده است

فکر پرواز گلستان دارد اندر سر کلیم

ساز راه گلشن کشمیر سامان کرده است

٭

نه همین میرمد آن نو گل خندان از من میکشد خار درین بادیه دامان از من

با من آميزش او الفت موج است و كنار   دمبدم با من و پيوسته گريزان از من

قمرى ريخته بالم، به پناه كه روم؟   تا بكى سركشىِ سرو خرامـــان از من؟

بتكلم، بخموشى، بتبسم، به نگاه   ميتوان برد بهر شيوه دلِ آسان از من

نيست پرهيز من از زهد كه خاكم بر سر   ترسم آلوده شود دامنِ عصيـان از من

اشكِ بيهوده مريز اينهمه از ديده، كليم،   گردِ غمِ را نتوان شستِ بطوفان از من

SÂ'IB
صائب

Mîrzâ Muhammad-Alî Sâ'ib Tabrîzî (1601–1678) was born and raised in
Isfahan. He travelled twice to India during Shahjahan's reign (1628–57)
and was received with accolades before he finally returned to Iran to be-
come Shah Abbas II's poet-laureate.

Author of an anthology and of a large corpus of poetry, Sâ'ib brings
to fruition the apophthegmatic style that had been cultivated particu-
larly by Kalîm. The ingenuity and cerebral juggling of sufistic and
pseudo-philosophical themes characteristic of the "Indian" style reach
their climax with Sâ'ib, whose poetry continued to exert great influence
on the poets of the Ottoman and Mughal empires for another century
and a half, whereas in Iran a reaction against the excessive intellectualiza-
tion of poetry, and in particular the ghazal, set in after Sâ'ib.

بزير چرخ دلِ شادمان نمى‌باشد   گلى شكفته درين بوستان نمى‌باشد

بهر كه مى‌نگرى همچو غنچه دلتنگست   مگر نسيم درين گلستان[1] نمى‌باشد؟

بچشم زنده‌دلان خوشترست خلوتِ گور   ز خانۀ كه دران ميهمان نمى‌باشد

خروش سيل حوادث بلند ميگويد كه "خواب امن از درين خاكدان نمى‌باشد"

هزار بلبل اگر در چمن شود پيدا   يكى، چو صائب، آتش‌بيان نمى‌باشد

*

اين ناكسان كه فخر باجداد ميكنند   چون سگ باستخوان دلِ خود شاد ميكنند

عشقِ مجاز[2] ابجدِ عشق حقيقتست   در عالمى كه اهلِ دل ارشاد ميكنند

گل بسته است راه به سرگوشىِ نسيم   اين بلبلان خام چه فرياد ميكنند؟

آينده‌را قياس كن از حال خود ببين   كز رفتگان بخير كرا ياد ميكنند؟

در مكتبى كه عشق اديبست، كودكان   مشقِ ستم بخامۀ فولاد ميكنند

---

[1]For the meter, read *gul'stân* for *gulistân*.
[2]*Ishq-i majâz*, "metaphorical love," is human love, opposed to "real love," mys-
tical love.

صائب، جماعتی که سوارند بر سخن　　در کوهِ قاف¹ صیدِ پریزاد میکنند

٭

با کمالِ احتیاج، از خلق استغنا خوشست
با دهانِ تشنه مردن بر لبِ دریا خوشست

نیست پروا تلخکامان را ز تلخیهای عشق
آبِ دریا در مذاقِ ماهیِ دریا خوشست

روی بر راه آورد چون راهرو تنها شود
از دو عالَم دشت‌پیمای طلب تنها خوشست

خرقهٔ تزویر از بادِ غرور آبستنست
حق‌پرستی در لباسِ اطلسِ دیبا خوشست²

فکرِ شنبه تلخ دارد جمعهٔ اطفال را³
عشرتِ امروزِ بی‌اندیشهٔ فردا خوشست

بادبانِ کشتیِ می نعرهٔ مستانه است
های‌هوی میکشان در مجلسِ صهبا خوشست

برق را در خرمنِ مردم تماشا کرده است
آنکه پندارد که حالِ مردمِ دنیا خوشست؟

ماه را ابرِ تنک جولانِ دیگر میکند
چهرهٔ طاعت نهان در پردهٔ شبها خوشست

هرچه رفت از عمر، یادِ آن بنیکی میکند
چهرهٔ امروز از آئینهٔ فردا خوشست

هیچ کاری گرچه، صائب، بی‌تأمل خوب نیست
بی‌تأمل آستین افشاندن از دنیا خوشست

BEDIL
بیدل

Abu'l-Ma'âlî Mîrzâ Abdul-Qâdir Bêdil (1644–1721) was born in Patna
to a family of Barlas Turk descent and spent most of his life in Shah-

---

¹*Kôh-i Qâf,* Mt. Qaf, the mythical mountain surrounding the earth, inhabited
by fairies and other creatures.
²The Sufi cloak *(khirqa)* had become synonymous with corruption and hypoc-
risy. Better, says Sâ'ib, to be a true worshipper clad in silken brocade, the wearing of
which was considered impious.
³Friday is the weekly holiday from school in Islamic countries.

jahanabad in retirement from the world. Now little known in Iran, Bêdil is perhaps the most admired of all poets of Persian in Afghanistan and the subcontinent, where his poetry has a large and very devoted following. Bêdil's poetry is not easy: it sometimes requires a good deal of thought on the reader's part to comprehend the gist of his lines.

یک سبق شاگرد استغنا کن این ابرام را   در طلب تا چند ریزی آبروی کام را؟

پخته نتوان کَرد زآتش آرزوی خام را   داغ بودن در خمار مطلب نایاب چند

پیش از آروغست نفرت آه بی‌هنگام را   مگذر از موقع‌شناسی ورنه در عرض نیاز

قطع کن وهم و خیال قاصد و پیغام را   مانعِ سیرِ سبکرو پای خواب‌آلوده نیست

اینقدرها هم اثر می‌بوده‌است اوهام را   حسنِ مطلق داشتیم، خودبینیَم آئینه کرد

بُه که از دوش افگنی این جامهٔ احرام را   زندگی تا کی هلاک کعبه و دیرت کند؟

نشاه یکرنگست اینجا دُرد و صاف جام را   از تغافل تا نگاه چشم خوبان فرق نیست

مار نتواند جدا از زهر دیدن کام را   کی رود فکر مضرت از مزاج اهل کین؟

دود آه صید باشد سرمه چشم دام را   حلقهٔ آن زلف رونق از غبارِ دل گرفت

بیدل، از آئینه نتوان ساخت وضعِ جام را   عرض مطلب دیگر و اظهار صنعت دیگرست

*

مطلبی گر بود از هستی همین آزار بود
ورنه در کنج عدم آسودگی بسیار بود

حیرتِ دل این قَدَرها جوش نالیدن نداشت
ما همان یک‌ناله‌ایم، اما جهان کهسار بود

غنچه‌ای پیدا نشد، بوی گلی صورت نیست
هرچه دیدم زین چمن، یا ناله یا منقار بود

دستِ همت کرد از بی‌جراتی‌ها کوتهی
ورنه چون گل کسوت ما یک گریبانوار بود

عافیت در مشربِ من بار گنجایش نداشت
بسکه جامم چون شرار از سوختن سرشار بود

قصرِ گردون را ز پستی رفعتِ یکپایه نیست
گردنِ منصور[1] را حرف بلندش دار بود

شوخیِ نظاره بر آئینهٔ ما شد نفس
چشم برهم بسته، بیدل، خلوت دیدار بود

---

[1] Mansûr = Hallâj, see p. 67, note 2.

POETS OF THE AFSHAR, QAJAR, AND PAHLAVI PERIODS
IN IRAN AND THE LATER MUGHAL PERIOD IN INDIA

HAZÎN

Shaykh Muhammad-Alî Lâhîjî "Hazîn" (1691–1767) was born in Isfahan but migrated to India after Nadir Shah Afshar's take-over of Iran in 1736.

در دام مانده باشد ، صیاد رفته باشد ای وای بر اسیری کز یاد رفته باشد

در خون نشسته باشم چون باد رفته باشد آه از دمی که تنها با داغ او چو لاله

روزی که کوه ِ صبرم بر باد رفته باشد از آه دردناکی سازم خبر دلت را

شاید بخواب ِ شیرین فرهاد رفته باشد آواز تیشه امشب از بیستون نیامد

گو مشت خاک ِ ما هم بر باد رفته باشد شادم که از رقیبان دامن کشان گذشتی

پُرشور ازین ، حزین ، است امروز کوه و صحرا

مجنون گذشته باشد ، فرهاد رفته باشد

∗

غم جان نیست ، جانان می پرستم من آن غارتگر ِ جان می پرستم

هنوز آتشعذاران می پرستم برآمد گرچه از پروانه ام دود

همان چاک ِ گریبان می پرستم دمید از تربتم صبح ِ قیامت

من آن زلف ِ پریشان می پرستم سرم سودای جمعیت ندارد

خروشان عندلیبان می پرستم بگلبانگ ِ پریشان داده ام دل

من آن صفهای مژگان می پرستم بچشمم در نمی آید صف ِ حور

من آن خورشید ِ تابان می پرستم حزین از کوری ِ خفاش طبعان

ÂZAR
آذر

Lutf-Alî Beg Âzar Begdilî (d. 1780), along with Hâtif and others, was instrumental in the Bâzgasht-i Adabî, the "literary return" to the older, classical style in reaction against the hypercerebralization and euphuism of the "Indian" style. He was panegyrist to Nâdir Shah's successors and to Karîm Khan Zand (1750–79). Author of many masnavis, he also composed the *Âtashkada-i Âzar* (Âzar's Fire Temple), an anthology of Persian poetry with short biographies of the poets.

The first selection is from Âzar's version of *Yûsuf u Zulaykhâ*. The second selection is taken from a long qasida.

چنانست آدمی غافل ز انجام   درین منزل که کس را نیست آرام

بداند چون ازو گردون ستاند   که تا نعمت بود قدرش نداند

که فکرش را چو من کوتاهیی بود   بدریائی شناور ماهیی بود

نه رنجی از شکنج دام دیده   نه از صیاد تشویشی کشیده

نه دل سوزان ز داغ آفتابش   نه جان از تشنگی در اضطرابش

که می‌گویند مردم «آب». کو آب؟   درین اندیشه روزی گشت بی‌تاب

که باشد مرغ و ماهی را روانبخش   کدامست آخر آن اکسیر جانبخش

چرا ، یارب ، ز چشم من نهانست؟   گر آن گوهر متاع این جهانست،

در آب آسوده از آبش خبر نه   جز آبش در نظر شام و سحر نه

که موج افکندش از دریا بساحل   مگر از شکر نعمت گشت غافل

فکند آتش بجانش دوری آب   بر او تابید خورشید جهان‌تاب

بخاک افتاد و آب آمد بیادش   زبان از تشنگی بر لب فتادش

بروی خاک غلطیدی و گفتی   ز دور آواز دریا چون شنفتی

کامید¹ هستیم بی‌روی او نیست   که «اکنون یافتم آن کیمیا چیست

که دستم کوتهست اورا ز دامن»   دریغا دانم امروزش بها من

✳

بشیخِ شهر فقیری ز جوع برد پناه   بدان امید که از لطف خواهدش خوان داد

هزار مساله پرسیدش از مسائل و گفت   که «گر جواب نگفتی، نبایدت نان داد»

نداشت حالِ جدل آن فقیر، و شیخ غیور   ببرد آبش و نانش نداد تا جان داد

عجب که با همه دانائی، این نمی‌دانست   که حق به بنده نه روزی بشرطِ ایمان داد

من و ملازمتِ آستانِ پیرِ مغان   که جام می بکفِ کافر و مسلمان داد

---

¹Read *k'umêd* for *ki umêd*.

HÂTIF
هاتف

Another exponent of the Bâzgasht, Sayyid Ahmad Hâtif of Isfahan (d. 1783) wrote with equal facility in Arabic and Persian and was also learned in medicine. His chief work, and the one that has earned him lasting fame, is the visionary recital given here in its entirety, his *tarjî'-band*.

In lines 1–6 the poet expresses his devotion to the One Beloved in familiar terms of self-sacrifice. The transition in line 7 introduces the poet's disturbed state, which took him to the Magian tavern (line 8), the perennial repository of the wine of mystical intoxication inhabited by the Magus, the beautiful *mughbachchas*, the *sâqî*, and the minstrel. When given the wine of unity, the disturbed poet and seeker loses his rationality (line 20), which loss enables him to gain a glimpse outside the world of sensual phenomena and multiplicity into the "realm of reality and unity." In the second stanza the poet encounters a Christian girl (line 20) whom he chastises for profaning divine unity with the "shame of the Trinity," but he is told of the substantial union of the three members of the Trinity as the church bell rings out the refrain. In the vintnor's shop in the third stanza help is sought from a *pîr*, who tells the poet that he is still in reason's chains, and to break them he quaffs wine and is given glad tidings by the Zoroastrian angel Surosh. The essence of the resulting vision is contained in stanza four, and the last stanza is addressed to the reader.

ای فدای تو هم دل و هم جان — وی نثار رهت هم این و هم آن

دل فدای تو، چون تونی دلبر — جان نثار تو، چون تونی جانان

دل رهاندن ز دست تو مشکل — جان فشاندن بپای تو آسان

راه وصل تو راه پرآسیب — درد عشق تو درد بی‌درمان

بندگانیم جان و دل بر کف — چشم بر حکم و گوش بر فرمان ٥

گر دل صلح داری، اینک دل — ور سر جنگ داری، اینک جان

دوش از سوز عشق و جذبهٔ شوق — هر طرف می‌شتافتم حیران

آخر کار شوق دیدارم — سوی دیر مغان کشید عنان

چشم بد دور، خلوتی دیدم — روشن از نور حق، نه از نیران

هر طرف دیدم آتشی کآن شب — دیده در طور موسی عمران ١٠

پیری آنجا به آتش‌افروزی — به ادب گرد پیر مغبچگان

همه سیمین‌عذار و گلرخسار — همه شیرین‌زبان و تنگ‌دهان

عود و چنگ و دف و نی و بریط — شمع و نقل و گل و می و ریحان

ساقی ماهروی مشکین‌موی — مطرب بذله‌گوی خوش‌الحان

مغ و مغزاده، موبد و دستور — خدمتش را تمام بسته میان ۱۵

من شرمنده از مسلمانی — شدم آنجا به گوشهٔ پنهان

پیر پرسید «کیست این؟» گفتند — «عاشقی بیقرار و سرگردان»

گفت «جامی دهیدش از می ناب — گرچه ناخوانده باشد این مهمان»

ساقی آتش‌پرست و آتش‌دست — ریخت در ساغر آتش سوزان

چون کشیدم نه عقل ماند و نه دین — سوخت هم کفر ازان و هم ایمان ۲۰

مست افتادم و درآن مستی — بزبانی که وصف آن نتوان

این سخن می‌شنیدم از اعضا — همه حتّی الورید والشریان[1]

که یکی هست و هیچ نیست جز او

وَحْـــدَهُ لا إلَـــهَ إلّا هُـــو[2]

از تو، ای دوست، نگسلم پیوند — ور به تیغم بُرند بند از بند

الحق ارزان بُوَد ز ما صد جان — وز دهانِ تو نَیَم شکّرخند ۲۵

ای پدر، پند کم ده از عشقم — که نخواهد شد اهلِ این فرزند

من ره کوی عافیت دانم — چه کنم؟ کاوفتاده‌ام بکمند

پند آنان دهند خلق، ای کاش — که ز عشق تو می‌دهندم پند

در کلیسا بدختری ترسا — گفتم «ای دل بدام تو در بند

ای که دارد به تار زنّارت — هر سرموی من جدا پیوند ۳۰

ره بوحدت نیافتن تا کی؟ — ننگ تثلیث بر یکی تا چند؟

نام حقّ یگانه چون شاید — که اب و ابن و روح قدس نهند»

لبِ شیرین گشود و با من گفت — وز شکرخنده ریخت آب از قند

که «گر از سرّ وحدت آگاهی — تهمت کافری به ما مپسند

در سه آئینه شاهدِ ازلی — پرتو از روی تابناک افکند ۳۵

سه نگردد بریشم ار اورا — پرنیان خوانی و حریر و پرند»

ما در این گفتگو که از یک سو — شد ز ناقوس این ترانه بلند

که یکی هست و هیچ نیست جز او

وَحْـــدَهُ لا إلَــهَ إلّا هُـــو

دوش رفتم بکوی باده‌فروش — زآتشِ عشق دل بجوش و خروش

محفلی نغز دیدم و روشن — میرِ آن بزم پیرِ باده‌فروش ۴۰

---

[1]Hatta'l-warîdi wa'sh-sharayân (Arabic): "down to the veins and arteries."
[2]Wahdahu lâ ilâha illâ hû (Arabic): "He alone, there is no god but He."

چاکران ایستاده صف در صف   باده‌خواران نشسته دوش بدوش

پیر در صدر و می‌کشان گردش   پارهٔ مست و پارهٔ مدهوش

سینه بی‌کینه و درون صافی   دل پر از گفتگو و لب خاموش

همه را از عنایت ازلی   چشم حق‌بین و گوش راست‌نیوش

سخنِ این بآن «هنیّاً لك»۱   پاسخ این بآن که «بادت نوش» ۴۵

گوش بر چنگ و چشم بر ساغر   آرزوی دو کون در آغوش

به ادب پیش رفتم و گفتم   «ای ترا دل قرارگاه سروش

عاشقم دردمند و حاجتمند   دردِ من بنگر و بدرمانِ کوش»

پیر خندان بطنز با من گفت   «کای ترا پیر عقل حلقه بگوش

تو کجا؟ ما کجا؟ ای از شرمت   دختر رز نشسته برقع‌پوش ۵۰

گفتمش «سوخت جانم. آبی ده!   وآتشِ من ز فرونشان از جوش

دوش می‌سوختم از این آتش   آه اگر امشبم بود چون دوش»

گفت خندان که «هین، پیاله بگیر»   ستدم. گفت «هان زیاده منوش»

جرعه درکشیدم و گشتم   فارغ از رنجِ عقل و زحمتِ هوش

چون بهوش آمدم یکی دیدم   مابقی سر بسر خطوط و نقوش ۵۵

ناگهان از صوامعِ ملکوت   این حدیثم سروش گفت بگوش

که یکی هست و هیچ نیست جز او

وَحْـــدَهُ لا إِلـــهَ إِلّا هُـــو

چشم دل باز کن که جان بینی   آنچه نادیدنیست آن بینی

گر به اقلیم عشق روی آری   همه آفاق گلستان بینی

بر همه اهل آن زمین بمراد   گردشِ دورِ آسمان بینی ۶۰

آنچه بینی دلت همان خواهد   وآنچه خواهدِ دلت همان بینی

بی سر و پا، گدای آنجارا   سر ز ملكِ جهان گران بینی

هم درانِ پابرهنه جمعی‌را   پای بر فرقِ فرقدان بینی

هم درانِ سربرهنه قومی‌را   بر سر از عرشِ سایبان بینی

گاه وجد و سماع هر یكدرا   بر دو کون آستین‌فشان بینی ۶۵

دل هر ذرّه که بشکافی   آفتابیش در میان بینی

هرچه داری اگر به عشق دهی   کافرم گر جوی زیان بینی

جان گدازی اگر بآتش عشق   عشق‌را کیمیای جان بینی

آنچه نشنیده گوشت، آن شنوی   وآنچه نادیده چشمت، آن بینی

تا بجائی رساندت که یکی   از جهان و جهانیان بینی ۷۰

---

[1] Haniyan lak (Ar.), "cheers."

با یکی عشق ورز از دل و جان   تا بعین‌الیقین عیان بینی

که یکی هست و هیچ نیست جز او

وَحْـــدَهٗ لا إِلٰـهَ إِلّا هُـــو

یار بی‌پرده از در و دیوار   در تجلیست، یا ولی‌الابصار¹

شمع جویی و آفتاب بلند   روز بس روشن و تو در شب تار

گر ز ظلمات خود رهی بینی   همه عالم مشارق‌الانوار² ۷۵

کورروش قائد و عصا طلبی   بهر این راه روشن هموار

چشم بگشا بگلستان³ و ببین   جلوهٔ آب صاف در گل و خار

زآب بی‌رنگ صد هزاران رنگ   لاله و گل نگر درین گلزار

پا براه طلب نه از ره عشق   بهر این راه توشهٔ بردار

شود آسان ز عشق کاری چند   که بود نزد عقل بس دشوار ۸۰

یار گو بالغدو والآصال   یار جو بالعشی والابکار⁴

صد رهت «لن ترانی»⁵ ار گوید   باز میدار دیده بر دیدار

تا بجانی رسی که می‌نرسد   پای اوهام و پایهٔ افکار

یار یابی بمحفلی کآنجا   جبرئیل امین ندارد بار

این ره آن زاد راه و آن منزل   مرد راهی اگر، بیا و بیار ۸۵

ور نئی مرد راه چون دگران   یار میگوی و پشت سر می‌خار⁶

هاتف، ارباب معرفت که گهی   مست خوانندشان و گه هشیار

از می و بزم و ساقی و مطرب   روز مغ و دیر و شاهد و زنار

قصد ایشان نهفته اسراریست   گه به ایما کنند، گاه اظهار

پی بری گر برازشان، دانی   که همینست سرّ آن اسرار ۹۰

که یکی هست و هیچ نیست جز او

وَحْـــدَهٗ لا إِلٰـهَ إِلّا هُـــو

---

¹Yâ walî'l-absâr (Ar.), "O possessor of insight."

²Mashâriqu'l-anwâr (Ar.), "the dawning places of lights," the points at which the light of dawn break through.

³For the meter, read gul'stân.

⁴Bi'l-ghudûwi wa'l-âsâl (Ar.), "in the morning and in the evening." Bi'l-'ashîyi wa'l-abkâr (Ar.), "in the evening and in the morning."

⁵Lan tarânî (Kor. 7:143), "you will never see me," God's reply to Moses when Moses asked God to reveal himself.

⁶Mîkhâr, a continuous imperative, "keep scratching."

VISÂL
وصال

Mîrzâ Muhammad-Shafi' of Shiraz (1782–1845), known as Mîrzâ Kû-chik, was particularly adept at incorporating classicisms from the older poets into his work. Like an expert copier of Old Master paintings, he could reproduce to perfection the style and idiom of classical models like Sa'dî.

زین بیشتر بباد مده مده آبروی ما　　　گشتیم خاك و پا ننهادی بروی ما

تا عشق جرعۀ دهدت از سبوی ما　　　تن خاك كرد باید و خاكش پیاله ساخت

بیچاره‌تر كسی كه برد آرزوی ما　　　بیچاره ما در آرزوی یك نگاه تو

این قطره می كه بی‌تو رود در گلوی ما　　　این طرفه بین كه مایۀ یك دجله خون شود

وقتست ساقیا كه دهی شستشوی ما　　　ناداده غسل، توبه دهد شیخمان ز می

ساقی؟ كه بار دیگرش آرد بجوی ما　　　عمر گذشته آب ز جو رفته شد. كجاست

كاو عیب ما چو آینه گوید بروی ما　　　گردیم خاك درگه روشندلی، وصال،

❋

من ایستاده‌ام، ای دوست، تا چه فرمایی　　　اگر كُشی و گر از مرحمت ببخشایی

دریغ كای شب وصل آنقدر نمی‌پایی　　　بسی شكایتم از روزگار هجرانست

كه آفتاب فلك را بگل بیندایی　　　بصبر عشق نهفتن بدل بدان ماند

كه هركه بیند پنداردت شكرخایی　　　چنان كنی سخن تلخ از ان لب شیرین

اگر ز مهر ببالین خستگان آیی　　　عیان شود كه چه می‌آید از لب لعلت

چنان بود كه ز ما عاشقان شكیبایی　　　وصال از دل خوبان وفا طلب كردن

FURÛGHÎ
فروغی

Mîrzâ Abbâs "Furûghî" of Bistâm (1798–1857), a prolific poet, was pan-egyrist to Furûghu'd-dawla, son of the governor of Khurasan and Kirman from whom he took his pen name, and to three consecutive Qajar shahs. Later in life he abandoned his official post and, withdrawing into contemplative retirement, devoted himself to Sufism.

كافروختهٔ‌رخ آمد و افراخته قامت　　　امروز ندارم غم فردای قیامت

یعنی كه مجو در طلبش راه سلامت　　　در كوی وفا چاره بجز دادن جان نیست

تا سینه نكردم هدف تیر ملامت　　　تیری ز كمانخانهٔ ابروش نخوردم

فرخنده مقامیست سرِ کوی تو لیکن   از رشکِ رقیبان نبود جای اقامت

چون دعوی خون با تو کنم در صف محشر؟   کز مستِ معربد نتوان خواست غرامت

تا محشر اگر خاک زمین را بشکافند   از خونِ شهیدان تو یابند علامت

با حلقهٔ زنارِ سرِ زلفِ تو، زاهد   تسبیح زِ هم بگسلد از دست ندامت

من پیرِو شیخیّ که زِ خاصیت مستی   در پای خُم انداخته دستارِ امامت

کیفیتِ پیمانه گر اینست، فروغی،   چونست سبوکش نزند لافِ کَرامت؟

YAGHMÂ
یغما

Abu'l-Hasan "Yaghmâ" (1782–1859) of Jandaq, north of Yazd, spent a good deal of his life as a wandering dervish, although he also held provincial offices from time to time. He was known for his excessively satirical verse, which caused his dismissal more than once.

نگاه کن که نریزد ، دهی چو باده بدستم

فدای چشم تو، ساقی، بهوش باش که مستم

کنم مصالحه یکسر بصالحان می کوثر

بشرط آنکه نگیرند این پیاله ز دستم

زِ سنگ حادثه تا ساغرم درست بماند

بوجهِ خیر و تصدق هزار توبه شکستم

چنین که سجده برم بی‌حفاظ پیشِ جمال

بعالمی شده روشن که آفتاب پرستم

کمندِ زلفِ بتی گردنم ببست بموئی

چنان کشید که زنجیرِ صد علاقه گسستم

نه شیخ میدهدم توبه ونه پیر مغان می

ز بس که توبه نمودم، ز بس که توبه شکستم

ز گریه آخرم این شد نتیجه در پی زلفش

که در میان دو دریای خون فتاده نشستم

زِ قامتش چو گرفتم قیاسِ روزِ قیامت

نشست و گفت «قیامت بقامتیست که هستم»

حرام گشت به یغما بهشت روی تو روزی

که دل بگندمِ آدم[1] فریبِ خالِ تو بستم

---

[1]Gandum-i Âdam: see p. 63, note 3.

٭

صوفیان را دگر امروز نه هایست و نه هوئی
آسمان باز همانا زده سنگی بسبوئی

نه بدستی زده‌ام چاك گریبان سلامت
گر ملامت کشم از کرده، توان کرد رفوئی

بر سرم چون گذری، دستهٔ گل بر سر خاری
پا بچشمم چو نهی، سرو روان بر لب جوئی

من که صد سلسله چون حلقهٔ مویی بگسستم
حلقهٔ سلسلهٔ زلف تو ام بست بموئی

زاهد ار اهل بهشتست، خدایا مفرستم
جز بدوزخ. چو منی ظلم بود یار چو اوئی

زین همه شنعت بیهوده‌ات، ای شیخ، چه حاصل؟
رو، بدست آر، چو مردانِ خدا، سیرت و خوئی

ای خوش آن دل که ز ترکان پریچهره چو یغما
نشود شیفتهٔ رنگی و آشفتهٔ بوئی

GHÂLIB
غالب

Mîrzâ Asadullâh Khan Ghâlib (1796–1869), born in Agra, went to Delhi
during his youth and remained there for the rest of his life. Better
known these days for his Urdu poetry, Ghâlib was much prouder of
his achievements in and knowledge of Persian. Ghâlib was connected
with the last Mughal emperor, Bahâdur Shâh II "Zafar" (r. 1837–58).

دل برد و حق آنست که دلبر نتوان گفت   بیداد توان دید و ستمگر نتوان گفت
در رزمگهش ناچخ و خنجر نتوان برد   در بزمگهش باده و ساغر نتوان گفت
پیوسته دهد باده و ساقی نتوان خواند   همواره تراشد بت و آزر نتوان گفت
هنگامه سرآمد، چه زنی لاف تظلم؟   گر خود ستمی رفت، بمحشر نتوان گفت
آن راز که در سینه نهانست و نه وعظست   بر دار توان گفت و بمنبر نتوان گفت
کاری عجب افتاد بدین شیفته مارا   مؤمن نبود غالب و کافر نتوان گفت

٭

ای ذوق نواسنجی بازم بخروش آور   غوغای شبیخونی بر بُنگِ هوش آور

گر خود نجهد از سر از دیده فرو بارم

دل خون کن و آن خون را در سینه بجوش آور

هان همدم فرزانه، دانی ره ویرانه؟   شمعی که نخواهد شد از باد خموش آور

شورابهٔ این وادی تلخست. اگر رادی   از شهر بسوی من سرچشمهٔ نوش آور

دانم که زری داری، هرجا گذری داری   می کر ندهد سلطان، از باده‌فروش آور

ریحان دمد از مینا، رامش چکد از قلقل

آن در ره چشم افکن، وین از پی گوش آور

گاهی بسبکدستی از باده ز خویشم بر[1]   گاهی بسیه‌مستی از نغمه بهوش آور

غالب که بقایش باد همپای تو کر ناید   باری غزلی فردی زآن موبینه‌پوش آور

QÂ'ÂNÎ
قاآنی

"Hassânu'l-'ajam" Mîrzâ Habîbullâh Qâ'ânî of Shiraz (1808–1854) was educated in his native Shiraz and in Khurasan, but he spent most of his professional life in Tehran as panegyrist to Muhammad Shah (r. 1834–48) and Alî-Qulî Mîrzâ I'tizâdu's-saltana during Nâsiruddîn Shah Qajar (r. 1848–96)'s reign.

A master of the traditional formal idiom of poetry, Qâ'ânî's themes range from the lascivious and obscene to the moribund and sentimental. Although he had some acquaintance with European literature, it had little influence on his writing, which seems to be caught in the nineteenth-century ambivalence characteristic of Iranian society at the time. The traditional forms and idiom still prevailed, yet they appear to have lost the vibrance they had formerly imparted to poetry.

The second poem given here is a *mukhammas*, a strophic form that consists of stanzas of five hemistiches each.

بهار آمد که از گلبن همی بانگ هزار آید

بهر ساعت خروش مرغ زار از مرغزار آید

تو گوئی ارغنون بستند بر هر شاخ و هر برگی

ز بس بانگ تذرو و صلصل و درّاج و سار آید

بجوشد مغز جان چون بوی گل از بوستان خیزد

بپرد مرغ دل چون بانگ مرغ از شاخسار آید

خروش عندلیب و صوت ساز و نالهٔ قمری

---

[1] *Zi khwêsh-am bar*: "take me away from myself."

گهی از گل ، گهی از سروین ، گاه از چنار آید

تو گوئی ساحت بستان بهشت عدن‌را ماند

ز بس غلمان و حور آنجا قطار اندر قطار آید

یکی بر کف نهد لاله که ترکیب قدح دارد

یکی بر گل کند تحسین کزو بوی نگار آید

یکی بیند چمن‌را بی‌تأمل «مرحبا» گوید

یکی بوید سمن‌را ، مات صنع کردگار آید

یکی بر لاله پا کوبد که هی هی رنگ می‌دارد

یکی از گل بوجد آید که بخ بخ بوی یار آید

یکی بر سبزه می‌غلطد ، یکی در لاله می‌رقصد

یکی گاهی رود از هُش ، یکی که هوشیار آید

ز هر سوئی نوای ارغنون و چنگ نی خیزد

ز هر کوئی نوای بربط و طنبور و تار آید

✳

باز برآمد به کوه رایت ابر بهار　　　　سیل فرو ریخت سنگ از زیر کوهسار

باز بجوش آمدند مرغان از هر کنار　　　　فاخته و بواللیح ، صلصل و کبك و هزار

طوطی و طاووس و بط ، سیره و سرخاب و سار

هست بنفشه مگر قاصد اردیبهشت　　　　کز همه گلها دمد پیشتر از طرف کشت

وز نفسش جویبار گشته چو باغ بهشت　　　　گوئی با غالیه بر رخش ایزد نوشت

کای گل مشکین‌نفس ، مژده بر از نوبهار

دیدهٔ نرگس بباغ باز پر از خواب شد　　　　طرهٔ سنبل براغ باز پر از تاب شد

آب فسرده چو سیم باز چو سیماب شد　　　　باد بهاری بجست ، زهرهٔ دی آب شد

نیمشبان بیخبر کرد ز بستان فرار

نرمك نرمك نسیم زیر گلان می‌خزد　　　　غبغب این می‌مکد ، عارض آن می‌مزد

گیسوی این می‌کشد ، گردن آن می‌گزد　　　　گه بچمن می‌چمد ، گه بسمن می‌وزد

گاه بشاخ درخت ، که بلب جویبار

لاله درآمد بباغ با رخ افروخته　　　　بهرش خیاط طبع سرخ قبا دوخته

سرخ قبایش به بر ، یك دو سه جا سوخته　　　　یا که ز دلدادگان عاشقی آموخته

کش شده دل غرق خون ، گشته جگر داغدار

طفل چو زاید ز مام گریه کند زودسر　　　　بهر تقاضای شیر وز پی قوت جگر

از پسِ گریه کند خنده بچندی دگر.   طفل شکوفه چرا خندد زان پیشتر[1]

کز پی تحصیلِ شیر گریه کند طفل‌وار؟

باغ چو از ایزدی جامه، مخلع شود   ظاهر از انواع گل شکل مضلع شود

یکی مخمس شود، یکی مربع شود   یکی مسدس شود، یکی مسبع شود

الحق بس نادرست هندسهٔ کردگار

نرگسك آن طشت سیم باز بسر بر نهاد   بر سر سیمینه طشت طاسك زر بر نهاد

در وسط طاس زد زرین پر بر نهاد   بر پر زرین او ژاله گهر بر نهاد

تا شود آن زر خشك از گهرش آبدار

کنیزکی چینی است بباغ در نسترن   سپید و سرخ و لطیف چو خواهرش یاسمن

ستارگانند خرد بهم شده مقترن   ریا گسسته ز مهر سپهر عقدِ پرن

نموده در نیمه‌شب بفرق نسرین نثار

دایرهٔ سرخ گل گشت مضرس چراست؟   بر تنش این ایزدی جامهٔ اطلس چراست؟

دیبهٔ او بی نورد، این همه املس چراست؟   بوته‌صفت در میانش زر مکلس چراست؟

بهر چه تکلیس کرد این همه زرّ عیار؟

بلبلکان زرج زرج زیر و بم انگیخته   صلصلکان فوج فوج خوش بهم آمیخته

پشت بهم داده حلق در نغم آویخته   تیغ تعنت ز قهر بر الم آهیخته

خورده بهم جامِ می با دف و طنبور و تار

ÎRAJ

ایرج

Jalâlu'l-mamâlik Îraj Mîrzâ (1874–1924) was a great-grandson of Fath-Alî Shah Qajar (r. 1797–1834). Fluent in Persian, Arabic, and French, Îraj Mîrzâ also knew Russian and Turkish.

His poetry is simple and colloquial in style, and Îraj borrowed much from European literature and transformed it into a quasi-classical Persian style. The beginning of his masnavi *Ârifnâma* on his friend Ârif, a masterpiece of ribald humor, is given here along with a fragment of a qasida and a short, humorous masnavi.

رفیق سابق طهرانم آمد   شنیدم من که عارف جانم آمد

نشاط و وجدِ بی‌اندازه کردم   شدم خوشوقت و جانی تازه کردم

که گر عارف رسد از در نرانند   به نوکرها سپردم تا بدانند

---

[1]A run-on line: *z' ân pêshtar ki…*

نگویند «این جنابِ مولوی کیست؟   فلانی۱ با چنین شخص آشنا نیست»

نهادم در اطاقش تختخوابی   چراغی، حوله‌یی، صابونی، آبی   ۵

عرقهائی که با دقت کشیدم   به دست خود درونِ گنجه چیدم

مهیا کردمش قرطاس و خامه   برای رفتنِ حمّامْ جامه

فراوان جوجه و تیهو خریدم   دوتائی احتیاطاً سر بریدم

نشستم منتظر کز در درآید   ز دیدارش مرا شادان نماید

نمی‌دانستم، ای نامردِ کونی،   که منزل می‌کنی در باغ خونی   ۱۰

نمی‌جویی نشان دوستانت   نمی‌خواهی که کس جوید نشانت

وگر گاهی به شهر آیی ز منزل   نبینم جای پایت نیز در گل

بری با خود نشان جای پارا   کنی تقلید مرغان هوارا

برو، عارف، که واقع حرف مفتی.   مگر بختی که روی از من نهفتی؟

مگر یاد آمد از سی سال پیشت   که بر عارض نبود آثار ریشت   ۱۵

مگر از منزل خود قهر کردی؟   که منزل در کنار شهر کردی

مگر نسرین‌تنی داری در آغوش؟   که کردی صحبت مارا فراموش

مگر با سروقدان آرمیدی؟   که پیوند از تهی‌دستان بریدی

چرا در پرده می‌گویم سخن را؟   چرا بر زنده می‌پوشم کفن را؟

بگویم صاف پاک و پوست‌کنده   که علت چیست می‌ترسی ز بنده   ۲۰

ترا من می‌شناسم بهتر از خویش   ترا من آوریدستم به این ریش

خبر دارم ز اعماق خیالت   به من یک ذره مخفی نیست حالت

تو از کون‌های گرد لاله‌زاری۲   یکی‌را این سفر همراه داری

کنار رستوران قلا نمودی   ز کون‌کنهای تهران در ربودی

چو آن گربه که دنبه از سر شام   همی وردارد و ورمالد از بام   ۲۵

کنون ترسی که گر سوی من آنی   کنی با من چو سابق آشنائی

منت آن دنبه از دندان بگیرم   خیالت غیر از اینه۳؟ من بمیرم

تو میخواهی بگریی دیرجوشی؟   به من هم هیزم تر می‌فروشی؟

تو مارا بسکه صاف و ساده دانی،   فلان کون را برادرزاده خوانی؟

چرا هر جا که یک بی‌ریش باشد   ترا فی‌الفور قوم و خویش باشد؟   ۳۰

چرا در روی یک خویش تو مو نیست؟   چرا هرکس که خویش تست کونیست؟

برو، عارف، که اینجا خبط کردی   مرین اندیشه‌را بی‌ربط کردی

۱Fulâni (so-and-so) here refers to Îraj.

۲Lâlazâr, the red-light district of Tehran.

۳Khiyâl-at ghayr az în-e? (colloquial) "Do you think any different?"

*

که کسبِ روزی با چشمِ اشك یاب كند

شنیده‌ام که بدریای هند جانوریست

دو دیده خیره برخسار برخسار آفتاب كند

بساحل آید و بی‌حس بروی خاك افتد

برای جلب مگس دیده پر لعاب كند

شود ز تابشِ خور چشم او پر از قی و اشك

بهم نهد مژه و سر بزیر آب كند

چو گشت كاسة چشمش پر از ذباب و هوام

تن ذباب و دلِ پشّه‌را كباب كند

بآب دیده سوزنده‌تر ز آتش تیز

مرو، که صیدِ تو چون پشّه و ذباب كند

چو اشك این حیوانست اشك دیدة شیخ

*

ویا از قصه‌پردازی شنیدم

ندانم در كجا این قصه دیدم

بهم بودند عمری یار و همسر

كه دو روبه، یكی ماده، یكی نر

كشیدند آن دو روبه‌را بزنجیر

ملك با خیل تازان شد بنخچیر

عیان شد روز روز ختم آشنائی

چو پیدا گشت آغاز جدائی

یكی مویه‌كنان با جفت خود گفت كه «دیگر در كجا خواهیم شد جفت؟»

جوابش داد آن یك از سر سوز «همانا در دكان پوستین‌دوز»

PARVÎN
پروین

At an early age Parvîn I'tisâmî (1906–1941) began composing sensitive
poetry that was popular in her own time and has remained critically ac-
claimed until today. She often adopts the tone of a mother telling her
child a story and couches her narrative in the form of a dialogue.

كه «ز ایام دلت زود آزُرد

غنچه‌ای گفت به پژمرده گلی

ز چه رو كاستی و گشتی خرد؟

آب افزون و بزرگست فضا

نفتاد و نشكست و نفسرد»

زینهمه سبزه و گل جز تو كسی

نه چنانست كه دانند سترد

گفت «زنگی كه در آینة ماست

صاف خوردیم و رسیدیم بدُرد

در می هستیِ ما صافی بود

بگرفتش ز من و بر تو سپرد

خیره نگرفت جهان رونقِ من

باغبان فلكم سخت فشرد

تا كند جای برای تو فراخ

چه توان كرد چو می‌باید مرد؟

چه توان گفت بیغمارِ دهر؟

آنكه آورد ترا، مارا برد

تو بباغ آمدی و ما رفتیم

اندرین دفتر پیروزه سپهر آنچه را ما نشمردیم شمرد٠

غنچه تا آب و هوا دید شکفت چه خبر داشت که خواهد پژمرد؟

ساقیِ میکدۀ دهر قضاست همه کس باده ازین ساغر خورد[1]

✳

لاله‌ای با نرگسی پژمرده گفت «بین که ما رخساره چون افروختیم»

گفت «ما نیز آن متاع بی‌بدل شب خریدیم و سحر بفروختیم

آسمان روزی بیاموزد ترا نکته‌هائی را که ما آموختیم

خرّمی کردیم وقت خرّمی چون زمانِ سوختن شد، سوختیم

تا سفر کردیم بر ملک وجود توشۀ پژمردگی اندوختیم

درزیِ ایام زآن ره می‌شکافت آنچه را زین راه ما می‌دوختیم

BAHÂR
بهار

Poet, scholar, author, and journalist, Maliku'sh-shu'arâ Muhammad-Taqî Bahâr (1886–1951) was a member of the turn-of-the-century educated elite of Iran and was actively involved in political and social reform. While maintaining traditional poetic forms—for which reason he can be included here as a "classical" poet—he broke away from the narrow strictures of traditional content and used the poetical tongue to convey his modernist views. His satirical qasida on religious intolerance and superstition, the first selection here, is indicative of his method of criticism, as is the second selection, his *mustazâd* lampooning "oriental fatalism" and complacency in the face of Western material superiority. In contrast to his contemporary, Iqbâl of Lahore, who used Persian as a medium of communication throughout the Indo-Iranian world, Bahâr's concern is solely for the Iran of his day, whereas his message is in many respects similar to Iqbal's. Both called for an awakening of Muslims from their centuries-long slumber in complacency.

Bahâr's *Sabkshinâsî* is a masterly critique of and introduction to Persian prose stylistics, and his dialect poetry is admired by Khurasanis and even by many from without this dialect area. His knowledge of ancient Iranian languages led him to introduce into his poetry many new compounds, the possibility for which had long since been passed over in favor of Arabic derivatives, and colloquial idioms.

---

[1]Read with the modern pronunciation, *khurd*.

ترسم من از جهنم و آتشفشان او — وان مالک عذاب و عمود گران او

آن اژدهای او که دمش هست صد ذراع — وان آدمی که رفته میان دهان او

آن کرکسی که هست تنش همچو کوه قاف — بر شاخهٔ درخت جحیم آشیان او

آن رود آتشین که درو بگذرد سعیر — وان مار هشت‌پا و نهنگ کلان او

۵ آن آتشین درخت کز آتش دمیده است — وان میوه‌های چون سر اهریمنان او

وان کاسه شراب حمیمی که هرکه خورد — از ناف مشتعل شودش تا زبان او

آن گرز آتشین که فرود آید از هوا — بر مغز شخص عاصی و بر استخوان او

آن چاه و پل در طبقهٔ هفتمین که هست — تابوت دشمنان علی در میان او

آن عقربی که خلق گریزند سوی مار — از زخم نیش پرخطر جانستان او

۱۰ جان میدهد خدا به گنهکار هر دمی — تا هر دمی ازو بستانند جان او

از مو ضعیفتر بود ، از تیغ تیزتر — آن پل که داده‌اند بدروزخ نشان او

جز چند تن ز ما علما، جمله کاینات — هستند غرق لجّهٔ آتشفشان او

جز شیعه هرکه هست بعالم خداپرست — در دوزخست روز قیامت مکان او

وز شیعه نیز هرکه فُکُل بست و شیک شد — سوزد بنار هیکل چون پرنیان او

۱۵ وانکس که با عمامهٔ سر موی سر گذاشت — مندیل اوست سوی درک ریسمان او

وانکس که کرد کار ادارات دولتی — سوزد به پشت میز جهنم روان او

وانکس که شد وکیل و ز مشروطه حرف زد — دوزخ بود به روز جزا پارلان او

وانکس که روزنامه‌نویس است و چیزفهم — آتش فتد بدفتر و کلک و بنان او

وان عالمی که کرد به مشروطه خدمتی — سوزد به حشر جان و تن ناتوان او

۲۰ وان تاجری که رد مظالم به ما نداد — مسکن کند به قصر سقر کاروان او

وان کاسب فضول که پالان او کج است — فردا کشند سوی جهنم عنان او

مشکل به جز من و تو به روز جزا کسی — زان گود آتشین بجهد مادیان او

تنها برای ما و تو یزدان درست کرد — خلد برین و آن چمن بیکران او

موقوفهٔ بهشت برین را بنام ما — بنموده وقف واقف جنت‌مکان او

۲۵ آن باغهای پر گل و انهار پر شراب — وان قصرهای عالی و آب روان او

آن خانه‌های خلوت و غلمان و حور عین — وان قابهای پر پلو و زعفران او

القصّه، کار دنیا و عقبا بکام ماست — بدبخت آنکه خوب نشد امتحان او

فردا من و جناب تو و جوی انگبین — وان کوثری که جفت زنم در میان او

باشد یقین ما که بدوزخ رود بهار — زیرا بحقّ ما و تو بد شد گمان او

✳

این دود سیه‌فام که از بام وطن خاست   از ماست که بر ماست¹

وین شعله سوزان که برآمد ز چپ و راست   از ماست که بر ماست

جان گر بلب ما رسد ، از غیر ننالیم   با کس نسگالیم

از خویش بنالیم که جان سخن اینجاست   از ماست که بر ماست

یك تن چو موافق شد ، یك دشت سپاهست   با تاج و کلاهست

ملکی چو نفاق آورد او یکه و تنهاست   از ماست که بر ماست

ما کهنه چناریم که از باد ننالیم   بر خاك ببالیم

لیکن چه کنیم؟ آتش ما در شکم ماست   از ماست که بر ماست

اسلام گر این روز چنین زار و ضعیف است   زین قوم شریف است

نه جرم ز عیسی ، نه تعدی ز کلیساست   از ماست که بر ماست

ده سال به یك مدرسه گفتیم و شنفتیم   تا روز نخفتیم

وامروز بدیدیم که آن جمله معمّاست   از ماست که بر ماست

گوئیم که بیدار شدیم ، این چه خیالیست؟   بیداری ما چیست؟

بیداری طفلیست که محتاج به لالاست   از ماست که بر ماست

از شیمی و جغرافی و تاریخ نفوریم   از فلسفه دوریم

وز قال و اِن قُلت² بهر مدرسه غوغاست   از ماست که بر ماست

گویند بهار از دل و جان عاشق غربی است   یا کافر حربی است

ما بحث نرانیم در آن نکته که پیداست   از ماست که بر ماست

---

¹For the source of the refrain, see p. 22, line 10 of *Rôz-i zi sar-i sang*.

²*Qâla wa-in qult* (Ar., he said and if you said), the style of the theological dialectic.

APPENDIX A: SCANSIONS OF POEMS

```
        ¯  ¯  ˘/  ¯   ˘  ¯  ˘/  ˘  ¯   ¯  ¯
page
 1     'ay ân kĭ gham gi nî ŭ sa ẓâ vâ rî

        ¯  ˘  ¯  ¯/  ˘   ¯  ˘  ¯/  ˘  ˘  ¯
       zin da gâ nî chĭ kû ta hŭ chĭ da râẓ

        ¯  ˘  ¯  ¯/  ¯  ˘  ¯  ¯/  ˘  ¯  ¯
 2     bû yĭ jû yĭ mû li yâ nâ yad ha mî

        ˘  ˘  ˘  ¯/  ˘  ¯  ˘  ¯/  ˘  ¯  ˘  ¯/  ˘ ˘ ¯
       sha bĭ si yâ hə ba dân ẓul fa kâ nĭ tŭ mâ nad

        ¯  ¯  ˘/  ˘  ¯  ˘  ¯/  ¯  ¯  ˘/  ˘  ¯  ¯
 3     bar khê ẓŭ ba raf râ ẓə ha lâ qib lă yĭ zar dusht

        ¯  ¯  ˘/  ¯  ˘  ˘  ¯/  ˘  ¯  ¯  ˘/  ¯  ˘  ¯
       'ay khû bə tar ẓi pay ka rĭ dê bâ yĭ 'ar ma nî

        ¯  ¯  ˘/  ˘  ¯  ˘  ¯/  ˘  ¯  ¯  ˘/  ¯  ˘  ¯
 4     nî lû fa rĭ ka bû də ni gah kun mi yâ nĭ 'âb

        ˘  ¯  ¯/  ˘  ¯  ¯/  ¯  ¯/  ˘  ¯
 5     chŭ rus tam ẓi chan gĭ va yâ ẓâ də gasht

        ¯  ˘  ¯  ¯/  ˘  ¯  ˘  ¯/  ˘  ¯  ¯/  ˘ ˘ ¯
 11    shah rĭ ghaẓ nî na ha mâ nas tə kĭ man dî dam pâr

        ¯  ˘  ¯  ¯/  ¯  ˘  ¯  ¯/  ˘  ¯  ¯/  ¯  ˘  ¯
 15    chun pa ran dĭ nî lə gûn bar rû yə pô shad mar ghə ẓâr

        ˘  ¯  ˘  ¯/  ˘  ¯  ¯  ¯/  ˘  ¯  ¯/  ˘  ¯  ¯
 16    ba gir dĭ mâ hə ba raz ghâ li yă hi sâ rə ki kard

        ¯  ˘  ¯  ¯/  ˘  ¯  ¯  ¯/  ˘ ˘ ¯
       but kĭ but gar ku nad shə dil bar nîst

        ˘  ¯  ¯  ¯/  ˘  ¯  ¯  ¯/  ˘  ¯  ¯
 17    sa dă jash nĭ mu lû kĭ nâ ma dâ rast
```

107

$$- \;\; - \;\; \breve{} \;/ \;\; - \;\; \breve{} \;\; - \;\; - \;\; \breve{} \;/ \;\; \breve{} \;\; - \;\; - \;\; - \;\; \breve{} \;/ \;\; - \;\; \breve{} \;\; -$$

'ay bâ 'a dû yĭ mâ gu za ran dă zi kû yĭ mâ

$$- \;\; - \;\; \breve{} \;/ \;\; \breve{} \;\; - \;\; - \;\; - \;\; \breve{} \;/ \;\; \breve{} \;\; - \;\; - \;\; - \;\; \breve{} \;/ \;\; \breve{} \;\; - \;\; -$$

'â mad sha bŭ 'az khâ bə ma râ ran jŭ 'a zâ bast

$$\breve{} \;\; - \;\; \breve{} \;\; - \;/ \;\; \breve{} \;\; \breve{} \;\; - \;\; - \;/ \;\; \breve{} \;\; - \;\; - \;\; \breve{} \;\; - \;/ \;\; \breve{} \;\; \breve{} \;\; -$$

18 ja hâ nĭ mâ sa gĭ shô khas tə mar tu râ bi ga zad

$$- \;\; \breve{} \;\; - \;\; - \;/ \;\; - \;\; \breve{} \;\; - \;\; - \;/ \;\; - \;\; \breve{} \;\; - \;\; - \;/ \;\; - \;\; \breve{} \;\; -$$

19 jâ ba jâ 'ab řĭ si pê dan dar ha vâ bîn khur də khurd

$$- \;\; \breve{} \;\; - \;\; - \;/ \;\; - \;\; \breve{} \;\; - \;\; - \;/ \;\; - \;\; \breve{} \;\; - \;\; - \;/ \;\; - \;\; \breve{} \;\; -$$

bin ga řî nab řĭ gi rân yâ zân ba gar dûn bar sa buk

$$- \;\; \breve{} \;\; - \;\; - \;/ \;\; \breve{} \;\; \breve{} \;\; - \;\; - \;/ \;\; \breve{} \;\; \breve{} \;\; - \;\; - \;/ \;\; - \;\; \breve{} \;\; -$$

21 dar di lam tâ ba sa har gâ hə sha bĭ dô shîn

$$- \;\; \breve{} \;\; - \;\; - \;/ \;\; - \;\; \breve{} \;\; - \;\; \breve{} \;/ \;\; - \;\; \breve{} \;\; \breve{} \;\; - \;/ \;\; -$$

bâ zĭ ja hân tê zə par řŭ khal qə shi kâ rast

$$- \;\; - \;\; \breve{} \;/ \;\; \breve{} \;\; - \;\; - \;\; - \;\; \breve{} \;/ \;\; \breve{} \;\; - \;\; - \;\; \breve{} \;/ \;\; \breve{} \;\; - \;\; -$$

22 rô zî zi sa řî san gə 'u qâ bî ba ha vâ khâst

$$\breve{} \;\; - \;\; \breve{} \;\; - \;/ \;\; \breve{} \;\; \breve{} \;\; - \;\; - \;// \;\; \breve{} \;\; - \;\; - \;\; \breve{} \;/ \;\; \breve{} \;\; \breve{} \;\; -$$

23 chu nân bi gir yam kam dush ma nân bi bakh shâ yand

$$- \;\; - \;\; \breve{} \;\; - \;/ \;\; - \;\; - \;\; \breve{} \;\; - \;/ \;\; - \;\; - \;\; \breve{} \;\; - \;/ \;\; - \;\; \breve{} \;\; -$$

24 'ay sâ rə bân man zil ma kun juz dar di yâ řĭ yâ řĭ man

$$- \;\; - \;\; \breve{} \;/ \;\; \breve{} \;\; - \;\; - \;\; \breve{} \;/ \;\; \breve{} \;\; - \;\; - \;\; - \;\; \breve{} \;/ \;\; -$$

25 pê shaz ma nŭ tŭ lay lŭ na hâ rî bû dast

$$- \;\; - \;\; \breve{} \;/ \;\; \breve{} \;\; - \;\; - \;\; \breve{} \;/ \;\; \breve{} \;\; - \;\; - \;\; - \;\; \breve{} \;/ \;\; -$$

'în yak dŭ sĭ rô ză naw ba tĭ 'um rə gu zasht

$$- \;\; - \;\; \breve{} \;/ \;\; \breve{} \;\; - \;\; - \;\; \breve{} \;/ \;\; \breve{} \;\; - \;\; - \;\; - \;\; \breve{} \;/ \;\; -$$

dar kâ rə ga hĭ kû ză ga řî raf tam dôsh

$$\breve{} \;\; - \;\; \breve{} \;\; - \;/ \;\; \breve{} \;\; \breve{} \;\; - \;\; - \;/ \;\; \breve{} \;\; - \;\; - \;\; \breve{} \;\; - \;/ \;\; \breve{} \;\; -$$

shi kas tă zul fâ 'ah dĭ vi sâ lĭ man ma shi kan

$$\breve{} \;\; - \;\; \breve{} \;\; - \;/ \;\; \breve{} \;\; \breve{} \;\; - \;\; - \;/ \;\; \breve{} \;\; - \;\; - \;\; \breve{} \;\; - \;/ \;\; \breve{} \;\; \breve{} \;\; -$$

26 da rîn ja hân kĭ sa râ yĭ gha mas tŭ tâ să ŭ tâb

$$\breve{} \;\; - \;\; \breve{} \;\; - \;/ \;\; \breve{} \;\; \breve{} \;\; - \;\; - \;/ \;\; \breve{} \;\; - \;\; - \;\; \breve{} \;\; - \;/ \;\; \breve{} \;\; \breve{} \;\; -$$

chŭ shâ hĭ zan gə ba râ vur də lash ka raz mak man

28   bâ zîn chǐ ja vâ nî ǔ ja mâ las tə ja hân râ

29   hâ nay di lǐ 'ib rat bîn 'az dî dǎ na zar kun hân

32   shar tas tə kǐ vaq tǐ bar gə rê zân

37   qis sǎ î yâ də dâ ra maz pi da rân

38   bas kǐ shi nî dî si fa tǐ rû mǔ chîn

39   gum shu dam dar khudchu nân kaz khê shə nâ pay dâ shu dam

     pa gah mî raf tə 'us tâ dî mi hî nǎ

40   'ay ham na fa sân tâ 'a ja lâ mad ba sa rǐ man

41   man mas tǔ tǔ dê vâ nǎ mâ râ ki ba rad khâ nǎ

42   bin mâ yə rukh kǐ bâ ghǔ gu lis tâ na mâ rə zûst

     'ay qaw mǐ bi haj raf tǎ ku jâ 'î də ku jâ 'îd

43   'aq lə 'â mad 'â shi qâ khud râ bi pôsh

     bish na waz nay chun hi kâ yat mî ku nad

45   na khus tîn bâ dǎ kan dar jâ mə kar dand

46   khân ǎ hâ yǐ ta naz da rî chǎ yǐ jân

47   sha bî yâ də dâ ram kǐ chashmam na khuft

48   bakh tĭ 'â yî nă na dâ ram kĭ da rû mî ni ga rî

yak rô zə ba shay dâ 'î dar zul fĭ tŭ 'â vê zam

49   'ay sâ rə bâ nâ has tă rân kâ râ mĭ jâ nam mî ra vad

50   kâ ra vâ nî shi ka raz mis rə ba shî râ zâ yad

51   chŭ tur kĭ mas tĭ man har lah ză î sŭ yĭ di gar ghal tad

'ab rə mî bâ ra dŭ man mî sha va maz yâ rə ju dâ

52   'ay chih ră yĭ zê bâ yĭ tŭ rash kĭ bu tâ nĭ 'â za rî

'ay pî rə khâ kĭ pâ yĭ tŭ nû rĭ sa 'â da tast

53   chan dîn chĭ nâ zâ mô khə tî 'ân gham ză yĭ gham mâ zə râ

bâ man na mî sâ zî da mî 'ay yâ dĭ tŭ dam sâ zĭ man

54   'ay khi rad man dĭ 'â qi lŭ dâ nâ

57   'ay sâ rə bân kĭ ran jə ka shî dî zi râ hĭ dûr

58   dil khas tă ha mî bâ shad zîn shah rĭ ba ham raf tă

59   sham 'ĭ mâ sham 'îs tə kû man zû rĭ har par vâ nă nîst

zi chash mĭ mas tĭ tŭ 'ân hâ kĭ 'â ga hî dâ rand

60   pê shĭ sâ hib na za rân mul ki su lay mân bâ dast

˘ − − − / ˘ − − − / ˘ − − −

61 shi nî dam 'az ma lak khô yî pa rî chihr

− ˘ − − / ˘ ˘ − − / ˘ ˘ − − / ˘ ˘ −

62 mâ ba sî tĭ ka ra mat 'az ra hĭ dû râ ma da 'îm

− ˘ − − / − ˘ − − / − ˘ − − / − − ˘ −

suh ba tî khush dar gi rif tim shab mi yâ nĭ sham 'ŭ man

− ˘ − − / ˘ ˘ − − / ˘ ˘ − − / ˘ ˘ −

63 dar 'a zal 'ak sĭ ma yĭ la' lĭ tŭ dar jâ muf tâd

˘ − − − / ˘ − − − / ˘ − − − / ˘ − − −

64 'a gar 'ân tur kĭ shî râ zî ba das tâ rad di lĭ mâ râ

− ˘ − − / ˘ ˘ − − / ˘ ˘ − − / ˘ ˘ −

65 dô shə dî dâm kĭ ma lâ yik da rĭ may khâ nă za dand

− − ˘ − / ˘ ˘ − − / − ˘ − − / ˘ − ˘ −

yû su fî gum gash tă bâ zâ yad ba kan 'ân gham ma khur

− − ˘ − / ˘ ˘ − − / ˘ ˘ − − / ˘ ˘ −

66 zul fə 'â shuf tă ŭ khuy kar dă ŭ khan dân la bŭ mast

− − ˘ − / ˘ ˘ − − / ˘ ˘ − − / ˘ ˘ −

67 sâ lə hâ dil ta la bĭ jâ mĭ ja maz mâ mî kard

˘ − ˘ − / ˘ ˘ − − / ˘ − ˘ − / ˘ ˘ −

bi yâ kĭ qas rĭ 'a mal sakh tə sus tə bun yâ dast

− ˘ − − / − ˘ − − / − ˘ − − / ˘ ˘ −

68 man zi lĭ jâ nĭ ja hân bar da rĭ jâ nâ nă yĭ mâst

− ˘ − − / − ˘ − − / − ˘ − − / ˘ − ˘ −

jân chĭ bâ shad gar na bâ shad 'â shi qĭ jân par va rî

− ˘ − − / − ˘ − − / − ˘ − − / ˘ − ˘ −

69 rah bi yâ bâ nas tŭ shab tâ rî kŭ pâ yam dar gi last

˘ − − − / ˘ ˘ − − // ˘ − − − / ˘ ˘ −

zi chash mĭ gô shă ni shî nân ni shâ nĭ saw dâ purs

− ˘ − − / ˘ ˘ − − / − ˘ − − / ˘ − ˘ −

70 gar na mî sô zad di lam 'î nâ hĭ dar dâ lû də chîst

˘ − ˘ − / ˘ ˘ − − / ˘ − − − / ˘ − ˘ −

ba yak ki rish mă kĭ bar jân za dî zi das tə shu dam

     –   –   ˘ /   –   –   ˘   –   –   ˘ /   ˘   –   –   –   ˘ /   –   –   ˘   –   –

     har   sub   hə   dam   mu   sav   vi   rĭ   'în   char   khĭ   'akh   za   rî

     ˘   –   – /   ˘   –   – /   ˘   –   – /   ˘   –

72   ya   kî   khâ   dĭ   mur ghĭ   ha   vâ   'î   shi   kâr

     –   ˘   –   – /   ˘   ˘   –   – /   ˘˘   –

73   sû   fi   yî   râ   hĭ   ya   qîn   mî   pay mûd

     –   ˘   –   – /   –   ˘   –   – /   –   ˘   –   – /   –   ˘   –

74   khâs   tə   har   sû   fit   nă   gû   'î   fit   nă   jû   yĭ   man   ra   sîd

     –   ˘   –   – /   ˘   ˘   –   – /   ˘   ˘   –   – /   ˘˘   –

     par   ta   wĭ   sham   ĭ   ru   khat   'ak   sə   ba   raf   lâ   kandâkht

     –   –   ˘ /   ˘   –   –   – //   –   –   ˘ /   ˘   –   –   –   –

75   rê   zam   zi   mu   zhă kaw   kab   bê   mâ   hĭ   ru   khat shab   hâ

     –   –   – /   –   ˘   –   – /   –   ˘   –   – /   –

76   yâ   rĭ   mâ   har   giz   na   yâ   zâ   rad   di   lĭ   'agh   yâr

     –   ˘   –   – /   –   ˘   –   – /   –   ˘   –   – /   –   ˘   –

     shî   shă   yĭ   may   dû   ra   zân   lab   hâ   yĭ   may   gûn   mî   gi   rîst

     –   ˘   –   – /   –   ˘   –   – /   –   ˘   –   – /   –   ˘   –

77   'ak   nûn   kĭ   tan   hâ   dî   da   mat   lut   far   na   'â   zâ   rî   bi   kun

     –   –   ˘ /   –   –   ˘   –   –   ˘ /   ˘   –   –   –   ˘ /   –   ˘   –

     'ân   sham   ĭ   gul   ru   khân   kĭ   ru   khash   lâ   lă   zâ   rĭ   mâst

     –   ˘   –   – /   ˘   ˘   –   – /   –   ˘   –   – /   ˘   –

78   dô   sə   tân   shar   hĭ   pa   rê   shâ   ni   yĭ   man   gô   shə   ku   nîd

     –   –   ˘ /   –   –   –   ˘ /   ˘   –   –   ˘ /   –   ˘   –

79   bâ   zîn   chĭ   shô   ri   shas   tə   kĭ   dar   khal   qĭ   'â   la   mast

     ˘   –   –   – /   ˘   –   –   – /   ˘   –   –   – /   ˘   –   –   –

82   fa   lak   zîn   kaj   ra   vî   hâ   yat   na   mî   gû   yam   kĭ   bar   gar   dî

     ˘   –   ˘   – /   ˘   ˘   –   – /   ˘   ˘   –   – /   ˘   –

83   ja   hân   bi   gash   ta   mŭ   dar   dâ   bi   hê   chə   shah   rŭ   di   yâr

     –   ˘   ˘   – /   ˘   –   ˘   – /   –   ˘   ˘   – /   ˘   –   ˘   –

84   khê   zŭ   sha   râ   bĭ   hay   ra   tam   zân   qa   dĭ   jil   va   sâ   zə   dih

     ˘   –   –   – /   ˘   –   –   – /   ˘   –   –   – /   ˘   –   –   –

85   ha   mâ   nâ   tur   kĭ   mas   tî   sŭ   yĭ   'în   vê   râ   nă   mî   â   yad

```
  –    –   ˘/    –    –   ˘   –   ˘/    ˘   –   –   –   ˘/    –   ˘   –
  pî   rî  ra   sî  dŭmaw  si  mĭ  tab  ĭ̆  ja  vân  gu  ɀasht

      –   ˘   –    –/    –    –   ˘   –    –/    –    –   ˘   –    –/    –    –   ˘   –
86  dij  lă   yĭ  'ash kaɀ  ba  hâ   rĭ shaw qə tugh yân  kar  da  'ast

      ˘   ˘   –    –/    ˘   ˘   –    –/    ˘   ˘   –    –/    ˘˘   –
    na  ha  mîn  mî  ra  sa  dân naw  gu  lĭ  khan  dâ  naz man

      ˘   –   ˘    –/    ˘   ˘   –    –/    ˘   –   –   ˘    –/    ˘˘   –
87  ba   ɀê   rĭ char khə  di  lî  shâ  di  mân  na  mî  bâ shad

      –    –   ˘/    –    ˘   –   ˘/    ˘   –   –   –   ˘/    –   ˘   –
    'în  nâ  ka  sân  kĭ fakh  rə  ba  'aj  dâ  də  mî  ku nand

      –   ˘   –    –/    –    –   ˘   –    –/    –    –   ˘   –    –/    –    –   ˘   –
88  bâ  ka  mâ  lĭ  'ih  ti  yâ  jaz khal qə  'is tigh  nâ  khu shast

      –    –   ˘    –/    ˘   –   ˘   –/    ˘   –   –   ˘    –/    –    –   ˘   –
    'aɀ  ta  lab  tâ chan də  rê  ɀî  'â  bĭ  rû  yĭ  kâ  mə  râ

      –    ˘   –    –/    –    –   ˘   –    –/    ˘   –   –   ˘    –/    –    ˘   –
89  mat  la  bî  gar  bû  də  'aɀ  has tî  ha  mî  nâ  ɀâ  rə  bûd

      –    –   ˘/    –    –   ˘   –    –/    –    –   ˘/    –   ˘   –    –
90  'ay  vâ  yə  bar  'a  sî  rî kaɀ  yâ  də raf  tă  bâ shad

      ˘   –   –   –/    –    ˘   –   –/    ˘   –   –   –
    ma nân ghâ  rat  ga  rĭ jân  mî  pa  ras tam

      ˘   –   –   –/    ˘   –   –   –/    ˘   –   –
91  da rîn man ɀil  kĭ kas  râ  nîs  tə  'â  râm

      ˘   –   ˘    –/    ˘   ˘   –    –/    ˘   –   –   ˘    –/    ˘   ˘   –
    ba shay khĭ shah  rə  fa  qî   rî  ɀi  jû  'ə  bur  də  pa  nâh

      –    –   ˘/    –    ˘   –   ˘/    ˘   –   –   ˘/    ˘˘   –
92  'ay  fi  dâ   yĭ  tŭ ham  di  lŭ ham jân

      –    –   ˘/    –    –   ˘   –   ˘/    ˘   –   –   –   ˘/    –   ˘   –
96  gash  tî  mə  khâ  kŭ pâ  na  ni  hâ  dî  ba  rû  yĭ  mâ

      ˘   –   ˘    –/    ˘   ˘   –    –/    ˘   –   –   ˘    –/    ˘˘   –
    'a  gar ku  shî  ŭ   ga  raɀ mar  ha  mat  bi bakh shâ  yî

      –    –   ˘/    ˘   –   –   ˘/    ˘   –   –   ˘/    ˘   –   –
    'im  rô  ɀə  na  dâ ram gha  mĭ  far  dâ  yĭ  qi  yâ mat
```

˘   -   ˘   - /   ˘   ˘   -   - /   ˘   -   ˘   - /   ˘   ˘   -   -

97   ni   gâ   hə   kun   kĭ   na   rê   zad   di   hî   chŭ   bâ   da   ba   das   tam

-   ˘   -   - /   ˘   ˘   -   - /   ˘   ˘   -   - /   ˘   ˘   -   -

98   sû   fi   yân   râ   di   ga   rim   rô   zə   na   hâ   yas   tŭ   na   hû   'î

-   -   ˘ /   ˘   -   -   ˘ /   ˘   -   -   ˘ /   ˘   -   -   -

dil   bur   dŭ   ha   qâ   nas   tə   kĭ   dil   bar   na   ta   vân   guft

-   -   ˘ /   ˘   -   -   - /   -   -   ˘ /   ˘   -   -   -

'ay   shaw   qĭ   na   vâ   san   jî   bâ   ʒam   ba   khu   rô   shâ   var

˘   -   -   - /   ˘   -   -   - /   ˘   -   - /   ˘   -   -   -

99   ba   hâ   râ   mad   kĭ   az   gul   bun   ha   mî   bân   gĭ   ha   zâ   râ   yad

-   ˘   ˘   - /   -   ˘   - //   -   ˘   ˘   - /   -   ˘   -

100   bâ   zə   ba   râ   mad   ba   kôh   râ   ya   tĭ   'ab   rĭ   ba   hâr

˘   -   -   - /   ˘   -   -   - /   ˘   -   -

101   shi   nî   dam   man   kĭ   'â   rif   jâ   na   mâ   mad

˘   -   ˘   - /   ˘   -   -   - /   ˘   -   ˘   - /   ˘   ˘   -

103   shi   nî   dĕ   'am   kĭ   ba   dar   yâ   yĭ   hin   də   jâ   na   va   rîst

˘   -   -   - /   ˘   -   -   - /   ˘   -   -

na   dâ   nam   dar   ku   jâ   'în   qis   sĕ   dî   dam

-   ˘   -   - /   ˘   ˘   -   - /   ˘   ˘   -

ghun   chĕ   î   guf   tə   ba   piʒh   mur   dĕ   gu   lî

-   ˘   -   - /   -   ˘   -   - /   -   ˘   -

104   lâ   lĕ   î   bâ   nar   gi   sî   piʒh   mur   dĕ   guft

-   -   ˘ /   -   ˘   -   ˘ /   ˘   -   -   ˘ /   -   ˘   -

105   tar   sam   ma   naʒ   ja   han   na   mŭ   'â   tash   fi   shâ   nĭ   'û

-   -   ˘ /   ˘   -   -   ˘ /   ˘   -   -   ˘ /   ˘   -   -   //

106   'în   dû   dĭ   si   yah   fâ   mə   kĭ   'az   bâ   mĭ   va   tan   khâst

-   -   ˘ /   ˘   -   -

'az   mâs   tə   kĭ   bar   mâst

VOCABULARY

Verbs are given in the infinitive in Persian; in the transcription the past and present stems are given. Regular verbs in -*îdan* are given in the infinitive only. Compounds are listed by the first element of the compound. The vowel qualities *ê* and *ô* (see *ITP* §78) are indicated here; in modern Iran they are pronounced *î* and *û* respectively. The sequence *khwâ-* is pronounced *khâ-*, as in *khwâb* (pronounced *khâb*) and *khwâst* (pronounced *khâst*); the sequence *khwa-* is pronounced *khu-*, as in *khwash* (pronounced *khush*).

Abbreviations: adj = adjective, conj = conjunction, cont = contraction, impt = imperative, int = intransitive, pl = plural, prep = preposition, trs = transitive.

آب *âb* water; tears; ~*dâda* watered (sword); ~*dâr* watery, moist; dazzling (jewel); ~*gîna* glass, crystal; ~*gîr* pool; ~*gûn* bright (sword); ~*khwar* watering-place, pond, pool

آباد *âbâd* flourishing

آبرو *âb(i)rû* honor, dignity; ~*rêkhtan* to lose one's dignity

آبستن *âbistan* pregnant

آبله *âbla* blister

آتش *âtash* fire; ~*afrozî* the act of kindling fire; ~*bayân* fiery of expression; ~*dân* brazier; ~*dast* one with a fiery "touch"; ~*fishân* volcano; ~*în* fiery; ~*'izâr* with fiery countenance; ~*kada* fire temple; ~*parast* fire-worshipper

آخر *âkhir* finally, at last

آدم *âdam* Adam; ~*î* human being; ~*iyyat* humanity

آذر *âzar* fire, spark

آر *âr-* → *âvurdan*

آراستن *ârâst-/ârâ-* to adorn; array (army, troops); *ârâsta* decorated, adorned

آرام *ârâm* rest, repose; ~*-giriftan* to calm down; ~*îdan* to rest

آرزو *ârzû* wish, desire; ~*-kardan* to make a wish; ~*mand* wishful, desirous

آرمیدن *âramîd-* = *ârâmîd-*

آروغ *ârûgh* belch

آری *ârê* yes, yea

آز *âz* desire, greed

آزاد *âzâd* free, free-moving, graceful; loose, unencumbered; ~*-gashtan* to get free, escape; ~*î* freedom, release

آزار *âzâr* affliction; ~*îdan* = *âzardan*

آزر *âzar* Azer, Abraham's father, who manufactured and served Nimrod's idols; ~*î* pertaining to Azer; ~*îvâr* Azerish, like something Azer made

آزردن *âzardan* to inflict harm upon; *âzurdan* to be wounded

آزرده *âzarda* wounded; ~*dil* with wounded heart

آژدن *âzhadan* to scratch, pierce

آسان *âsân* easy

آسای *âsây* → *âsûdan*

آسایش *âsâyish* rest, repose

آستان *âstân, âsitân* threshold

آستین *âstîn* sleeve; ~-*afshândan* to shake (*az* something) off the sleeve, get rid of (*az* of); ~*fishân* shaking the sleeve, getting rid of

آسمان *âsmân* sky, heaven

آسودگی *âsûdagî* rest, repose

آسودن *âsûd-/âsây-* to rest, repose

آسیا *âsyâ* mill

آسیب *âsîb* tragedy, affliction

آشفتن *âshuft-/âshôb-* to put in disarray, confuse

آشفته *âshufta* in disarray, tangled

آشکار *âshkâr,* ~*a,* ~*â* plain, clear; ~*san'at* obvious as to maker

آشنا *âshnâ* acquainted, friend

آشوب *âshôb* tumult, commotion; *âshôb-* → *âshuftan*

آشیان *âshyân* nest

آغاز *âghâz* beginning

آغوش *âghôsh* embrace

آفاق *âfâq* horizon

آفت *âfat* affliction

آفتاب *âftâb* sun, sunlight; ~*parast* sun worshipper

آفریدن *âfarîd-/âfarîn-* to create; *âfarîda* creature, created being

آفرین *âfarîn* bravo, well done; *âfarîn-* → *âfarîdan*

آگاه *âgâh* aware, enlightened

آگه *âgah* = *âgâh;* ~*î* awareness, enlightenment

آل *âl* family; ~-*i abâ* the family of (the Prophet's) mantle, the immediate family of the Prophet Muhammad

آلایش *âlâyish* defilement

آلودگی *âlûdagî* defilement

آلودن *âlûd-/âlây-* to defile, sully; mix

آموی *Âmû(y)* the Oxus River

آموختن *âmôkht-/âmôz-* to learn, to teach

آمیختن *âmêkht-/âmêz-* to mix, mingle

آمیز *âmêz* → *âmêkhtan*

آمیزش *âmêzish* mingling, converse

آنچه *ânchi* that which (note that *ânchi* never refers to a person; see *ânki*)

آندم *ândam* → *dam*

آنك *ânk'* = *ânki;* ¶ *ânak* there...is, *voilà*

آنكه *ânki* he who, that which

آرا *âvâ* = *âvâz*

آرار *âvâr,* ~*a* wanderer, wandering; ~*agî* wandering

آراز *âvâz,* ~*a* sound; song, singing; ~-*dâdan* to cry out

آوردگه *âvardgah* battlefield

آوردن *âvurd-/â(va)r-* to bring

آوریدن *âvarîdan* = *âvurdan*

آویختن *âvêkht-/âvêz-* to hang, suspend

آویز *âvêz* → *âvêkhtan*

آه *âh* sigh, cry; ~-*kardan* to sigh; ~ *u dardâ* alas and alack

آهسته *âhasta* slowly, gently; ~*gî* slowness; ~*kâr* slow-moving

آهن âhan iron; ~dil iron-hearted, hardhearted; ~sây iron-piercing; ~în made of iron

آهنگ âhang outset; ~-kardan to set out for, begin to

آهو âhû gazelle, deer; ~bara fawn

آهيختن âhêkht-/âhêz- to draw, un-sheathe (sword)

آيت âyat sign; verse of the Koran

آينده âyanda coming, future

آينه âyina = âîna

آئين âîn custom, ritual

آئينه âîna mirror

اب ab (Ar.) father

ابا abâ = bâ

ابجد abjad the alphabet; rudiments

ابد abad everlasting, eternal

ابر abr cloud

ابرام ibrâm importuning

ابراهيم Ibrâhîm Abraham

ابرو abrû eyebrow

ابل ibil camel

ابله ablah fool; ~âna foolish; ~î foolishness, stupidity

ابن ibn (Ar.) son

اثر asar pl âsâr trace, footprint; bar ~-i on the heels of

آثار âsâr pl of asar

اثير asîr ether, one of the layers between the earth and the celestial spheres

اجداد ajdâd ancestors

اجرام ajrâm pl of jirm body

اجزا ajzâ pl of juzv part

اجسام ajsâm pl of jism body

اجل ajal fate; moment of death, death

احتياج ihtiyâj need, neediness

احتياط ihtiyât precaution; ~an as a precautionary measure, just in case

احرار ahrâr free men

احرام ihrâm pilgrimage garb; ~-bastan to put on pilgrimage garb

احزان ahzân sorrows

احسان ihsân beneficence

احوال ahvâl condition; ~-pursîdan to inquire after

اختر akhtar star; ~shinâs astrologer

اختيار ikhtiyâr free will

اخضر akhzar dark green, dark blue

اخگر akhgar embers

اخوان ikhvân brethren

ادارات idârât bureaux

ادب adab etiquette, manners

ادراك idrâk comprehension

اديب adîb schoolmaster

ار ar = agar

ارادت irâdat devotion, discipleship

ارباب arbâb lords, masters

ارديبهشت urdîbihisht second month of the Persian year, Taurus

ارز arz → arzîdan

ارزان arzân worthy; cheap

ارزيدن arzîdan to be worth

ارشاد irshâd guidance

ارض arz the earth

ارغنون arghanûn ὄργανον, musical instrument

ارغوان *arghavân* a vermillion red flower, red-bud, Judas tree

اركان *arkân* pillars, ministers of state

ارم *Iram* the Garden of Iram, a legendary garden of great splendor in South Arabia

ارمنى *armanî* Armenian

ارواح *arvâh* pl of *rûh* spirit

از *az* from

ازار *izâr* trousers

ازل *azal* (pre)eternity, eternity backwards from the present; ~*î* eternal

اژدها *azhdahâ* dragon, serpent; ~*khû* with the disposition of a dragon

اساس *asâs* foundation

اسب *asb, asp* horse; knight (in chess)

اسباب *asbâb* pl of *sabab* cause

اسپرى *isparî* destroyed, annihilated

است *ast* is; ¶ *ist-* → *îstâdan*

استاد *ustâd* teacher, master

استادن *istâdan* = *îstâdan*

استبرق *istabraq* silk brocade shot with gold

استخوان *ustakhân* bone

استغنا *istighnâ* ability to dispense (*az* with)

استفادت *istifâdat* benefit

استوار *ustuvâr* stable, faithful, true

اسرار *asrâr* pl of *sirr* secret

اسلام *islâm* Islam

اسير *asîr* prisoner, captive

اشتياق *ishtiyâq* longing, yearning

اشرف *ashraf* most noble

اشك *ashk* tears; ~*bâr* tear-raining; ~*yâb* tear-producing

اشيا *ashyâ* things, items

اصحاب *ashâb* friends, companions

اصطرلاب *usturlâb* astrolabe

اصطلاح *istilâh* idiom, jargon

اصفر *asfar* yellow

اصل *asl* root, origin

اضطراب *iztirâb* agitation

اطاق *utâq* room

اطراف *atrâf* parts, sides, directions

اطفال *atfâl* children

اطلال *atlâl* ruins of former habitations

اطلس *atlas* silk brocade

اطول *atval* (Ar.) longer

اظهار *izhâr* manifestation; ~-*kardan* to make manifest, show

اعدا *a'dâ* enemies

اعزاز *i'zâz* honor, welcome

اعضا *a'zâ* members, limbs

اعظم *a'zam* great(est)

اعلام *i'lâm-kardan* to inform

اعماق *a'mâq* pl of *umq* depth

اغبر *aghbar* dusty

اغيار *aghyâr* pl of *ghayr* other, stranger

افتادن *uftâd-/uft-* to fall, befall

افراشتن *afrâsht-/afrâz-* to raise

افروختن *afrôkht-/afrôz-* to light, kindle

افريدون *Afrêdûn* Fredun, Faridun, an Iranian king

افزون *afzûn* more, better

افسانه *afsâna* tale, fable

افسر *afsar* crown

افسردن *afsurd-/afsur-* to congeal, freeze (int)

افسوس *afsôs* alas, pity

افسون *afsûn* incantation, spell

افشاندن‎ afshând-/afshân- to strew, scatter

افشردن‎ afshurdan to press, squeeze

افشره‎ afshura juice, sherbet

افغان‎ afghân cry, lament; alas

افكار‎ afkâr thoughts, ideas

افكندن‎ afkand-/afkan- to throw, toss; overthrow, overcome

افگار‎ afgâr afflicted, sore

افگندن‎ afgandan = afkandan

افلاطون‎ Aflâtûn Plato

افلاك‎ aflâk pl of falak celestial orb

اقامت‎ iqâmat residence, dwelling

اقبال‎ iqbâl good fortune

اقل‎ aqal(l) less

اقلام‎ aqlâm pl of qalam pen

اقليم‎ iqlîm clime

اكثر‎ aksar more

اكسير‎ iksîr elixir

اكنون‎ aknûn now

اگر‎ agar if; ~chi although, even though

الّا‎ illâ except

الحان‎ alhân pl of lahn melody

الحق‎ alhaq(q) truly, verily

الرحمن‎ arrahmân the Merciful, epithet of God

الست‎ alast (Ar.) "am I not [your Lord]?" (Kor. 7:172)

العطش‎ al'atash (Ar.) thirst

الف‎ alif first letter of the alphabet, alpha

الفت‎ ulfat intimacy

القصه‎ alqissa in short

الم‎ alam pain

الماس‎ almâs diamond; ~rêza diamond dust

الوان‎ alvân types, sorts

الها‎ ilâhâ → bâr-i ilâhâ

الهى‎ ilâhî divine, godly

اما‎ ammâ but, however

امام‎ imâm imam, prayer leader; in Shiism, one of the eleven lineal descendants of Muhammad through Ali and Fatima

امامت‎ imâmat imamship, leadership of prayer

امان‎ amân security

امانت‎ amânat trust, covenant

امت‎ ummat community

امتحان‎ imtihân trial, test

امتياز‎ imtiyâz discrimination, discernment

امروز‎ imrôz today

امسال‎ imsâl this year

امل‎ amal hope

املس‎ amlas smooth, sleek

امن‎ amn security

اميد‎ um(m)êd hope, aspiration

امير‎ amîr prince, commander

امين‎ amîn faithful; rûh-i ~, rûhu'l~ Gabriel

انار‎ anâr pomegranate

انبار‎ ambâr store, storehouse; ambâr- → ambâshtan

انبازى‎ ambâzî partnership

انباشتن‎ ambâsht-/ambâr- to store up; to sprinkle

انبيا‎ ambiyâ prophets

انتظار‎ intizâr waiting, expectation

انجام‎ anjâm end, conclusion

انجم‎ anjum pl of najm star

انجمن‎ anjuman assembly, gathering

انجير‎ anjîr fig

انداختن *andâkht-/andâz-* to cast,
scatter

اندازه *andâza* measure; ~ *bar-
giriftan* to size up

اندام *andâm* body

انداى *andây-* → *andûdan*

اندر *andar* in, = *dar*

اندرز *andarz* advice

اندك *andak* little, little bit; ~-*î* a
little, somewhat

اندوختن *andôkht-/andôz-* to store
up

اندودن *andûd-/andây-* to encrust,
cover over

اندوه *andôh* grief

انده *anduh* = *andôh*

اندیشه *andêsha* worry, concern;
thought

انس *uns* familiarity; ~-*giriftan* to
become familiar

انسان *insân* human being

انگبین *angabîn* honey; ~*lab* with
lips of honey; ~*yâr* fond of
honey

انگشت *angusht* finger; ~*gazân* bit-
ing the fingers (from grief,
anxiety, surprise, &c.); ~*kash*
notorious, famous; ¶ *angisht*
charcoal

انگیختن *angêkht-/angêz-* to stir up

انواع *anvâ'* types, sorts, kinds

انور *anvar* most luminous

انهار *anhâr* pl of *nahr* river,
stream

اوج *awj* zenith

اول *avval* first, first of all

اولاد *awlâd* offspring, progeny

اولوم *olum* (Tk.) "may I be"

اولیا *awliyâ* saints

اوهام *awhâm* pl of *vahm* imagin-
ing

اهریمن *Ahrîman* Ahriman, Zoro-
astrian principle of darkness

اهل *ahl* people; worthy; ~-*i bayt*
the people of the Prophet's
house; ~-*i dil* "people of the
heart," metaphorically used
for Sufis; ~*iyyat* worthiness

اى *ay* O (vocative particle)

ایام *ayyâm* days, time (in the ab-
stract)

ایدون *aydûn, îdûn* only in *gar* ~
ki if

ایزد *îzad* God; ~*î* divine

ایست *îst* stopping, standing still; ¶
îst- → *îstâdan*

ایستادن *îstâd-/îst-* to stand, stop

ایلچی *îlchî* ambassador

ایلخان *îlkhân* (tribal) chieftain

ایما *îmâ* allusion

ایمان *îmân* faith

ایمنی *aymanî* security

اینك *înak* here is, *voici*

ایوان *ayvân, êvân* portico, palace

ب *ba* to, with, for; ¶ *bi-* with,
at, in

با *bâ* with; despite, in spite of;
~ *ânki* inasmuch as, because,
despite the fact that

بابزن *bâbzan* spit

بابل *Bâbil* Babylon

باخبر *bâkhabar* aware

باختن *bâkht-/bâz-* to play; to lose

باخود *bâkhwad* sober; in one's
right mind; self-aware

باد *bâd* wind, breeze; pride; *ba*
~ *dâdan* to scatter to the

winds; bar ~ rafta gone with the wind; ¶ bâd let it be, may it be

بادام bâdâm almond

باده bâda wine; ~nôsh wine-drinker; ~parast devoted, addicted to wine; ~khwar wine drinker; ~furôsh wine seller

بادیه bâdiya desert

بار bâr fruit, load, burden; audience, court; time, occasion; ~-dâdan to give audience, hold court; ~-i ilâhâ O divine court; ~-kashîdan to bear a load; ~gâh court; ba~ fruit-laden; ¶ bâr- → bârîdan

باران bârân rain

بارش bârish raining

بارگاه bârgâh court

باره bâra rampart, city-wall

باری bâ´rî yea; ¶ bârî = bârîk

باریدن bârîdan to rain, rain down

باریك bârîk slender, thin; ~bînî sharp eyesight; insight

باز bâz again, still; open; falcon, hawk; ~-âvurdan to bring back, recapture; ~-dâshtan to keep back, withhold; arrest; ~-mândan to lag behind, be deprived; ~-pêchîdan to turn aside (trs.); ~-shudan to return; ~-yâftan to regain; ~pas behind, turn around, backwards; ¶ bâz- → bâkhtan

بازار bâzâr bazaar, market

بازو bâzû arm, forearm

بازی bâzî play, jest, game

باطل bâtil cancelled, nullified

باعث bâ'is cause, impetus

باغ bâgh garden; ~bân gardener

باقی bâqî rest, the rest, remainder

باك bâk care, concern; náyâmad-ash ~, ~-ash náyâmad he didn't care

بال bâl wing; ~-ârâstan to spread the wings

بالا bâlâ up, above; stature; ~-yi over

بالان bâlân moving, growing

بالش bâlish pillow

بالیدن bâlîdan to grow great

بالین bâlîn pillow, headrest

بام bâm roof

بامداد bâmdâd dawn, at dawn

بان bân myrobalan, a tree resembling the tamarisk, from which fine balsam is extracted

بانگ bâng cry, shout

بانو bânû -ân lady

باور bâvar-kardan to believe

باید bâyad it is necessary

ببار babâr → bâr

بت but idol; ~gar idol carver, idol maker; ~parast idol worshipper

بتر batar (= badtar) worse

بچه bachcha child

بحث bahs-rândan to deliberate

بحر bahr sea; poetic meter

بحق bihaqq-i → haqq

بخار bukhâr pl -ât vapor, steam, smoke; "hot air"

بخارا Bukhârâ Bukhara, city in Transoxiana

بخ بخ bakh-bakh exalamation of pleasure

بخت bakht luck, fortune

بخش bakhsh portion, lot

بخشیدن *bakhshîdan* to give, bestow; forgive

بخل *bukhl* avarice

بخود *bakhwad* = *bâkhwad*

بد *bad* bad, evil; *~andêsh* malicious; *~bakht* out of luck, unlucky; *~hâl* one whose condition is bad; *~khwâh* malevolent; *~khwayî* viciousness, malice; *~sigâl* malevolent, ill-wisher; *~kunish* malefactor; *~nâm* villified, slandered; *~nâmî* disrepute, slander; ¶ *bud* a shortened, poetic form of *bûd*

بدخشان *Badakhshân* Badakhshan, region of modern Afghanistan famed for its rubies

بدخشی *badakhshî* of Badakhshan

بدر *badr* the full moon

بدر افتادن *ba dar uftâdan* → *dar*

بدر آمدن *ba dar âmadan* → *dar*

بدل *badal* change, exchange, stead; *~ az* instead of

بدن *badan* body

بدو *badû* = *ba û*

بدیع *badi'* marvellous; *~badan* of a marvellous physique

بدین *badîn* = *ba în*

بدیهه *badîha* extemporaneous

بذله‌گوی *bazlagûy* comical, jokester

بر *bar* (prep) over, above, against; *az ~-i* over, above; ¶ *bar* breast, embrace; *az ~ khwândan* to recite from memory; ¶ *bar-* → *burdan*; ¶ *bur-* → *burîdan*; for all compounds with *bar-*, see alphabetically

برادر *barâdar* brother; *~zâda* nephew

برافروختن *bar-afrôkhtan* to light up

بران *barân* = *bar ân*; ¶ *burrân* sharp, cutting

برانگیختن *bar-angêkhtan* to stir up, foment

برآوردن *bar-âvurdan* to bring forth, produce (fruit)

بربستن *bar-bastan* to seal, shut up

بربط *barbat* harp, lute; *~zan* harpist, lutanist

برپای *bar pây* standing

برپریدن *bar-parîdan* to fly away, fly off

برتاختن *bar-tâkhtan* to charge forth

برخاستن *bar-khâstan* to rise up, get up, go away; *az sar-i jân ~* to despair of one's life

برخواندن *bar-khwândan* to recite out loud

برخوردار *barkhwardâr az* enjoying, taking advantage of

برخوردن *bar-khwardan* to enjoy the fruit of

بردادن *bar-dâdan* to give up, let loose

برداشتن *bar-dâshtan* to take up, pick up, raise up

بردریدن *bar-darîdan* to rip open, slice through, rip apart

بردمیدن *bar-damîdan* to puff up

بردن *burd-/bar-* to take, carry

برز *burz* greatness

برزدن *bar-zadan* to beat the breast; to beat out (with drums)

برزن *barzan* open plain, desert

برف *barf* snow

برفروختن *bar-furôkhtan* = *bar-afrôkhtan*

برق *barq* lightning, flash

برقع *burqa'* veil; *~pôsh* veiled

برکردن *bar-kardan* to raise; *sar* ~ to rear the head

برکشیدن *bar-kashîdan* to draw (sword); to draw up, across; to pluck the fruit; to gird the waist (with a sword, &c., for battle, service, &c.)

برکندن *bar-kandan* to uproot; *bunyâd* ~ to destroy the foundation

برگ *barg* leaf; care, solicitude; ~*rêzân* autumn

برگردانیدن *bar-gardânîdan* to turn back (trs)

برگرفتن *bar-giriftan* to pull back, lift (veil)

برگزیدن *bar-guzîdan* to choose, select

برگشودن *bar-gushûdan* to let loose, let down (hair)

برو *barû* = *bar û*

برون *burûn* = *bêrûn*

بره *bar(r)a* lamb, Aries; ¶ *ba rah* on the road, on the way

برهم *barham* jumbled; ~-*zadan* to jumble, destroy order

برهمن *barhaman, birahman* Brahmin

برهنه *birahna, barhana* naked

بریان *biryân* roasted, cooked; ~-*shudan* to be roasted

بریدن *bur(r)îdan* to cut, sever; be cut

بریشم *barêsham* silk

برین *barîn* = *bar în*; ¶ *barîn* sublime

بزرگ *buzurg* big, great; ~*mardî* virtue, magnanimity; ~*vâr* great

بزم *bazm* banquet; ~*gah* banquet hall

بس *bas* many a; enough; surely; ~-*î* (+ sing.) many a; *az* ~-*ki* so much so

بساط *bisât* carpet

بسان *ba sân-i* → *sân*

بستان *bustân* garden, orchard

بستر *bistar* bed, sick bed

بستن *bast-/band-* to tie up, bind

بسیار *bisyâr* very; much, many

بسیط *basît* carpet; ~-*i arz* the flat earth

بصر *basar* vision, ability to see

بصیرت *basîrat* inner vision, insight

بط *bat(t)* duck

بعید *ba'îd* unlikely, remote

بعین *bi ayn* → *'ayn*

بغداد *Baghdâd* Baghdad

بغل *baghal* armpit; embrace

بقا *baqâ* immortality, eternity

بقیع *Baqî'* the Baqi' al-Gharqad Cemetary in Medina, where Fatimah and a number of the Prophet's family and Companions are buried

بلا *balâ* affliction, calamity

بلبل *bulbul* nightingale; ~*ak* little nightingale

بلعجب *bul'ajab* astonishing, marvellous

بلکه *balki* rather, on the other hand

بلند *buland* high, tall, sublime; ~-*shudan* to rise up; ~-*î* exaltedness, greatness; ~*nazar* one whose gaze is fixed on lofty things

بلور *bulûr* crystal; ~*în* crystaline

بم *bam* bass note

بن *bun* root; bottom; *az ~-i dandân* with all one's mind; *~âgôsh* area behind the ear; *~gah* rear of the army

بنا *binâ* structure, edifice

بنان *banân* fingers

بند *band-* → *bastan*; *band* band, strap; fetters, enchained; joint; *~ az ~* from limb to limb

بندگی *bandagî* slavery, servitude

بنده *banda* slave, servant; I, me

بنفشه *banafsha* violet, pansy; *~khatt* with dark down on the upper lip; *~zulf* with tresses like violets

بنیاد *bunyâd* foundation; *~ barkandan* to destroy the foundation

بو *bô = bôy*; ¶ *baw = buvad*

بوالملیح *bulmalîh* type of song bird

بوته *bôta* shrub; *~sifat* resembling a bush, bush-like

بود *bûd* being, existence

بوس *bôs* kiss

بوستان *bôstân* garden, orchard

بوسه *bôsa* kiss

بوسیدن *bôsîdan* to kiss

بوقلمون *bûqal(a)mûn* chameleon; *~numây* iridescent

بوی *bôy* scent, aroma

بوئیدن *bôîdan* to smell, sniff

به *ba* with, to, by, at; ¶ *bih* better, best; *~î* superiority

بها *bahâ* price, worth

بهار *bahâr* spring; ¶ *bihâr* a Buddhist temple

بهانه *bahâna* excuse, pretext

بهر *ba har* for/to every; ¶ *bahr: az ~-i* for the sake of

بهرام گور *Bahrâm-i Gôr* Bahram Gor (Varahran V)

بهره *bahra* portion, share

بهشت *bihisht* heaven, paradise; *~î* heavenly

بهم *baham* together; *~ raftan* to collapse, go to ruin; *~ rasânîdan* to procure, get together; *~ zadan* to disrupt; *~ kardan* to throw together

بهمن *bahman* midwinter month, Aquarius; *~î* related to the month of Bahman

بهی *bihî* → *bih*

بی *bê* without (see compounds below, alphabetically)

بیابان *biyâbân, bêâbân* wilderness, desert, arid plain

بی اختیار *bêikhtiyâr* spontaneous, involuntary

بی آشنا *bêâshnâ* friendless

بیان *bayân* explanation, explication; exposition, wording

بی اندازه *bêandâza* without measure

بی بدل *bêbadal* unique, peerless

بی بصری *bêbasarî* lack of vision

بی بنیاد *bêbunyâd* without foundation

بیت *bayt* line of poetry

بی توش *bêtôsh* powerless, weak

بیجاده *bîjâda* ruby; *~bâr* ruby-raining

بی جراتی *bêjur'atî* lack of boldness, timidity

بیچاره *bêchâra* poor, pitiful

بی حس *bêhis(s)* unconscious

بی حضور *bêhuzûr* without presence of mind, distracted

بیخ *bîkh* root

بی خبر *bêkhabar* unaware, uninformed

بیختن *bêkht-/bêz-* to sift

بی‌خطر *bêkhatar* without danger, safe

بی‌خواب *bêkhwâb* sleepless

بی‌خرد *bêkhwad* deranged, out of one's mind/senses, beside oneself

بید *bêd* willow

بیداد *bêdâd* unjust; ~*î* injustice

بیدار *bîdâr* awake, aware; ~*dil* alert; ~*î* wakefulness, awareness

بی‌درمان *bêdarmân* remediless

بی‌دل *bêdil* one who has lost his heart, forlorn

بی‌ربط *bêrabt* extraneous, beside the point

بی‌روزی *bêrôzî* without sustenance

بیرون *bêrûn* out, outside; ~*-i* out of

بی‌ریش *bêrîsh* beardless, beardless youth

بیز *bêz* → *bêkhtan*

بیژن *Bêzhan* Bezhan, beloved of Manizha

بی‌ساز *bêsâz* useless, ill-equipped

بیستون *Bêsutûn* Bihistun, the mountain Farhâd carved for Shîrîn

بی‌سروپا *bêsarupâ* destitute; confused, in a dither

بی‌سروسامان *bêsarusâmân* destitute; ~*î* destitution

بیش *bêsh* more; ~*tar* more

بی‌صورت *bêsûrat* formless

بیضا *bayzâ* white

بیضه *bayza* egg; pellet, ball

بی‌طاقتی *bêtâqatî* inability to endure

بی‌فایده *bêfâyida* useless, in vain

بی‌قرار *bêqarâr* disturbed, restless

بی‌قوتی *bêqûtî* hunger

بی‌کران *bêkirân* shoreless, endless

بی‌کس *bêkas* all alone

بیگانه *bêgâna* stranger, foreigner

بیگاه *bêgâh* timeless; at the wrong time

بی‌گناه *bêgunâh* innocent, not at fault; ~*î* sinlessness, innocence

بی‌لنگر *bêlangar* without anchor, untethered

بیم *bîm* fear

بیمار *bîmâr* sick, ill, patient; ~*î* illness

بی‌موقع *bêmawqi'* untimely, out of season

بین *bîn-* → *dîdan*

بینا *bînâ* sighted

بی‌نشان *bênishân* traceless

بی‌نصیب *bênasîb* hapless

بی‌نوا *bênavâ* dispossessed, destitute

بی‌نورد *bênavard* wrinkle-free

بی‌وفا *bêvafâ* faithless, unreliable; ~*î* faithlessness

بی‌هنگام *bêhangâm* inopportune, at the wrong time

بیهوده *bêhûda* vain, useless

بی‌هوش *bêhôsh* unconscious; not sober

پا *pâ* foot; ~*-birahna* with naked, uncovered feet; ~*-kashîdan* to withdraw; ~*-kôbîdan* to dance

پادشاه *pâdishâh* emperor, ruler

پار *pâr* = *pârsâl*

پارسال *pârsâl* last year

پارلمان *pârlimân* parliament

پاره *pâra* torn, broken to pieces

پاس *pâs* watch, guard; ~-*dâsh-tan* to keep, protect

پاسخ *pâsukh* answer, reply; ~-*dâdan* to answer, reply

پاك *pâk* pure; completely, utterly

پاکیزه *pâkîza* pure; ~*gawhar* pure in substance; ~*sirisht* sanctimonious

پالان *pâlân* pack saddle; ~-*ash kaj-ast* "he's not quite honest"

پالودن *pâlûd-/pâlây-* to wipe clean

پای *pây* = *pâ*; ~*band*, ~*bast* chained to, adherent of; ~*mâl* trampled underfoot; ¶ *pây-* → *pâyîdan*

پایان *pâyân* end

پایه *pâya* stair, rung

پاییدن *pâyîdan* to last, remain

پخته *pukhta* ripe, mature, cooked; ~-*kardan* to cook, make ripe

پدرود *padrûd-kardan* to bid farewell

پدید *padîd* visible, apparent; ~-*âmadan* to appear, become visible

پذیر *pazîr-* → *pazîruftan*

پذیرا *pazîrâ* acceptable, received

پذیرفتن *pazîruft-/pazîr-* to take, receive, accept

پر *par* feather, blade, petal; ~ *u bâl ârâstan* to spread the wings; ~ *u bâl zadan* to flap the wings; ¶ *pur* full (see compounds alphabetically below)

پرآسیب *pur-âsîb* steep, hilly; full of ups and downs

پراکنده *parâkanda* dispersed, torn down

پراندیشه *pur-andêsha* troubled, full of worry

پرتو *partaw* ray

پرخطر *pur-khatar* dangerous

پرخون *pur-khûn* bloody, bloodstained

پرداختن *pardâkht-/pardâz-* to accomplish

پردرم *pur-diram* full of dirhems, full of coins, full of scales (fish)

پرده *parda* veil, curtain; canvass; musical note; ~-*darîdan* to rip a veil, to dishonor, scandalize (*bar* someone); ~*dâr* modest; ~*dar* slanderous, one who reveals secrets; ~*sarây* tent, pavilion; ~*nishîn* secluded, shrouded, chaste, one whose actions are hidden

پرستنده *parastanda* servant

پرستیدن *parastîdan* to serve, worship

پرسیدن *pursîdan* to ask

پرشکایت *pur-shikâyat* complaining, full of complaint

پرشکست *pur-shikast* curly, tangled (tress)

پرشکن *pur-shikan* tossed, curly

پرقصور *pur-qusûr* faulty, full of mistakes

پرگار *pargâr* compass

پرگل *pur-gil* muddy

پرگله *pur-gila* full of complaint

پرمایه *pur-mâya* dear

پرن *paran* the Pleiades

پرنار *pur-nâr* full of fire

پرنور *pur-nûr* full of light

پرند *parand* silk

پرنگار *pur-nigâr* full of beauties

پرنیان parniyân silk

پروا parvâ fear; ¶ parvâ = parvâz

پرواز parvâz flight; ~-kardan to fly

پروانه parvâna moth; ~sifat moth-like

پروردگار parvard(i)gâr provider, nourisher

پروردن parvard-/parvar- to nurture, nourish

پرورش parvarish nurture, upbringing

پرویز Parvêz Chosroës Parvez

پرهنر pur-hunar artful, crafty

پرهیختن parhêkht-/parhêz- to abstain

پرهیز parhêz abstinance; parhêz- → parhêkhtan

پری parî fairy, peri; ~chihr beautiful; ~rukh, ~rûy with a face like a fairy, beautiful; ~zâd fairy, peri; ~zada possessed, mad

پریدن parîdan, parrîdan to fly

پریشان parîshân distraught, upset; ~î distress, consternation

پزشك pizishk physician

پژمردن pizhmurd-/pizhmur- to wither, wilt

پژمریدن pizhmurîdan = pizhmurdan

پس pas behind, then; az ân ~ afterwards; az ân ~ ki after (conj.)

پسته pista pistachio

پسندیدن pasandîdan to be pleased with

پشت pusht back; ~-i on top of; ~î support, instigation; ~shikan back-breaking

پشته pushta patch, clump, hill; ~pusht with a back like a hill (camel)

پشه pashsha mosquito, gnat

پگاه pagâh dawn, early in the morning

پگه pagah = pagâh

پل pul bridge

پلنگ palang leopard

پلو pilaw, pulaw pilaff, cooked rice

پناه panâh refuge, asylum; ~burdan to take refuge

پنجه panja hand, grasp

پند pand advice, good counsel

پندار pindâr advice, counsel, thought; → pindâshtan

پنداشتن pindâsht-/pindâr- to think, believe

پنهان pinhân hidden, invisible, concealed; ~î concealment

پنیر panêr cheese

پود pûd weft

پور pûr son, boy; ~â O my son

پوز pôz snout

پوست pôst skin; ~în skin; ~indôz furrier; ~kanda skinned, peeled; frankly

پوشیدن pôshîdan to put on, wear, cover up

پولاد pûlâd steel

پوییدن pûyîdan to run, trot; ba farq ~ to run pell-mell

پهلو pahlû side, direction; az ~-i by means of, from the direction of; ¶ pahlaw = pahlavân

پهلوان pahlavân hero, champion

پی *pay* foot; ~*-i* after, on the heels of; *dar* ~ *âmadan* to come after; ~*-burdan ba* to follow, trace, track; ~*-kardan* to follow, trace; ~*-nihâdan bar* to trample on; ~*â~* continuously

پیاده *piyâda* on foot; pawn (chess)

پیاله *piyâla* cup, goblet, phial

پیچ *pêch* twist, turn; ~*â~* twisted, complicated; ~*ân* twisting, turning

پیچیدن *pêchîdan* to twist, turn, writhe

پیدا *paydâ* found; ~*-kardan* to find

پیر *pîr* old (man); pir, Sufi master; ~*âna* like an old person; ~*î* old age

پیرار *pîrâr* year before last

پیراهن *pîrâhan* shirt, undergarment

پیروزی *pîrôzî* victory

پیرهن *pîrahan* = *pîrâhan*

پی سپر *pay-sipur* trampled

پیش *pêsh* fore; ~*-i* before, in front of; ~*-âmadan* to come forward, up; ~*kash* present, gift

پیغام *payghâm* message; ~*bar* messenger, apostle

پیغمبر *payghambar* messenger, apostle

پیکار *paykâr* stature, body

پیکان *paykân* arrow, shaft, dart; ~*-zadan* to shoot (arrow), cast (spear)

پیکر *paykar* = *paykâr*

پیگار *paygâr* combat, battle

پیل *pîl* elephant; bishop (chess); ~*-i mast* mad elephant; ~*tan* epithet of Rustam; ~*kirdâr* huge, built like an elephant

پیمان *paymân* promise, pact

پیمانه *paymâna* large drinking cup, goblet, bumper

پیمای *paymây-* → *paymûdan*

پیمبر *payambar* = *payghambar*

پیمودن *paymûd-/paymâ(y)-* to traverse

پیوسته *payvasta* continual(ly)

پیوند *payvand* link, connection

تا *tâ* (prep) until, up to; (conj) in order that, until; (+ past) ever since; (+ subj) in order that; (+ negative) until; (+ *mî*) as long as

تاب *tâb* strength; brilliance; wrath, heat; *tâb-* → *tâftan*

تابان *tâbân* shining

تابش *tâbish* shining, burning

تابناك *tâbnâk* brilliant

تابنده *tâbanda* shining

تابوت *tâbût* bier, coffin

تابیدن *tâbîdan* = *tâftan*

تاثیر *ta'sîr* influence

تاج *tâj* crown

تاجر *tâjir* merchant

تاجور *tâjvar* crowned, crowned head

تاختن *tâkht-/tâz-* to charge, gallop, hasten

تار *târ* dark; curl, thread, string; warp; stringed instrument

تاراج *târâj* plunder, pillage

تاریخ *târîkh* history

تاریك *târîk* dark

تاز *tâz-* → *tâkhtan*

تازان *tâzân* charging, attacking

تازه *tâza* fresh; ~-*kardan* to refresh; ~*nihâl* young sprout, fresh sapling

تاسه *tâsa* anxiety, grief

تافتن *tâft-/tâb-* to shine; to twist, turn away; *sar-~* to turn the head away

تاك *tâk* vineyard, grape vine

تام *tâm(m)* full (moon)

تامل *ta'ammul* reflection, pondering

تائب *tâ'ib* penitent

تایید *ta'yîd* support, affirmation

تب *tab* heat

تبار *tabâr* family, kindred

تباه *tabâh* ruined; ~*î* ruination

تبخاله *tabkhâla* fever blister

تبریز *Tabrîz* Tabriz, city in Azerbaijan, NW Iran

تبسم *tabassum* smile, laughter

تبلرزه *tab-larza* convulsive fever

تبیره *tabîra* drum

تپانچه *tapâncha* billow, wave

تثلیث *taslîs* trinity

تجرد *tajarrud* abstraction, disengagement

تجلی *tajallî* manifestation

تحت *taht* below

تحسین *tahsîn* praise, laud

تحصیل *tahsîl* acquisition

تحفه *tuhfa* rare object; gift, present

تحقیق *tahqîq* actuality; *bi~* really, actually

تحمل *tahammul* endurance

تخت *takht* throne; ~*ikhwâb* bed

تخته *takhta* board, slate

تخم *tukhm* seed; ~-*kâshtan* to sow seeds; ~*a* race, stock

تدارك *tadâruk* muster; ~-*kardan* to muster troops

تدبیر *tadbîr* remedy; strategem

تذرو *tazarv* partridge

تر *tar* wet, damp; fresh; ~*dâman* disgraced; ~*î*, *tarrî* wetness, dampness

تراز *Tarâz* Taraz, city in Turkistan famed for its beauties; ~*î* of Taraz

تراشیدن *tarâshîdan* to carve

ترانه *tarâna* tune

تربت *turbat* dust; grave, tomb

تربیت *tarbiyat* training, education

ترسا *tarsâ* Christian

ترسیدن *tarsîdan az* to be afraid of

ترش *tur(u)sh* sour

ترشح *tarashshuh* secretion, exudation

ترك *turk* Turk, Turanian (in Shâhnâma); ~*tâz* plundering excursion; blandishments; ~*istân* Turkistan; ¶ *tark-kardan* to leave, abandon

ترکیب *tarkîb* shape

ترنج *turanj, turunj* citron

تره *tara* leek

تریاق *taryâq* antidote

تزاحم *tazâhum* crowded state

تزویر *tazvîr* dissimilation, sanctimoniousness

تزیین *tazyîn* decoration, ornamentation; ~-*dâdan* to decorate

تسبیح *tasbîh* rosary, prayer beads

تسخر *tasakhkhur-zadan* to be snide

تسليم *taslîm* surrender

تشبيه *tashbîh* likening, comparison

تشنه *tishna* thirsty; ~*gî* thirst; ~*lab* thirsty-lipped

تشوير *tashvîr* confusion

تشويش *tashvîsh* trouble; ~*-kashîdan* to have trouble

تصدق *tasadduq* almsgiving

تضرع *tazarru'* supplication, entreaty

تظلم *tazallum* suffering oppression

تعجب *ta'ajjub* astonishment

تعدى *ta'addî* hostility

تعظيم *ta'zîm* reverence, veneration

تعلق *ta'alluq* attachment (to material things)

تعليم *ta'lîm* instruction

تعنت *ta'annut* fault-finding

تعنيف *ta'nîf* reproach

تغافل *taghâful* feigned ignorance

تف *taf(f)* heat

تفاؤل *tafâ'ul* reading, augury; ~*-kardan* to take an augury

تفسير *tafsîr* explanation

تفكر *tafakkur* meditation

تقاضا *taqâzâ* supplication

تقدير *taqdîr* fate, destiny; apportionment

تقرب *taqarrub* nearness (to God)

تقليد *taqlîd* imitation; ~*-kardan* to imitate, follow

تقوى *taqvâ* piety

تك *tak* bottom

تكاو *Takâv* Takaw, name of a village

تكبير *takbîr* exaltation, pronouncement of the formula *Allâhu akbar*

تكلم *takallum* conversation

تكليس *taklîs* calcination

تكمه *tukma* button

تلافى *talâfî-kardan* to take revenge

تلخ *talkh* bitter; ~*î* bitterness; ~*kâm* one a bitter taste in his mouth, with bitter experiences

تلقين *talqîn* instruction, indoctrination

تلون *talavvun* multicoloration, fickleness

تماشا *tamâshâ* spectacle, promenade; ~*-kardan* to witness, watch (a spectacle); ~*î* spectacular

تمام *tamâm* whole, complete; ~*at* totality, whole; ~*î* totality, all

تمثال *timsâl* idol, statue

تمكين *tamkîn* stabilization, empowerment

تمنا *tamannâ* desire, wish; ~*-kardan* to desire, entreat

تموز *tam(m)ûz* July, midsummer

تن *tan* body; strength; ~*durust* in good health

تند *tund* fast, quick; ~*î* speed, severity; ~*î-kardan* to go quickly; ~*khway* harsh

تنگ *tang* narrow; ~*dahân* with a small mouth

تنومند *tanûmand* enormous, strong

تنها *tanhâ* only, alone, lonely; ~*î* loneliness, solitude

تواضع *tavâzu'* humility

توان *tavân* strength

توانستن *tavânist-/tavân-* to be able

توبه *tawba* repentance, vow of abstinence; ~-*dâdan* to make someone (-*râ*) swear a vow of repentance (*az* from something); ~-*shikastan* to break a vow of abstinence

توده *tôda* heap, pile

توسن *tawsan* steed

توش *tôsh* strength

توشه *tôsha* provisions

توقع *tavaqqu'* expectation

توکل *tavakkul* trust (in the Lord)

ته *tah* bottom, root (of hair); ~*î* see alphabetically

تهمت *tuhmat* accusation

تهمتن *tahamtan* enormous in body, one of Rustam's epithets

تهنیت *tahniyat* congratulations; ~-*guftan* to congratulate

تهویل *tahvîl* frightening away

تهی *tahî, tuhî* empty; ~*dast* empty-handed, poor; ~*mi'-dagî* starvation

تیر *tîr* arrow, dart; ~-*gushâdan* to let an arrow fly; ~-*khwar-dan* to be hit by an arrow; ~*andâz* archer; ~*bârân-kardan* to shower with arrows

تیره *tîra* dark, obscure; ~*dil* dark, unfathomable; ~*rôz* despondent; ~*rûy* with clouded countenance; ~*shab* dark night; ~*vash* darkish

تیز *têz* swift, sharp; ~*par* swift of wing; ~*î* swiftness

تیشه *têsha* axe

تیغ *têgh* sword, blade

تیمار *tîmâr* sorrow

تیهو *tayhû, tîhû* quail

ثریا *surayyâ* the Pleiades

ثمر *samar* fruit

ثمین *samîn* valuable, priceless

ثنا *sanâ* praise

جالینوس *Jâlînûs* Galen

جام *jâm* cup, goblet

جامه *jâma* clothing, garment

جان *jân* life, soul; ~-*burdan* to escape with one's life; ~-*dâ-dan* to give up one's life; ~-*kandan* to agonize, suffer; ~-*sipurdan* to give up one's life; ~*ân* beloved; ~*âna* beloved; ~*bakhsh* life-giving; ~*bâz* one who is ready to lose his life; ~*fazâ* soul-increasing; ~*par-var* soul-nourishing; ~*rafta* one whose soul has departed; ~*sitân* deadly, lethal; ~*sôz* devastating

جانور *jânivar* animal

جاویدان *jâvêdân* eternal

جایگه *jâygah* place

جبار *jabbâr* tyrant

جبرئیل *Jibrâîl, Jibrîl* Gabriel

جبین *jabîn* forehead

جحیم *jahîm* Jahim, a layer of hell

جدا *judâ* separate, separated; ~*î* separation

جدل *jadal* disputation

جدول *jadval* rule, marginal rule; a garden water-course

جدی *jady* Capricorn

جذبه *jazba* attraction, magnetism

جرات *jur'at* boldness

جراح *jarrâh* surgeon

جرس *jaras* caravan bell

جرعه *jur'a* gulp, draught

جرم *jurm* crime; ¶ *jirm* body

جریده *jarîda* register

جز *juz* except

جزا *jazâ* retribution

جزع *jaz'* shell

جزو *juzv* pl *ajzâ* part, section

جستجو *justujû* search, quandry

جستن *jast-/jih-* to jump, leap; ¶ *just-/jû(y)-* to seek, search for

جسم *jism* body

جشن *jashn* celebrations, festival

جعد *ja'd* lock of hair

جعفری *ja'farî* related to Ja'far; *zar-i ~* pure gold

جغد *jughd* owl

جغرافی *jughrâfî* geography

جفا *jafâ* cruelty; *~pêsha* cruel

جفت *juft* mate; pair; *~~* in pairs; *~jû(y)* seeking a mate; *~zadan* to fly, to dive

جگر *jigar* liver; *~dôz* bowel-splitting; *~gôsha* beloved, object of affection, child; *~sôz* agonizing

جلال *jalâl* magnificence

جلب *jalb* attraction

جلوه *jilva* manifestation, beauty; *~sâz* of consummate splendor; *~gar* conspicuous

جم Jam Jamshed, legendary king of Iran

جمازه *jum(m)âza* swift (camel)

جماعت *jamâ'at* group

جمال *jamâl* beauty; fascination

جمره *jamra* ember

جمع *jam'* gathering, gathered; *~âvarî* collecting, assembling

جمعه *jum'a* Friday

جمعیت *jam'iyyat* gathering, group of people; collectedness; *~-i dil* peace of mind

جمله *jumla* all; altogether

جن *jinn* the djinn

جناب *janâb* excellency; *~-i mawlavî* his lordship

جنان *jinân* pl of *jannat* garden, paradise

جنبش *jumbish* motion

جنبیدن *jumbîdan* to move, stir

جنت *jannat* pl *jinân* garden, paradise; *~makân* the late, deceased

جنس *jins* sort, kind

جنگ *jang* war, battle; *~î* warlike, pugnacious; *~jûy* pugnacious, battle-seeking

جو *jaw* barley grain; iota; ¶ *jû → jûy*

جواب *javâb* answer, reply

جوان *javân* young; youth; *~î* youth; *~mard* of good birth, of noble station

جوجه *jûja* chicken

جوش *jôsh* tumult(uousness); *~ândil* with embroiled heart, aflame; *~ish* tumultuousness, ferment

جوشن *jawshan* breastplate, coat of mail

جوع *jû'* hunger

جولان *jawlân* circuit (of a polo field on a horse), prancing

جوی *jûy* stream, brook; *~bâr* stream, canal; ¶ *jûy- → justan*

جویا *jûyâ* searching for, seeking out

جه *jih- → jastan*

جهان jahân, jihân the world;
~ârâ world-adorning, splendid; ~âfarîn world-creating,
world creator; ~bîn world-seeing, world-revealing; ~dâr
master of the world; ~dîda
experienced in the world;
~parast worldly, devoted to
worldly things; ~sôz world-destroying; ¶ jihân leaping,
jumping

جهانيدن jihânîdan to make leap
(horse, e.g.)

جهت jihat direction; shish ~ all
directions

جهل jahl ignorance

جهنم jahannam hell

جيب jîb, jayb opening at the neck
of a shirt

جيحون Jayhûn the Oxus River

چادر châdur canopy, covering,
tent

چار châr = chahâr

چاره châra way out, remedy

چاك châk torn, rent; ~-âvurdan
to be split

چاكر châkar servant

چالاك châlâk nimble

چاه châh well, pit

چپ chap left (opp. of right)

چتر chatr parasol

چراغ chirâgh lamp

چرب charb fat, grease; ~guftâr of
smooth speech

چرخ charkh wheel, (celestial) orb,
wheel of fortune

چرخشت charkhusht wine press

چسان chisân in what manner?,
how?

چش chash- → chashîdan

چشاندن chashând-/chashân- to give
to taste

چشم chashm eye; ~-dâshtan to
expect, wait for; ~-i bad the
evil eye; ~a eye (of a needle),
spring; ~ak wink, beautiful
little eye; ~ bar râh expectant,
waiting; ~zada struck by the
evil eye; dar ~-i kas-î âmadan
to have value for someone

چشيدن chashîdan to taste

چفته chafta bent

چكاندن chikândan to drip (trs)

چكيدن chikîdan to drip (int)

چگونه chigûna how?

چمن chaman meadow

چميدن chamîdan to strut

چنار chanâr plane tree

چنان chunân thus; so much, so
many

چنبر chambar hoop; ~î hoop-like, shaped like a hoop

چند chand how much?, how
many?, how often?; ~în so
much; tâ ba ~ until when, for
how long

چنگ chang claw, clutches, talon;
harp

چنگال changâl claw, talon

چنگل changal = changâl

چو chu = chun

چوب chôb wood; ~în wooden

چوگان chawgân polo-stick, polo;
~bâzî polo, polo playing

چون chun when, if, because,
since; how?; (prep) like

چه chi what?; ¶ chah = châh

چهره chihra face, countenance;
~gushâ portraitist

چيدن chîd-/chîn- to take up, pick
up, pluck; to arrange, set out

چیز chîz thing; ~fahm one who "understands a thing or two"

چین chîn China; curl; furrow (in the brow); ~î Chinese; chîn- → chîdan

حاجب hâjib chamberlain

حاجت hâjat need, necessity; ~mand needy

حاجی hâjjî pilgrim

حادثه hâdisa temporality, temporal event, untoward event

حاشالله hâshâlillâh God forbid

حاصل hâsil crop, gain

حال hâl condition, state; ~at state, condition; ~gardân one who causes conditions to change

حب habb grains, seeds

حباب habâb bubble; ~vâr bubble-like

حب الوطن hubbulvatan patriotism, love of one's native land

حبذا habbazâ bravo, well done

حبس habs prison, imprisonment; ~gâh prison, jail

حبل المتین hablulmatîn (Ar.) "the strong rope," the rope with which God tugs on mystics

حج haj(j) pilgrimage to Mecca

حجاب hijâb veil; humiliation

حجره hujra chamber, room, specifically an upper room

حجله hijla bridal chamber

حد had(d) boundary, limit, extent; tâ ba ~î ki insofar as

حدی hudâ a song that makes camels travel fast; ~sâzî singing the hudâ

حدیث hadîs talk, tale

حذر hazar precaution

حرام harâm illicit; ~-gashtan ba kas-î to be forbidden to someone

حرب harb battle; ~gâh battle-field; ~î bellicose

حرص hirs greed, avarice

حرف harf letter of the alphabet; word; ~-zadan to speak

حرکت harakat motion, movement

حرم haram sanctuary; harem

حرمان hirmân disappointment, deprivation; ~zada deprived

حرمت hirmat deprivation, disappointment; ¶ hurmat respect, reverence

حریر harîr silk

حریص harîs greedy, avaricious

حریف harîf partner; rival

حریم harîm right, privilege

حزن huzn, hazan sorrow, remorse

حزین hazîn sad, mournful

حساب hisâb reckoning

حسد hasad envy; ~-burdan to be envious

حسرت hasrat regret

حسن husn beauty; ¶ hasan beautiful; Hasan-i Mujtabâ Hasan the Chosen, Second Imam of the Shia

حسین Husayn Husayn ibn Ali, Third Imam of the Shia

حشر hashr resurrection

حشم hasham retinue

حصار hisâr fortress; ~î besieged, blockaded, entombed

حضرت hazrat presence; title of great respect

حضور huzûr presence, presence of mind

حظيره hazîra grave enclosure, grating

حفاظ hifâz screen

حق haq(q) ultimate reality, verity; God; bi~-i concerning; ~bîn God-seeing; ~parastî worship of the divine truth

حقارت haqârat misery, being despicable

حقه huqqa coconut shell used in the shell-and-pea game; ~bâz trickster, shell-and-pea game artist

حقيقت haqîqat truth, verity

حكايت hikâyat tale, narration

حكم hukm order, command; law; force

حكمت hikmat wisdom

حكيم hakîm sage, wise

حل hall-kardan to solve

حلق halq throat

حلقه halqa ring; ~bagôsh slave, in bondage

حلم hilm clemency

حمام hammâm bath, public bath

حمايل hamâyil shoulder sword-belt

حمدالله hamdullâh praise be to God

حمل hamal Aries

حمله hamla attack; ~-burdan bar to attack

حميم hamîm hot water

حنوت hanût sweet herbs strewn over a corpse prior to burial

جوادث havâdis temporal events, untoward events

حواصل havâsil pelican

حوت hût Pisces

حور hûr houris, beauties; ~î houri, maiden of paradise

حوض hawz pond, pool

حوله hawla towel

حى hayy tribe

حيات hayât life

حيران hayrân perplexed, confused; ~î perplexity, confusion

حيرت hayrat perplexity, confusion

حيوان hayavân animals, animal

خاتم khâtim, khâtam seal, seal ring

خاتون khâtûn lady, mistress

خاد khâd kite (bird)

خار khâr thorn, thistle; ¶ khâr = khâra; ¶ khâr- → khârîdan

خاره khâra flint, granite

خاريدن khârîdan to scratch

خاستن khâst-/khêz- to rise

خاشاك khâshâk chip, shaving; twig

خاص khâss, khâs elite; ~iyyat property, special quality

خاطر khâtir mind; bahr-i ~-i for the sake of

خاقان khâqân ruler, emperor (especially of Turkistan)

خاك khâk dust, dirt; ground, earth; ~ bar sar dust on the head, a sign of mourning; ~dân dust heap; ~î dusty, made of dust, earthling; ~sâr dusty, humble; bâ ~ shuda yaksân leveled to the ground

خال khâl mole; maternal uncle

خالق khâliq creator

خالى khâlî empty, void; ~-kardan to empty

خام khâm unripe, raw, immature

خامش khâmush = khâmôsh

خاموش khâmôsh silent

خامه khâma pen

خانه khâna house, home

خاور khâvar east, orient; ~î eastern, oriental

خبر khabar news; ~-kardan to inform

خبط khabt mistake; ~-kardan to be mistaken, make a mistake

ختم khatm end, finish

ختن Khutan Khotan, city in Turkistan famed for its musk and its beauties

خجسته khujasta auspicious; ~pay one who leaves auspicious traces behind

خجل khajil ashamed

خدا khudâ lord, God; ~dâd God-given; ~parast God-fearing; ~vand lord, master; ~y = khudâ

خدمت khidmat service

خدنگ khadang arrow

خذلان khizlân distress

خر khar donkey, ass

خراب kharâb destroyed, broken, useless; ~âbâd ruined place, metaphor for the world; ~ât tavern

خراس kharâs mill turned by a donkey

خراسان Khurâsân Khurasan

خرامان khirâmân strutting, walking gracefully

خراميدن khirâmîdan to strut, walk gracefully

خرج kharj expenditure

خرد khirad wisdom; ~mand wise; ¶ khurd small, little, minute, insignificant; ~-shikastan to break into little pieces

خرده khurda trifle; ~-giriftan bar to find fault with, cavile

خرسند khursand happy, satisfied; ~î happiness

خرقه khirqa patched cloak, Sufi cloak

خرگاه khargâh trellis tent, domed tent

خرگ khargah = khargâh; yâr-i ~î "tent companion," lover at a camp site

خرم khurram fresh, joyful; ~dil happy, fortunate; ~î rejoicing

خرما khurmâ date

خرمن khirman haystack, harvest, heap

خروش khurôsh cry, lamentation; ~ân weeping, wailing, crying out

خروشيدن khurôshîdan to cry out, shout, make a racket

خريدار kharîdâr customer, purchaser

خريدن kharîdan to buy

خزان khazân autumn

خزيدن khizîdan to crawl, creep

خزينه khazîna treasury; ~dârî office of the treasurer

خس khas straw

خسبيدن khusbîdan to sleep

خسپيدن khuspîdan = khusbîdan

خستن khastan to wound, be wounded

خسته khasta wounded; ~dil heart-sick

خسرو *khusraw* king, prince, Chosroës; ~*ânî* royal, regal; ~ *Parvêz* Chosroës Parvez

خشت *khisht* brick, brick slab used to cover the face at burial

خشك *khushk* dry; ~*lab* parched-lipped; ~*u tar* vicissitudes

خشم *khashm* rage, wrath

خصال *khisâl* qualities, properties

خصم *khasm* opponent

خضر *Khizr* Khizr, one of the immortals; identified as Alexander's cook, he is said to have fallen into the Fountain of Youth; ¶ *khazir* green, verdant

خضرا *khazrâ* dark green, dark blue

خط *khat(t)* down on the cheek; line of writing

خطا *khitâ* mistake; crime, sin; ¶ *Khatâ* Cathay

خطاب *khitâb* address, act of addressing someone

خطر *khatar* danger; ~*nâk* dangerous

خطوط *khutût* pl of *khatt* line

خطه *khitta* realm, region

خفا *khafâ* concealment

خفاش *khaffâsh* bat; ~*tab'* with a bat-like nature

خفتان *khaftân* vest

خفتن *khuft-/khwâb-* to sleep, lie down

خلاص *khalâs* liberty, release

خلاف *khilâf* fault; opposite

خلاق *khallâq* creator, creative

خلخى *khallukhî* related to the Qarluqs, a Turkic tribe; ~*nizhâd* of Qarluq descent

خلد *khuld* eternity, heaven

خلعت *khil'at* robe of honor

خلف *khalaf* offspring

خلفا *khulafâ* pl of *khalîfa* caliph

خلق *khalq* creation, creature, people; ~*shikâr* that which preys on people; ¶ *khulq*, *khuluq* nature, temperament

خلل *khalal* being marred

خلوت *khalvat* retreat, solitude; ~*nishîn* one who is on retreat, one who sits in solitude

خليفه *khalîfa* caliph; successor

خم *kham(m)* bent, bowed; noose; loop, curl; *ba*~ bent; *ba* ~ *âvurdan* to bend; ¶ *khum* vat; ~*khâna* wine house

خمار *khumâr* hangover; ¶ *khammâr* vintnor

خموش *khamôsh* = *khâmôsh*

خنجر *khanjar* dagger

خندان *khandân* laughing, smiling; ~*lab* laughing, smiling, smirking

خنده *khanda* laughter; slosh of wine in a goblet

خندیدن *khandîdan bar* to laugh at, smile at

خنك *khunak* cool; ~*jân* of a cold temperament

خنگ *khing* horse, steed

خو *khû* = *khway*

خواب *khwâb* sleep; *khwâb-* → *khuftan*

خواجگی *khwâjagî* dignity

خواجه *khwâja* khwaja, title of learning and distinction

خوار *khwâr* = *khwar*; ¶ *khwâr* wretched, mean, lowly, humble; ~*î* contempt, misery

خواستار *khwâstâr-kardan* to ask for, seek out

خواستن *khwâst-/khwâh-* to want, desire; beseech

خوان *khwân* banquet table; ~*cha* small table; ¶ *khwân-* → *khwândan*

خواندن *khwând-/khwân-* to call; to recite, read

خواهر *khwâhar* sister

خوب *khûb* good, beautiful; ~*rûy* beautiful; ~*î* beauty

خود *khwad* self; ~*bîn* conceited

خور *khwar* eating; ¶ *khwar* = *khwarshêd*

خورد *khward* food

خوردن *khward-/khwar-* to eat, drink, consume; suffer

خورش *khwarish* nourishment, food

خورشید *khwarshêd* sun; ~*rukh* one whose face is as splendid as the sun; ~*mahall* as highly placed as the sun

خوش *khwash* good (see compounds following); ~~ softly, delicately; ~*î* pleasure

خوشاب *khwash-âb* lustrous (pearl!)

خوش‌الحان *khwash-alhân* one who sing or plays nice tunes

خوش آوازی *khwash-âvâzî* ability to sing beautifully

خوش‌حال *khwashhâl* prosperous, in good condition

خوش‌خوان *khwashkhwân* beautiful of song

خوش‌سودا *khwashsawdâ* easily marketable

خوش‌عنان *khwash'inân* easy on the reins, tractile

خوش‌منظر *khwashmanzar* good-looking

خوش نغمه *khwashnaghma* sweet-songed

خوشوقت *khwashvaqt* happy

خوشه *khôsha* gleaning; ~*chîn* gleaner

خوف *khawf* fear

خون *khûn* blood; ~-*rêkhtan* to shed blood, to cry bitter tears; ~*bâr* blood-raining, tear-shedding; ~*chikân* blood-dripping; ~*garmî* hot-bloodedness, excitability; ~*khizâb* tinged with blood; ~*rêzî* bloodshed

خونابه *khûnâba* tears; vermillion

خوی *khôy* sweat, perspiration; ¶ *khway* habit, disposition

خویش *khwêsh* one's self; relative, kindred; ~*tan* one's self; ~*tansôz* self-immolating

خیاط *khayyât* tailor

خیال *khayâl* image, phantom, wraith

خیر *khayr* goodness, charity

خیره *khîra* dazed, confused; in vain, futile; ~-*mândan* to be dazzled; *ba* ~*khîr gashtan* to wander aimlessly

خیز *khêz-* → *khâstan*

خیزران *khayzurân* myrtle

خیل *khayl* cavalry, horses, troop

خیمه *khayma* tent; ~-*zadan* to pitch a tent

داد *dâd* justice; ~*gar* dispenser of justice

دادن *dâd-/dih-* to give

دار *dâr* gallows, gibbet; *dâr-* → *dâshtan*

دارو *dârû* antidote, medicine

داستان *dâstân* story, tale

داشتن *dâsht-/dâr-* to have, hold, keep

داغ *dâgh* scar, wound, brand; ~*dâr* scarred, branded; ~*gâh* branding place

دام *dâm* snare, trap; ~*gâh*, ~*gah* snare, trap

داماد *dâmâd* bridegroom

دامان *dâmân* skirt, train; tent flap; ~-*i chîz-î az dast guzâsh-tan, dâdan* to give up, abandon something; ~-*giriftan* to seize someone's skirt, coat-tails, to entreat; ~-*kashîdan* to drag the skirt, to pull in the skirt, avoid; *dast az* ~-*i chîz-î kûtâh bûdan* for something to be out of reach

دامن *dâman* = *dâmân*

دانا *dânâ* knowing, knowledge-able, wise; ~*î* wisdom

دانستن *dânist-/dân-* to know, realize, recognize

دانش *dânish* knowledge, wisdom

دانك *dânk* for *bîdân ki* know that...

دانه *dâna* seed, grain, trifle

داور *dâvar* arbiter, judge

دايره *dâyira* circle

دايگی *dâyagî* office of a wet-nurse

دايم ، دائم *dâyim, dâ'im* always, constant

دائما *dâ'iman* always

دجله *Dijla* the Tigris River

دخان *dukhân* steam, evaporation; smoke; ~*î* smoky

دخل *dakhl* income

دخمه *dakhma* Zoroastrian tomb tower

دد *dad* beasts of the wild

در *dar* in, inside; door, gate, court; *ba* ~ *âmadan* to come out; *ba* ~ *kardan* to put away, get rid of; *ba* ~ *uftâdan* to fall out of, escape from; for compounds with *dar-* see below alphabetically; ¶ *dar-* → *darîdan*; ¶ *dur(r)* pearl; ~-*suftan* to pierce a pearl, accomplish the impossible; ~*dâna* a pearl; ~*fishân* pearl-scattering, weeping

دراج *durrâj* francolin

دراز *darâz* long; ~'*umr* long-lived

درافتادن *dar-uftâdan* to fall, tumble down

درآميختن *dar-âmêkhtan* to admix

درآويختن *dar-âvêkhtan* to hang up

دربان *darbân* gatekeeper

درج *durj* jewel casket

درخت *darakht* tree

درخورد *darkhward* worthy

درخزيدن *dar-khizîdan* to creep into

درد *dard* pain; ~*â* alas, what a pity; ~*âlûd* painful; ~*mand* in pain, suffering; ~*mandî* suffering, pain; ~*nâk* pained, suffering; ~*nâkî* pain, being in pain; ¶ *durd* dregs; ~*kash* dreg-drinker

درربودن *dar-rubûdan* to snatch, carry off

درزی *darzî* tailor

درس *dars* study

درست *durust* right, correct, exact; ~-*kardan* to make, fix; ~*î* correctness

درشت *durusht* coarse; ~*î* coarse-ness

درشدن *dar-shudan* to go in, sink into

درشكستن *dar-shikastan* to break down, break in

درغلطيدن *dar-ghaltîdan* to roll around

درك *darak* a layer of hell

دركشيدن *dar-kashîdan* to draw across, to gulp down

درگذشتن *dar-guzashtan* to pass away

درگرفتن *dar-giriftan* to begin; to undertake, set out

درم *diram* dirhem, coin

درمان *darmân* remedy

درماندن *dar-mândan* to despair, fall into; to be left behind, get stuck

درنگ *dirang* hesitation; ~-*kardan* to wait, lie in expectation

درنه *dar-nih* impt of *dar-nihâdan*

درنهادن *dar-nihâdan* to place down, submit

درو *darû* = *dar û*; ¶ *diraw-* → *dirawîdan*

درود *durûd* greetings

دروغ *durôgh* lie

درون *darûn, durûn* inside; ~-*i* in, inside (prep.)

درويدن *dirawîdan* to reap

درويش *darvêsh* dervish, poor man; ~*âna* dervish-like

درهم *darham* in disarray, disordered

دريا *daryâ* sea, large river

دريافتن *dar-yâftan* to comprehend

دريچه *darîcha* small door, trap door; chink

دريدن *darîdan* to tear, rip

دريده *darîda* torn, ripped; ~*girîbân* with shirt torn open from grief

دريغ *dirêgh* regret; ~*â* alas, alack

دريوزه *daryûza* supplication

دزديدن *duzdîdan* to steal, pilfer

دژ *dizh* fortress, castle

دژم *dizham* dark, dejected

دست *dast* hand; ~*âs* hand mill; ~*burd* ability; attack; ~ *dar jân zadan* to risk one's life; ~*gâh* power, might; ~*tahî* empty-handed; ~ *u pâ zada dar khûn* drenched in blood from head to foot

دستار *dastâr* turban

دستان *Dastân* epithet of Zâl, Rustam's father; ~-*i Sâm* Zâl, son of Sâm; ~*sâz* melody-making

دستور *dastûr* permission, formula; canon; Zoroastrian priest

دسته *dasta* bouquet

دشت *dasht* field, plain, desert; ~*navard*, ~*paymâ* able to cross with desert with ease

دشمن *dushman* enemy

دشنام *dushnâm* defamed

دشنه *dashna* sword, blade

دشوار *dushvâr* difficult; ~*î* difficulty

دعا *du'â* expository prayer

دعوت *da'vat* invitation, summons

دعوى *da'vâ* claim, suit; ~-*kardan* to sue, bring a claim

دف *daf(f), duf(f)* drum, tambourine

دفتر *daftar* ledger

دفع *daf'* repelling, repulsion; ~-*guftan* to tell someone to go away

دقت *diqqat* care, precision

دقيق *daqîq* subtle, precise

دكان *duk(k)ân* shop

دگر‎ *digar = dígar;* ~*bâra* once again, once more; ~*gûn* of a different aspect; ~*gûna* different

دل‎ *dil* heart; ~ *ba dast âvurdan* to charm, accept as lover; ~*-bastan ba* to fix the heart on; ~*-giriftan az* to be weary of, find unpleasant; ~*gumâshtan bar* to set one's heart on; ~*ârâî* charm; ~*âvar* hero, warrior; ~*band* one whose heart is fixed on something; ~*bar* charming, sweetheart, charmer, mistress; ~*barî* charm, ability to steal one's heart away; ~*dâda* one who has lost his heart; ~*dâr* sweetheart, mistress; ~*gîr* noxious; ~*jûî* comfort, satisfaction; ~*jûy* comforting, consoling; ~*shâd* happy, gladhearted; ~*sitân* heart-stealer; ~*tang* sad, distressed, homesick

دلیر‎ *dilîr* bold

دلیل‎ *dalîl* proof

دم‎ *dam* breath; moment, instant; ~*-zadan* to breathe, utter a sound; ~*â*~, ~*ba*~ moment by moment; *ân*~ at that instant; ~*sâz* confidant, consort; ~*ak* an instant; ¶ *dum* tail

دماغ‎ *dimâgh* mind

دنبه‎ *dumba* sheep's fatty tail

دمدمه‎ *damdama* clamor

دمساز‎ *damsâz* consort, confidant, friend

دمن‎ *diman* traces of former dwellings

دمیدن‎ *damîdan* to break (dawn); to sprout (flower)

دندان‎ *dandân* tooth

دندانه‎ *dandâna* crenellation, battlement

دنیا‎ *dunyâ* this world

دو‎ *du* two

دوا‎ *davâ* remedy, medicine

دوات‎ *davât* inkpot

دوال‎ *davâl* belt, band

دوختن‎ *dôkht-/dôz-* to sew, stitch

درد‎ *dûd* smoke; ~ *ba sar raftan* to suffer anguish, perish

درر‎ *dûr* far; ~*andâz* powerful archer; ~*bâsh* a club or mace used to keep crowds back; ¶ *dawr* revolution; era; ~*-i* around

دوران‎ *dawrân* age, epoch

دوز‎ *dôz-* → *dôkhtan*

دوزخ‎ *dôzakh* hell

دوست‎ *dôst* friend, beloved; ~*dâr* adherent, admirer

دوش‎ *dôsh* shoulder, back; last night

دوشویه‎ *du-shôya* having two spouses

دوشین‎ *dôshîn* last night

دوصد‎ *dosad* two hundred (archaic and dialect)

دوکون‎ *du-kawn* this world and the next

دولت‎ *dawlat* fortune, wealth; ~*î* governmental

دوم‎ *duvum* second

دومغز‎ *du-maghz* two-kernelled

دویدن‎ *dawîdan, davîdan* to run

دویم‎ *duyum* second

ده‎ *dah* ten; ¶ *dih-* → *dâdan*

دهان‎ *dahân* mouth

دهر‎ *dahr* time, Father Time; era

دهقان *dihqân* farmer, peasant; village head

دهل *duhul* drum

دهن *dahan* = *dahân*; ~*darîda* with the mouth torn

دى *day* Day, the midwinter month, Capricorn; ¶ *dê* yesterday

ديار *diyâr* realm, region; ¶ *day-yâr* householder, inhabitant

ديبا *dêbâ* brocade

ديبه *dêba* gold tissue

ديد *dîd* sight, ability to see

ديدار *dîdâr* rendezvous; vision

ديدن *dîd-/bîn-* to see

ديده *dîda* eye; vision

دير *dêr* late, long (of time); ~*zîs-tan* to live for a long time; ~*îna* old, of long standing; ~*jôsh* slow to boil, slow to make friends; ¶ *dayr* monastery

ديگ *dêg* pot

ديلم *daylam* slave

دين *dîn* religion

ديو *dêv* devil, demon

ديوار *dîvâr* wall

ديوان *dîvân* office, bureau; divan, a poet's collected works

ديوانه *dêvâna* mad, madman

ذات عماد *zât-i imâd* "possessed of pillars," epithet of the Garden of Iram

ذباب *zubâb* flies

ذرات *zarrât* → *zarra*

ذراع *zirâ'* cubit

ذره *zarra* pl -*ât* iota, atom, particle, dust mote

ذوالقرنين *Zulqarnayn* "he of the two horns," epithet of Alexander the Great

ذوالمنن *zulminan* "possessor of obligations," epithet of God

ذوق *zawq* taste, desire, experience

راحت *râhat* ease, comfort

راد *râd* liberal, munificent

راز *râz* secret, mystery; ~*gushâdan* to reveal a secret; ~*dâr* keeper of secrets, confidant

راست *râst* straight, right; directly, immediately; ~*pindâshtan* to think something is exactly (like something else); ~*î* truth; ~*niyûsh* attuned to the truth

راغ *râgh* meadow

راكع *râki'* kneeling

رام *râm* tame

رامش *râmish* cheer, cheerfulness

راندن *ránd-/rân-* to drive, drive forward, make go

راه *râh* way, road; musical mode; ~*zadan* to waylay, engage in highway robbery; ~*i kasî zadan* to waylay someone; ~*bar* guide, leader; ~*ni-shîn* one who sits in the road; ~*raw* wayfarer; ~*tôsha* travel provisions

راهب *râhib* monk

راى *rây* free will, mind

رايت *râyat* banner

رباب *rubâb* rebec, lute

رباط *ribât* caravanserai

رباى *rubây-* → *rubûdan*

ربط *rabt* bond, connection

ربع‎ *rab'* halting place, camping ground (particularly in the spring)

ربودن‎ *rubûd-/rubâ-* to snatch

رحلت‎ *rihlat* journey; death

رحم‎ *rahm* mercy, clemency; ~-*kardan bar* to have mercy on

رحمان‎ *rahmân* merciful

رحمت‎ *rahmat* mercy; ~-*âvurdan bar* to have mercy on

رخ‎ *rukh* cheek; rook (chess); ~-*numûdan* to reveal the face, unveil the face; ~*sâra* cheek

رخت‎ *rakht* baggage

رخش‎ *Rakhsh* Rakhsh, Rustam's horse

رخشان‎ *rakhshân* shining, bright

رخنه‎ *rakhna* chink, crack

رد‎ *rad(d)* rejection, disputation; ~-*kardan* to contradict; to cross over; ~-*i mazâlem dâdan* to redress wrongdoing, to pay "conscience money"

ردا‎ *ridâ* cloak

رز‎ *raz* the vine; ~*bun* vine

رزق‎ *rizq* daily sustenance

رزم‎ *razm* battle; ~*gah* battlefield

رسالت‎ *risâlat* apostleship, message

رساندن‎ *rasândan* to make arrive, deliver

رستاخیز‎ *rustâkhêz* resurrection, tumult

رستخیز‎ *rustakhêz = rustâkhêz*

رستم‎ *Rustam* Rustam; ~*âna* Rustam-like

رستن‎ *rast-/rah-* to escape, be delivered; ¶ *rust-/rôy-* to grow, sprout

رستوران‎ *restorân* restaurant

رسته‎ *rasta* street

رسم‎ *rasm* custom, habit

رسن‎ *rasan* rope

رسوائی‎ *rusvâî* scandal, dishonor

رسول‎ *rasûl* messenger, envoy

رسیدن‎ *rasîdan* to arrive, come about; ripen

رشت‎ *Rasht* Rasht, capital of Gilan

رشته‎ *rishta* thread

رشك‎ *rashk* jealousy; object of jealousy

رضا‎ *rizâ* pleasure, contentment; ~-*dâdan ba* to be content with

رطل‎ *ratl* bumper, large measure

رعنا‎ *ra'nâ* fresh; ~*î* freshness, loveliness

رفتن‎ *raft-/raw-* to go; ¶ *ruft-/rû(y)-* to sweep

رفرف‎ *rafraf* carpet, floor covering

رفو‎ *rufû* repair, darn; ~-*kardan* to repair (torn fabric)

رفیع‎ *rafî'* high, lofty

رفیق‎ *rafîq* comrade; ~-*î-kardan* to accompany, be a comrade

رقاص‎ *raqqâs* dancer

رقص‎ *raqs* dance, dancing; ~-*kardan* to dance

رقم‎ *raqam* cipher; ~-*kashîdan* to obliterate, cross out; ~-*zadan* to calculate, to obliterate; ~*sanj* measuring every cipher, exacting

رقیب‎ *raqîb* guardian; rival

رکاب‎ *rikâb* stirrup

رکناباد‎ *Ruknâbâd*, Ruknabad, a waterway in Shiraz

رکوع‎ *rukû'* kneeling, being prostrate

رمز *ramz* innuendo; enigma

رمل *ramal* the poetic meter *ra-mal*; geomancy

رميدن *ramîdan* to shy away, flee

رنج *ranj* pain, trouble; ~*ûr* pained, in pain; ~*ûrî* ailment

رنجانيدن *ranjânîdan* to cause hurt

رنجيدن *ranjîdan* to pain, hurt (trs)

رند *rind* scoundrel, antinomian dervish

رنگ *rang* color; ~-*dâdan* to tint; ~*în* colored, varied

رو *raw* → *raftan*; *rô* → *rôy*, *rustan*; *rû-* → *ruftan*

روا *ravâ* fitting, suitable, permissible; ~-*dâshtan* to allow; ¶ *rivâ* narration

روان *ravân* soul; running, flowing; ~-*kardan* to make go, launch; ~(*a*)-*shudan* to leave, go, flow; ~*bakhsh* life-giving; *sarv-i* ~ elegant, flowing cypress

روباه *rûbâh* fox

روبه *rûbah* = *rûbâh*

رويس *rûpas* looking back; ~-*kardan* to look back

روح *rûh* spirit; ~*ul'amîn*, ~-*i amîn* Gabriel; ~*ulquds*, ~-*i quds* the Holy Ghost; ~*vâr* spirit-like

روحانى *rûhânî* spiritual

رود *rûd* river; ¶ *rôd* bow string; ~-*navâkhtan* to play (a string instrument); ~*navâz* one who plucks a string

روده *rôda* bow string

رودابه *Rûdâba* Rudaba, Rustam's mother

روز *rôz* day; ~*afzûn* daily increasing; ~*gâr* time, period of time; fate; ~*gârî* for ages; ~*î* sustenance, daily bread

روزن *rawzan* skylight, small window

روزنامه *rôznâma* newspaper; ~*nivîs* journalist

روزه *rûza* fast, fasting

روستا *rôstâ* village

روسياه *rû-siyâh* disgraced

روش *ravish* flow

روشن *rawshan* bright, clear, splendid, enlightened; ~*bîn* clearsighted, clairvoyant; ~*dil* bright-hearted; ~*gar* polisher

روضه *rawza* garden

روم *Rûm* Byzantium

رونق *rawnaq* splendor

روى *rôy*, *rûy* face; ~-*bûdan* to happen, occur; ~-*nihâdan* to turn, face, head; ~*siyâh* disgraced; ¶ *rûy-* → *ruftan*; ¶ *rôy-* → *rustan*

رويت *ru'yat* vision

ره *rah* = *râh*; *rah-* → *rastan*

رهاندن *rahând-/rahân-* to free, deliver, drive off

رهآورد *rahâvard* gift brought back from a trip

رهبر *rahbar* leader, guide; ~*î* leadership, guidance

رهرو *rahraw* wayfarer, Sufi

رهنماى *rahnumây* guide; searching for

رهنمون *rahnamûn* guide

رهى *rahî* slave, servant

رى *Ray* the city of Ray

رياحين *rayâhîn* aromatic herbs

ريحان *rayhân* aromatic herb, basil

ریختن rêkht-/rêz- to spill, pour out, shed (tears); throw, cast away

ریز rêz- → rêkhtan; rêz small, insignificant; ~ân dropping, dripping

ریسمان rîsmân rope

ریش rêsh apprehensive; wound; wounded; ¶ rîsh beard

ریگ rêg sand

رئیس ra'îs head, chief

ز z', zi poetic contr. of az

زاد zâd = âzâd; ¶ zâd provisions

زادن zâd-/zây- to give birth; to be born

زار zâr mournful(ly); weeping; ~~ bitterly, mournfully; ~î wailing, moaning, entreaty; ~î-kardan to wail, bemoan; ¶ zâr = nizâr

زاغ zâgh raven

زال Zâl Zal, son of Sâm and father of Rustam; old man, old woman; ~ak contemptuous old man or woman

زان zân cont. of az ân; ~ki because

زانو zânû knee

زاویه zâviya pl zavâyâ corner, retreat

زاهد zâhid ascetic

زای zây- → zâdan

زائد ، زاید zâ'id, zâyid increasing; surplus; ~unnûr of great light

زاییدن zâyîdan = zâdan

زبان zabân tongue, language; ~ bar-kashîdan bar to revile, scold

زبر zibar-i above (prep)

زبرجد zabarjad emerald

زبسکه zi bas-ki → bas

زجاجه zujâja glass

زحل Zuhal Saturn

زحمت zahmat trouble

زخم zakhm wound; ~-khwar-dan to suffer a wound

زدای zadây- → zadûdan

زدن zad-/zan- to hit, strike, strike down; to block (road); to pitch (tent); to cast (pottery)

زدودن zadûd-/zadây- to polish

زر zar(r) gold; Zâl-i ~ Zal the Albino; ~âb gold wash, gilt; ~baft gold-spun; ~gar goldsmith; ~în, zarrîn golden; ~înnigâr painted in gold; ~kash-kardan to gild; ~nigâr gilded

زرد zard yellow, pale

زردشت Zardusht Zoroaster

زردهشت Zarduhusht = Zardusht

زره zirih chain-mail

زشت zisht hideous, heinous

زعفران za'farân saffron

زغال zughâl dogwood

زغن zaghan hawk

زکوة zakât alms, tithe; ~istân treasury where alms are housed; ~sitân tithe-taker, alms-collector

زلال zulâl pure water, limpid water

زلزله zilzila earthquake

زلف zulf tress; ~ak beautiful tress; ~ayn two tresses

زلیخا Zulaykhâ Zuleikha, wife of the biblical Potiphar

زمام zimâm reins; ~kash refractory, pulling on the reins

زمان zamân time, age, epoch

زمانه zamâna = zamân

زمرد zumurrud emerald

زمن zaman = zamân

زمین zamîn earth, ground

زن zan woman; ¶ zan- → zadan

زنار zunnâr Christian or Zoroastrian girdle, metaphorically applied to all non-Muslim peoples

زناشوئی zanâshôî marital state

زنجیر zanjîr chain

زنخ zanakh chin, dimple in the chin; ~zadan to wag the chin

زندان zindân prison

زندگانی zindagânî life

زنده zinda alive

زنگ zang rust, verdigris; Zanzibar; ~âr rust, verdigris; ~î Negro, black

زنهار zinhâr asylum; grief; beware

زوال zavâl perishing, annihilation

زوایا zavâya → zâviya

زوبین zûbîn spear, javelin, shaft

زوپین zûpîn = zûbîn

زوج zawj pair

زود zûd quick; ~î quickness, speed; ba ~î quickly, fast

زور zôr might, strength; ~dast strong of arm

زورق zawraq barque, ship

زهد zuhd asceticism

زهر zahr poison

زهرا Zahrâ epithet of Fatimah

زهره zahra bitter gall; ~ash âb shud he lost his nerve; ¶ Zuhra Venus

زی zî- → zîstan; ¶ zî toward

زیادت ziyâdat increase, waxing

زیان ziyân harm; (financial) loss

زیب zêb beauty; ¶ zêb- → zêbîdan

زیبا zêbâ beautiful; ~î beauty

زیبیدن zêbîdan to adorn

زیر zêr below; treble note; ~-i below, beneath (prep)

زیرا zîrâ because

زیرك zêrak clever

زیستن zîst-/zî- to live; dêr-~ to live for a long time

زین zîn = az în; ¶ zîn saddle; ~kardan to saddle

زینهار zînhâr = zinhâr

ژاله zhâla dew, dew drop

ژرف zharf deep; ~î depth

ژنده‌پیل zandapîl mad, enraged elephant

ژولیده zhûlîda dishevelled

سابق sâbiq past, former; ~-a-i lutf past favors

ساجد sâjid prostrating, bowing down in prostration

ساحت sâhat courtyard, open space

ساحل sâhil shore, seashore

ساختن sâkht-/sâz- to make, accomplish; ~ bâ to get along with, accomodate oneself to

ساده sâda plain, simple; ~dilî simplicity, foolishness

سار sâr starling

ساربان sârbân caravan leader

ساروان sârvân = sârbân

ساز sâz musical instrument; provisions; ~-ârâstan, ~-dâ-

dan to tune an instrument;
~-i râh provisions for a trip;
¶ sâz- → sâkhtan

ساعت sâ'at time, moment, hour

ساعد sâ'id arm, forearm

ساغر sâghar cup, bowl

ساقی sâqî saqi, cup-bearer

ساکن sâkin inhabitant, dweller

سالار sâlâr leader; ~î leadership, greatness

سام Sâm Sâm, father of Zâl

سامان sâmân belongings; state of order; ~-kardan to get in order

سامری sâmirî Samaritan, the maker of the golden calf

سان sân manner; ba~-i like, as (prep); badân~-ki just as (conj); chi~ how?

سای sây- → suftan, sûdan, sâî-dan

سایبان sâyabân shady, trellised

سایه sâya shade, shadow

سائیدن sâîdan to rub

سبب sabab pl asbâb cause, reason

سبحه subha rosary

سبز sabz green; dark; ~a greenery, verdure

سبق sabaq precedence; lesson

سبک sabuk quick, sudden; light; ~bâr lightly-burdened; ~dastî dexterity; ~raw speedy, fast

سبو sabû pitcher, glass, goblet

سپار sipâr- → sipurdan

سپاه sipâh army

سپر sipar shield

سپردن sipurd-/sipâr- to entrust, turn over

سپری siparî annihilated

سپس sipas later, then

سپند sipand rue (burned as purifying incense)

سپه sipah = sipâh; ~bad commander; ~dâr commander

سپهر sipihr celestial sphere, celestial orb

سپید sipêd white, bright, brilliant; ~a dawn; ~abrû white-browed

ستادن sitâdan = sitadan, îstâdan

ستاره sitâra star

ستان sitân- → sitadan

ستایش sitâyish praise

ستدن sitad-/sitân- to take, take away

ستر sitr being veiled, sanctity

ستردن siturdan to erase, scratch out

ستم sitam distress; oppression; ~gar oppressor; ~kâr oppressor, unjust

ستودن sitûd-/sitâ(y)- to celebrate, praise

ستیز sitêz spite; ~a = sitêz

سجده sijda prostration, prayer, worship; ~-burdan to prostrate oneself

سجین sijjîn dungeon of hell

سحر sahar dawn; ~gâh dawn; sihr magic, sorcery; ~-rândan to perform sorcery; ~numâ magician

سخت sakht tight, hard; ~-giriftan to be harsh; ~jânî hard-heartedness, inhumanity; ~kamân powerful archer; ~raftâr swift-paced; ~rânî severity, driving (animals) cruelly

سخن sukhan, sukhun speech, poetry; ~gûy speaking, poet,

possessed of rational speech;
~*sarâ* singer, reciter of poetry

سد *sad* dam; dammed, blocked
off

سدره *sidra* the Sidra tree that
grows next to the throne of
God; ~*nishîn* perched on the
Sidra tree

سده *sada* Sada, Iranian festival
of fire

سر *sar* head; end; ~ *ba jahân
dar-nihâdan* to wander off
into the wide world; ~-*i ...
dâshtan* to be intent upon;
~-*farâ-kârdan* to poke the
head out; ~*âpây* from head
to toe, all over; ~*â*~ all over,
from one end to the other; ~
u sâmân earthly goods; for all
compounds with *sar*, see al-
phabetically below

سر *sirr* secret, mystery

سراب *sarâb* mirage

سراپرده *sarâparda* tent, pavilion

سرادق *surâdiq* tent, pavilion

سراسیمه *sarâsîma* confounded,
dumbfounded

سرآمدن *sar-âmadan* to come to an
end

سرانداختن *sar-andâkhtan* to cut off
the head, lob off the head

سرای *sarây* house, palace, court

سراینده *sarâyanda* player of music,
singer

سرباختن *sar-bâkhtan* to lose one's
head, go crazy

سربرهنه *sarbirahna* with uncovered
head (sign of grief)

سربسته *sarbasta* closed, stoppered

سربلندی *sarbulandî* exaltedness,
pride

سربند *sarband* head covering

سرتافتن *sar-tâftan* to turn the head
away

سرچشمه *sarchashma* spring

سرخ *surkh* red; ~*âb* tears of
grief; a type of water fowl;
~*âbrukh* rosy-cheeked

سرد *sard* cool, cold

سررشته *sarrishta* end of a thread

سرزدن *sar-zadan* to arise

سرزنش *sarzanish* reproach; ~-
kardan to reproach,
admonish

سرسام *sarsâm* delirium

سرسبز *sarsabz* green, verdant

سرشار *sarshâr* brimful

سرشتن *sirisht-/sirîs-* to knead

سرشك *sirishk* tears; ~*dâna* tear
drop

سركش *sarkash* refractory; ~*î* re-
fractoriness

سرگذشت *sarguzasht* adventure

سرگردان *sargardân* confused

سرگشتن *sar-gashtan* to be perplexed

سرگشته *sargashta* bewildered, dis-
oriented; ~-*dil* confused

سرگوشی *sargôshî* whisper

سرمست *sarmast* dead drunk

سرمه *surma* collyrium, mascara

سرنگون *sarnigûn* upside down

سرنوشت *sarnivisht* fate, destiny

سرنهادن *sar-nihâdan ba* to begin,
set out to

سرو *sarv* cypress; ~-*i sahî* elegant
cypress, graceful walker;
~*qadd* tall and elegant

سروپا *sar-u-pâ* dignity, self-pos-
session

سرور *sarvar* leader; ¶ *surûr* joy,
happiness

سروش Surôsh Surosh, the Zoroastrian angel of glad tidings

سره sara good, excellent

سریر sarîr bed, couch

سرین sarîn forehead

سز saz- → sazîdan

سزاوار sazâvâr worthy

سزیدن sazîdan to be worthy

سست sust weak; ~'anâsir weak-natured; ~bunyâd, ~nihâd on weak foundations; ~nazm weak poet

سعادت sa'âdat felicity; ~mand happy, felicitous

سعدی Sa'dâ Arabic female name

سعیر Sa'îr Saïr, a layer of hell

سفتن suft-/sây- to pierce, bore through

سفر safar travel, journey; ~-kardan to travel

سفره sufra table, tablecloth

سفله sifla low, mean

سفلی suflâ inferior, lower

سفید sifêd white; good (luck)

سفیدار sifêdâr white poplar, aspen

سقر Saqar Saqar, a layer of hell

سکونت sukûnat rest, being at rest

سگ sag dog

سگالیدن sigâlîdan to speak ill of one who is absent

سلام salâm salaam, greeting

سلامت salâmat health, well-being

سلسبیل salsabîl a fountain in paradise

سلسله silsila chain; continuum; ~mû one with braided hair

سلطان sultân sultan

سلمی Salmâ Arabic female name

سلوت salvat remedy for grief

سلیمان Sulaymân Solomon

سم sum(m) hoof

سما samâ heaven

سماع samâ' mystic music-dance session

سماك simâk Arcturus

سمرقند Samarqand Samarkand

سمن saman jasmine; ~'ârizayn jasmine-cheeked; ~bar jasmine-bosomed

سمند samand charger, steed

سنان sinân spear

سنبل sumbul hyacinth

سنجیدن sanjîdan to weigh, compare

سنگ sang rock, stone

سنگین sangîn heavy; ~bâr heavy-laden; ~dil hard-hearted

سو sû direction; ~-yi toward

سواد savâd blackness

سوار savâr, suvâr mounted, rider, cavalier; ~-kardan to mount (trs); ~-shudan to mount (int)

سوختن sôkht-/sôz- to burn, be seared

سوخته sôkhta burned; ~kharman one whose harvest is burnt, devastated

سود sûd profit, advantage

سودا sawdâ melancholy

سودن sûd-/sây- to rub, polish

سوده‌گر sûdagar gem polisher

سور sôr, sûr festival, holiday

سوراخ sûrâkh hole, chink

سوری sûrî Syrian; gul-i ~ Damascene rose

سوز sôz burning; sôz- → sôkhtan; ~ân burning (adj); ~nâk burning, fiery

سوزن *sûzan* needle

سوگ *sôg* mourning; ~*vârî* mourning, bereavement

سوگند *sawgand* oath

سوهان *sawhân* file

سوی *sû(y)* direction; ~*-i* toward

سویدا *suvaydâ* the (black) core of the heart

سهی *sahî* elegant, graceful

سهل *sahl* flat, easy

سهیل *Suhayl* Canopus, a star renowned for its great beauty

سیاوش *Siyâvush* Siyavush

سیاه *siyâh* black; ~*chashm* black-eyed; ~*î* blackness, darkness; ~*khâna* nomadic tent; ~*fâm* black in color; ~*pistân* black-bosomed

سیب *sêb* apple

سیر *sayr* travel; ¶ *sêr* satiated; ~*âb* satiated with water

سیرت *sîrat* good conduct

سیره *sayra* a small songbird

سیف *sayf* sword

سیل *sayl* flood, torrent; ~*âb* torrent, tears; ~*rêz* torrent; *khâna-i* ~*rêz* path of a torrent

سیلان *sayalân* flowing, flood

سیلی *sîlî* slap; ~*-khwardan* to get slapped

سیم *sîm* silver; ~*âb* mercury, quicksilver; ~*badan* silvery-bodied; ~*în*, ~*îna* silvery; ~*înbar* silvery-breasted; ~*în'izâr* with a sparkling countenance; ~*ziqan* silvery-chinned

سیما *sîmâ* countenance

سینه *sîna* breast, chest

سیه *siyah* = *siyâh*

شاخ *shâkh* branch; ~*a*, ~*sâr* branch, limb, stem

شاد *shâd* happy, glad; ~*î* happiness, glee, joy; ~*ân-nimûdan* to make happy

شادروان *shâdurvân* canopy

شاگرد *shâgird* pupil, apprentice

شام *shâm* evening; Syria

شامل *shâmil* inclusive, incorporating

شان *shân* beehive; regard; *dar* ~*i* regarding, concerning

شانه *shâna* comb; ~*-zadan* to comb

شاه *shâh* king; ~*âna* royal, regal, kingly; ~*bâz* royal falcon; ~*râh* highway; ~*anshâhî* kingship; ~*vâr* kingly

شاهد *shâhid* witness; testimony; a young beauty; ~*bâz* one who 'toys' with young beauties

شایستن *shâyist-/shây-* to be fitting, be proper; *shâyad* it is proper

شای *shây-* → *shâyistan*

شب *shab* night; ~*afrôz* night-illuminating; ~*ânrôzî* day and night; ~*gûn* pitch black; ~*gîr* attacking by night, ambushing; ~*istân* a warm, dark place where one spends the winter; ~*nam* dew; ~*rang* black as night

شبه *shaba* jet; ~*gûn* jet black

شبیخون *shabîkhûn* surprise attack, ambush

شتاب *shitâb* haste; *shitâb-* → *shitâftan*

شتافتن *shitâft-/shitâb-* to hasten (int)

شتر *shutur* camel; ~*savâr* on camel back

شجر *shajar* trees

شجن *shajan* sorrow

شخص *shakhs* person

شداد Shaddâd Shaddâd ibn Âd, the legendary tyrant who built the Garden of Iram

شدآمد *shud-âmad* coming and going

شدت *shiddat* hardship, severity

شدن *shud-/shaw-* to become (for compounds, see first element); to go (in early New Persian *shudan* usually means to go unless it is in a compound)

شر *shar(r)* evil

شراب *sharâb* wine; ~*khâna* tavern

شرار *sharâr* spark; ~*a* spark; ~*î* fiery-natured

شربت *sharbat* potion

شرح *sharh* explanation; ~-*dâdan* to explain

شرحه *sharha* shred; ~~ mangled, ripped to shreds

شرط *shart* condition; inevitable; *bi-~-i ânki* on condition that, provided

شرف *sharaf* nobility, exaltedness

شرق *sharq* orient; rising (of the sun)

شرم *sharm* shame; ~-*dâshtan* to be ashamed; ~*anda* ashamed; ~*sâr* ashamed, humiliated

شریف *sharîf* noble

شست *shast* thumb, thumb-ring (archery); snare; sixty

شستشوی *shustushûy* washing

شستن *shust-/shôy-, shûy-* to wash

شط *shatt* river, riverbank

شعاع *shu'â'* ray

شعبده *shu'bada* prestidigitation, sleight-of-hand

شعر *sha'r* hair; ¶ *shi'r* poetry, lyric; ~-*sarâîdan* to recite poetry

شعرا *shi'râ* the Dog-star, Sirius

شعشعه *sha'sha'a* shine, splendor

شعله *shu'la* spark

شغب *shaghab* uproar; lament; mischief

شغل *shughl* job, work; diversion

شفا *shifâ* health, recovery; ~-*yâftan* to recover from an illness

شفق *shafaq* sunset

شفیع *shafî'* intercessor

شك *shakk* doubt

شكار *shikâr* hunt, hunting; prey

شكافتن *shikâft-/shikâf-* to split

شكایت *shikâyat* complaint, lament

شكر *shukr* thanks, gratitude; ~*âna* thankful(ly); ¶ *shikar, shikkar* sugar, metaphor for lips; ~*khâ* sugar-chewing, sweet; ~*khand* with a sweet smile

شكریدن *shikarîdan* to hunt down

شكست *shikast* wrinkles; ~-*giriftan* to become old and wrinkled; ~-*khwardan* to be broken, wrecked

شكستن *shikast-/shikan-* to break (trs & int); to get wrinkled

شكسته *shikasta* broken; ~*basta* jumbled, crooked; ~*dil* broken-hearted

شكفاندن *shikufândan* to make blossom, cause to bloom

شکفتن *shikuft-/shikuf-* to bloom, blossom

شکل *shakl* form

شکم *shikam* stomach, belly

شکن *shikan* twist, curl; *shikan-* → *shikastan*

شکنج *shikanj* torture

شکوفه *shikûfa, shukûfa* blossom, bloom

شکیبا *shakêbâ* patient; *~î* patience

شگفت *shigift* surprise, astonishment

شمار *shumâr* counting, accounting, number; *shumâr-* → *shumurdan*

شمامه *shamâma* scent, perfumed pastille

شمر *shumar* = *shumâr*

شمردن *shumurd-/shumâr-* to count, reckon, think

شمس *shams* sun

شمسه *shamsa* sunburst, luminary; figures woven in brocade

شمشاد *shamshâd* box tree

شمع *sham'* candle; *~î* waxen

شمن *shaman* idolater, shaman

شناختن *shinâkht-/shinâs-* to know, recognize

شناس *shinâs-* → *shinâkhtan*

شناور *shinâvar* swimming

شنبلید *shambalîd* fenugreek

شنبه *shamba* Saturday

شنعت *shun'at* baseness, brutality

شنفتن *shinuft-/shinaw-* to hear (variant of *shinîdan*)

شنیدن *shinîd-/shinaw-* to hear

شوخ *shôkh* playful, impudent, impish

شور *shôr* uproar, tumult, confusion; salty, brackish, barren (earth); *~âba* brackish water; *~ginî* saltiness

شورش *shôrish* unrest, inquietude; tumult, clamor

شوریده *shôrîda* in a commotion

شوق *shawq* longing, yearning

شوم *shûm, shu'm* inauspicious, ill

شوی *shôy* spouse; *du~a* having two spouses; ¶ *shûy-* → *shustan*

شه *shah* = *shâh*; *~mât* checkmate

شهاب *shihâb* shooting star

شهادت *shahâdat* profession of faith; martyrdom

شهدا *shuhadâ* martyrs

شهر *shahr* city; *~âshôb* one who casts a city into an uproar; *~yâr* prince

شهرت *shuhrat* fame, renown

شهره *shuhra* renowned

شهلا *shahlâ* eye with a sinister look

شهمات *shahmât* checkmate

شهوت *shahvat* passion, desire

شهید *shahîd* martyr

شیخ *shaykh* sheikh, old man

شیدا *shaydâ* infatuated, mad with love; *~î* infatuation

شیر *shêr* lion; *~i khudâ* "The Lion of God," Ali b. Abi-Talib; *~awzhan* lion-overthrowing, powerful; *~dam* ferocious as a lion; ¶ *shîr* milk

شیراز *Shîrâz* the city of Shiraz; *~î* native of Shiraz

شیرین *shîrîn* sweet; Shirin, Armenian princess beloved of and finally wed to Chosroës Parvez; ~*harakât* beautiful of movement; ~*kâr* delightful; ~*namak* sweet-natured; ~*nizhâd* of Shirin's lineage; ~*zabân* sweet-spoken

شیشه *shîsha* glass

شیعه *shî'a* the Shia, Shiites

شیفته *shêfta* upset, confused; ~*vâr* in a state of bewilderment

شیك *shîk* chic

شیمی *shîmî* chemistry

شیون *shêvan* moan, wail; ~*gar* wailer

شیوه *shêva* manner; amorous gesture

صابون *sâbûn* soap

صاحب *sâhib* master; ~*dil* courageous; ~*nazar* a person of insight

صادقی *sâdiqî-kardan* to be faithful

صاف *sâf* pure; ~*î* pure

صالح *sâlih* pious

صبا *sabâ* morning breeze, zephyr

صباح *sabâh* morning

صبح *subh* morning; ~*dam* dawn

صبر *sabr* patience; ~*-kardan* to be patient

صبوحی *sabûhî* morning draught; ~*zadan* to take a morning draught, usually as a remedy for a hangover

صبور *sabûr* patient; ~*î* patience

صحبت *suhbat* conversation; friendship

صحت *sihhat* health

صحرا *sahrâ* desert; ~*gard* able to cross the desert (camel)

صحیفه *sahîfa* page

صخره *sakhra* rock; ~*gudâz* rock-shattering

صدا *sadâ* sound, noise, voice, echo

صدر *sadr* chief, head, the most important place in a room

صدف *sadaf* oyster shell

صراحی *surâhî* flask, usually long-necked

صرصر *sarsar* the "cold wind" that destroyed the pre-Islamic nation of Âd

صرف *sarf-shudan* to be spent

صعود *su'ûd* ascent

صف *saf(f)* row, line, rank; ~*zanân* forming in ranks

صفاهان *Safâhân* Isfahan

صفت *sifat* quality, attribute

صفرا *safrâ* choler

صفه *suffa* dais, platform

صفیر *safîr* whistle; ~*zadan* to whistle for

صلا *salâ* invitation; ~*zadan* to invite

صلاح *salâh* rectitude, piety

صلح *sulh* peace, truce

صلصل *sulsul* pigeon; ~*ak* little pigeon

صندوق *sandûq* chest, coffer

صنع *san', sun'* handicraft, manufacture

صنعت *san'at* craft

صنم *sanam* idol

صنوبر *sanawbar* pine tree

صوامع *savâmi'* pl of *sawma'a* cell, chamber, monastery

صوب *sawb* path, track

صوت *sawt* sound, voice

صور *sûr* the trumpet that sounds Doomsday

صورت *sûrat* face, form; ~*bîn* that which sees only external form, superficial

صوفی *sûfî* Sufi, mystic

صومعه *sawma'a* pl *savâmi'* monastery

صهبا *sahbâ* wine

صیاد *sayyâd* hunter, fisherman

صیت *sît* fame, repute

صید *sayd* hunting, the hunt; prey; ~*-kardan* to hunt, snare; ~*-i haram* prohibited game

ضامن *zâmin* guarantor

ضحاک *Zahhâk* Zohak, the tyrannical usurper of the Iranian throne from whose shoulders grew serpents that fed on human brains

ضربت *zarbat* violent blow, slap

ضعف *za'f* weakness, impotence

ضعیف *za'îf* weak, thin

ضمان *zamân* surety, guarantee

ضمیر *zamîr* mind

ضیا *ziyâ* light

ضیمران *zaymurân* basil

طاس *tâs* cup, bowl; ~*ak* small bowl

طاعت *tâ'at* obedience; religoius exercise

طاق *tâq* arch

طاقت *tâqat* endurance; ~*-âvurdan* to endure

طالب *tâlib* aspirant, aspiring to

طالع *tâli'* ascendant (astrology), rising

طاووس *tâvûs, tâûs* peacock

طائر *tâ'ir* bird

طبع *tab'* nature, disposition, mood; ~*kôb* indigestible

طبق *tabaq* platter

طبقه *tabaqa* layer, stratum

طبل *tabl* drum

طبیب *tabîb* physician

طبیعت *tabî'at* nature

طپان *tapân* trembling (adj)

طپیدن *tapîdan* to tremble

طراز *Tarâz* Taraz, a city in Turkistan famed for the beauty of its inhabitants

طرب *tarab* entertainment; ~*zây* joy-producing, exciting

طرز *tarz* manner

طرف *taraf, tarf* edge, side

طرفه *turfa* marvellous, novelty

طره *turra* ringlet (of hair); crenellation (of a fortress); tendril (of a vine)

طری *tarî* fresh, green

طریق *tarîq* way, road

طریقت *tarîqat* the Sufi way, Sufi order

طشت *tasht* basin, kettle; ~*ak* small basin

طعمه *ta'ma* morsel

طعنه *ta'na* jab, pointed remark

طغیان *tughyân* wickedness; ~*-kardan* to transgress, overflow (river)

طفل *tifl* child; ~*vâr* childlike

طلاق *talâq* divorce; ~*-dâdan* to divorce; *si ~ dâdan* to divorce thrice, i.e., finally

طلایه *talâya* night watch

طلب *talab* search, quest; ~kâr creditor

طلبیدن *talabîdan* to search, seek out

طلعت *tal'at* countenance

طلوع *tulû'* rising (of the sun)

طمع *tam', tama'* desire, covet

طناب *tanâb* tent rope

طنبور *tambûr* drum

طنز *tanz* joke

طواف *tavâf* circumambulation

طوبی *tûbâ* the Tuba, a mythical tree in heaven

طور *Tûr* Sinai

طوطی *tûtî* parrot

طوفان *tûfân* deluge

طوق *tawq* collar, neck chain, necklace

طهران *Tihrân* older spelling of Tehran

طی *tay-kardan* to traverse

طیر *tayr* bird, fowl

طیران *tayarân* flight

ظرف *zarf* plate

ظریف *zarîf* fine

ظفر *zafar* victory

ظلم *zulm* tyranny, oppression

ظلمت *zulmat* darkness

ظن *zann* suspicion, (false) belief, notion

عاجز *âjiz* helpless, impotent; ~î helplessness, weakness

عاد *Âd* Âd, a pre-Islamic nation destroyed for its wickedness

عادت *âdat* custom, habit

عارض *âriz* cheek; ~ayn the two cheeks

عاشق *âshiq* pl *ushshâq* lover, in love; ~î the state of being a lover; ~î-kardan to act like a lover

عاصی *âsî* disobedient, sinful

عافیت *âfiyat* good health; ~guzîn opting for good health

عاقبت *âqibat* the end, conclusion; recompense; in the end, finally

عاقل *âqil* rational, reasonable

عالم *âlam* world, universe; ~î earthling, human being; ¶ *âlim* learned

عالی *âlî* high, sublime

عام *âm(m)* general

عامل *âmil* tax collector, government agent

عبادت *ibâdat* worship, devotion

عبث *abas* in vain

عبرت *ibrat* example, lesson; ~bîn capable of learning a lesson by example

عبقر *Abqar* Abqar, a town renowned for its marvellous textiles; ~î related to Abqar

عبهر *abhar* anemone

عبور *ubûr-kardan* to cross

عتاب *itâb* rebuke

عجایب *ajâyib* marvels

عجب *ajab* marvellous, amazing; ~-âmadan to be amazing; ~-dâshtan to be astonished; ~-mândan to be dumbfounded; ¶ *ujb* pride

عجز *ajz* helplessness

عجوزه *ajûza* old woman

عجیب *ajîb* marvellous

عدم *adam* non-existence; death

عدن *adan, adn* Eden; Aden, famed for its pearls

عذاب *azâb* torment, torture

عذر *uzr* excuse, forgiveness; ~-*i kas-î nihâdan* to excuse someone

عذرا *Azrâ* Azrâ, the beloved of Wâmiq; ~'*izâr* as beautiful of countenance as Azrâ

عرب *arab* Arab, Arabian

عربده *arbada* quarrel, brawl; ~*jûy* quarrelsome, looking for a fight

عرش *arsh* throne

عرصه *arsa* field

عرض *arz* presentation; muster, review (of troops); ~-*dâdan* to expose; ~-*kardan* to present

عرق *araq* liquor

عروس *arûs* bride, virgin; ~*vâr* bride-like

عز *izz* power, glory

عزا *azâ* mourning

عزت *izzat* power

عزرائیل *Azrâîl* Azrael, the angel of death

عزم *azm* determination

عزیز *azîz* dear, beloved, loved, loved one; ~*vâr* dearly

عسل *asal* honey

عشاق *ushshâq* pl of *âshiq* lover

عشرت *ishrat* pleasure

عشق *ishq* love

عشوه *ishva* amorous playfulness, coquetry; ~*gar* coquette

عصا *asâ* staff, cane

عصابه *isâba* turban, bandage

عصمت *ismat* inviolability, impeccability

عصیان *isyân* disobedience, transgression

عطر *itr, atr* perfume

عظیم *azîm* great; solemn (oath)

عفاف *afâf* chastity

عفاک الله *afâkallâh* "may God forgive you"

عفو *afv* forgiveness

عقاب *uqâb* eagle

عقبا *uqbâ* the next life, the world to come

عقد *aqd* marriage bond; ¶ *iqd* necklace, string of pearls

عقرب *aqrab* scorpion

عقل *aql* mind, reason

عقوبت *uqûbat* torment

عقیق *aqîq* carnelion, agate; ~*în* made of agate

عکس *aks* reflection; ~-*andâkhtan* to cast a reflection

علاج *ilâj* treatment, remedy

علاقه *alâqa* attachment; ¶ *ilâqa* link

علامت *alâmat* pl *alâmât* sign, symptom

علامه *allâma* master, a title of scholarship

علت *illat* disease, illness; cause

علقت *ulqat* suspension

علم *ilm* knowledge, learning; ¶ *alam* banner; ~-*zadan* to spring up

علما *ulamâ* the ulema, the learned in religion

علوی *ulvî* sublime, celestial

علی *Alî* Ali ibn Abi-Talib, First Imam of the Shia

عم‎ am(m) paternal uncle

عمارت‎ imârat structurally sound

عمارى‎ imârî howdah, camel litter

عمامه‎ amâma turban

عمان‎ um(m)ân sea

عمر‎ umr life, lifespan

عمران‎ Imrân Amram, father of Moses

عمل‎ amal deed, act, job; (fiscal) duty, tax collection; dar ~ âvurdan to put into practice

عمو‎ amû uncle, a familiar term of address

عمود‎ amûd cudgel, club

عنا‎ anâ distress, affliction

عناب‎ unnâb jujube

عنان‎ inân reins

عنايت‎ inâyat bounty

عنبر‎ ambar ambergris; ~bû scented with ambergris; bû-yi-~dih giving off the scent of ambergris

عندليب‎ andalîb nightingale

عنقا‎ anqâ the mythical Anqa bird

عود‎ ûd lute, oud; aloe, incense

عهد‎ ahd pact, promise; era; ~-bastan to make a covenant, conclude a pact; ~-shikastan to break a promise

عيار‎ iyâr touchstone

عيان‎ ayân clear, obvious

عيب‎ ayb fault

عيد‎ îd holiday, festival

عيسى‎ Îsâ Jesus

عيش‎ aysh pleasure

عين‎ ayn essence; eye; bi~ exactly; ~ulyaqîn "the eye of certitude," absolute conviction

عينك‎ aynak glasses

عيوق‎ ayyûq Capella

غارت‎ ghârat plunder; ~gar plunderer

غافل‎ ghâfil neglectful, heedless

غاليه‎ ghâliya a mixture of musk and ambergris used to perfume the hair

غائب‎ ghâ'ib absent, invisible

غايت‎ ghâyat extreme

غبار‎ ghubâr dust

غبغب‎ ghabghab double chin, roll of fat under the chin, a sign of beauty

غرامت‎ gharâmat fine

غران‎ ghurrân roaring

غرب‎ gharb west; ~î western

غربال‎ ghirbâl sieve

غربت‎ ghurbat exile

غرض‎ gharaz motive, ulterior motive

غرق‎ gharq drowned; steeped (in blood); ~a drowned; ~gah whirlpool

غرور‎ ghurûr pride, haughtiness

غره‎ gharra deceived, blinded by pride

غريب‎ gharîb poor, humble; stranger

غريدن‎ ghurrîdan to roar, shout

غريو‎ gharîv growl, shout, roar

غزا‎ ghazâ campaign, raid (on non-Muslims)

غزال‎ ghazâl gazelle

غزل‎ ghazal love poetry, ghazal; ~khwân singing, reciting love poetry

غزنی *Ghazní* Ghazni, Ghazna, south of Kabul, capital of the Ghaznavid empire

غسل *ghusl* washing, ritual cleansing; ~-*dâdan* to wash

غصه *ghussa* grief

غفلت *ghaflat* negligence, carelessness

غل *ghal(l)* fetters

غلام *ghulâm* pl *ghilmân* slaveboy, serving boy

غلطان *ghaltân* turning, revolving, roving (eye)

غلطیدن *ghaltîdan* to roll, writhe

غلغله *ghulghula* riot, uproar

غلمان *ghilmân* pl of *ghulâm* slaveboy, serving boy

غم *gham(m)* grief, sorrow; ~-*khwardan* to grieve; ~-*i kasî khwardan* to feel sorry for someone, sympathize with someone; ~-*dîda* having experienced grief; ~-*gin*, ~-*gîn* sorrowful; ~-*gusâr* comforter, consoler; ~-*khwar* griever, grieving; ~-*în* sad, sorrowful; *ba* ~-*i kasî nishastan* to become accustomed to the grief inflicted by someone

غماز *ghammâz* winking, flirtatious

غمزه *ghamza* amorous glance, wink; ~-*zan* winking, flirting

غنچه *ghuncha* rosebud

غنودن *ghunûd-/ghunaw-* to slumber

غواص *ghavvâs* diver, pearl diver

غورگاه *ghawrgâh* depth, abyss

غوغا *ghawghâ* chaos

غوك *ghôk* frog

غوی *ghavî* led astray

غیب *ghayb* the unseen realm

غیر *ghayr* pl *aghyâr* other; stranger; ~-*i*, ~ *az* other than

غیرت *ghayrat* zeal, jealousy

غیور *ghayûr* zealous

فاخته *fâkhta* ring-dove

فارس *fârs* Fars, province in SW Iran

فارغ *fârigh* free, unencumbered, released

فاش *fâsh* open, in public; ~-*kardan* to reveal, make public

فاقه *fâqa* poverty, need

فال *fâl* omen, augury

فانوس *fânûs* lantern

فتادن *futâdan* = *uftâdan*

فتح *fath* victory

فتراك *fitrâk* saddle strap, from which game is hung

فتنه *fitna* sedition; seductive; ~-*jû* seditious, seductive

فجر *fajr* dawn

فخار *fakhâr* boasting, vainglory

فخر *fakhr* pride

فدا *fadâ* ransom; *ay* ~-*yi tu* "may I be your ransom"; ¶ *fidâ* devotion; ~-*î* one who risks his life in service

فر *far(r)* splendor, aura of greatness

فرا *farâ-kardan* to put out, stick out (trs)

فرات *Furât* the Euphrates River

فراخ *farâkh* wide, spacious

فرار *farâr* flight; ~-*kardan* to flee; ~-*î* escapee

فراز *farâz* down; shut; ~-*i* upon

فراق *firâq* separation, act of separating

فراگوش *farâgôsh* next to the ear

فراموش *farâmôsh* forgotten; ~-*kar-dan* to forget

فراوان *farâvân* abundant

فرج *faraj* freedom from grief, relief

فرخ *farrukh* auspicious, happy; ~*hamâl* auspicious; name of King Mihrâb's castle in Kabul

فرخنده *farkhunda* auspicious

فرد *fard* individual, unique; odd (opposite of even); isolated

فردا *fardâ* tomorrow

فردوس *firdaws* paradise

فرزانه *farzâna* wise

فرزند *farzand* child, son

فرزین *farzîn* queen (in chess)

فرش *farsh* carpet, floor covering

فرشته *firishta* angel

فرصت *fursat* opportunity

فرع *far'* branch, subdivision

فرعون *Fir'awn* Pharaoh

فرغانه *Farghâna* the Fergana Valley (modern Uzbekistan)

فرق *farq* top of the head; *ba ~ pûyîdan* to run pell-mell

فرقت *firqat* separation, exile

فرقد *Farqad* a circumpolar star in Ursa Minor

فرمان *farmân* order, command; ~*bar* obedient

فرمای *farmây-* → *farmûdan*

فرمودن *farmûd-/farmâ-* to command

فرو *firô* down; ~-*bastan* to tie down; ~-*burdan* to take down; ~-*dawîdan* to run down (int); ~-*gardânîdan* to turn over (trs); ~-*gushâdan*

to pull down; ~-*hishtan* to let down (tent flap); ~-*kâstan* to drag down, pull down; ~-*khwardan* to gulp down, swallow; ~-*mândan* to lag behind, to be disabled; ~-*shustan* to wash off, rinse out

فروش *furôsh-* → *furôkhtan*

فروختن *furôkht-/furôsh-* to sell

فروغ *furûgh* splendor, brilliance

فره *farrah* magnificence; halo; ¶ *farih* active

فرهاد *Farhâd* Farhad, unrequited lover of Shirin who, at her request, performed the impossible task of chiseling a conduit for milk through a stone mountain, at the end of which labor he died of a broken heart

فریاد *faryâd* cry, wail

فریب *firêb, farîb* deception; ~-*khwardan* to be deceived

فریدون *Firêdûn* Fredun, a king of Iran

فزع *faza'* terror, fright

فزون *fuzûn* more, greater

فساد *fasâd* corruption

فسان *fasân* whetstone, flint

فسردن *fisurdan* = *afsurdan*

فسون *fusûn* spell, incantation

فشاندن *fishândan* = *afshândan*

فشردن *fishurdan* = *afshurdan*

فطان *fattân* intelligent

فضا *fazâ* space

فضل *fazl* excellence, superiority

فضول *fuzûl* meddling, impertinent

فغان *fighân* = *afghân*

فقر *faqr* poverty, spiritual poverty

نقیر *faqîr* poor man

فكر *fikr* thought, contemplation, concern

فكرت *fikrat* thought, idea

فكل *fukul* faux col, European-style collar

فكندن *fikandan = afkandan*

فگار *figâr* afflicted, sore

فكندن *fikandan = afkandan*

فلسفه *falsafa* philosophy

فلك *falak* celestial orb; ~*gardân* turner of the spheres; ~*î* celestial; ~*vash* spherical, like the celestial orb

فن *fan(n)* art, artifice, craft

فنا *fanâ* annihilation

فندق *funduq* hazel-nut; ball

فوج *fawj* troop, military unit; ~~ in droves

فوق *fawq* above

فولاد *fûlâd* steel

فهم *fahm* understanding

فى الفور *filfawr* immediately

فيروزه *fîrôza* turquoise

فيروزى *fîrôzî* victory, prosperity

فيض *fayz* divine grace; outpouring of grace

قاب *qâb* vessel, container

قابل *qâbil* capable, receptive

قاتل *qâtil* murderer

قار *qâr = qîr*

قاروره *qârûra* vial used by physicians to determine state of health by urine specimen

قاصد *qâsid* messenger, herald; headed toward a place

قاف *Qâf* Mount Qaf, mythical mountain that surrounds the earth and is inhabited by peris, djinn, the Huma, &c.

قاقم *qâqum* ermine

قالب *qâlib, qâlab* mold, form, body

قامت *qâmat* stature

قانع *qâni'* satisfied

قانون *qânûn* type of dulcimer; mode

قائد *qâ'id* guide, leader

قبا *qabâ* cloak

قبل *qabl* before; *az qibal-i* for, in the direction of

قبله *qibla* kiblah, the direction of prayer

قبول *qabûl* acceptance, receptivity; ~-*kardan* to accept, receive

قبه *qubba* dome

قحط *qaht* drought, famine

قد *qad(d)* stature

قدح *qadah* cup, goblet

قدر *qadr* destiny; power; ~-*dânistan* to appreciate; ¶ *qadar* amount

قدرت *qudrat* power, ability

قدس *quds, qudus* spirituality, sanctity, heaven; ~*î* blessed, sanctified being; *arvâh-i* ~ holy spirits, angels

قدم *qadam* foot, pace; ~ *dar-nihâdan dar* to step into; ~-*zadan* to set foot, step

قديم *qadîm* old, ancient; *az* ~ of old

قرار *qarâr* rest, stability; ~-*giriftan* to settle down, be quiet, be at rest; ~*gâh* station, resting-place

قراضه qurâza shavings, chips

قرآن qur'ân the Koran

قرب qurb proximity

قربان qurbân sacrifice

قرص qurs orb, disc

قرطاس qirtâs paper

قرعه qur'a cast of the die; ~-zadan to cast lots

قرمطى Qarmatî Qarmatian

قسم qism portion, lot

قسمت qismat portion, lot

قصب qasab reed; linen; ~-pôsh wrapped in linen

قصد qasd intention

قصر qasr palace, castle

قصور qusûr fault, shortcoming

قصه qissa tale, story; ~-pardâz storyteller

قضا qazâ fate, destiny

قطار qitâr rank, file, row, camel train

قطره qatra drop

قطع qat' cutting; ~-kardan to cut

قطعه qit'a fragment; a poetic form, a ghazal minus the first line

قفس qafas cage

قلا qullâ for qullâb (q.v.)

قلاب qullâb hook; ~-nimûdan to hook, snare, catch

قلاده qilâda neck chain, necklace

قلب qalb heart, middle, midst; center (battle array)

قلعه qal'a fortress, castle

قلقل qulqul glug, the sound of wine being poured from a bottle

قلم qalam pl aqlâm pen; ~-rafta traversed by the pen

قمر qamar moon

قمرى qumrî turtle-dove

قمل qummal louse

قناعت qinâ'at contentment; ~-kardan ba to content oneself with

قند qand lump sugar

قنديل qandîl lantern

قوا quvâ powers

قوت qût nourishment; ¶ quvvat power, faculty

قول qawl chatter, noise

قوم qawm people, nation, tribe; ~-u-khwêsh relative

قوه quvva = quvvat

قوى qavî strong, powerful; ~-haykal strong in body

قهر qahr wrath; ~-kardan to have a falling-out

قى qay vomit

قياس qiyâs analogy; ~-kardan to compare

قيام qiyâm rectitude, stability; ~-shudan to arise, be resurrected (on Doomsday)

قيامت qiyâmat resurrection, doomsday

قيد qayd bonds, fetters

قير qîr tar, pitch

قيس Qays-i Banî Âmir Qays of the Bani-Amir tribe, Majnun's real name

كابين kâbîn marriage portion, dowry

كاخ kâkh palace

کار *kâr* work, labor, deed, task; ~*gah* worshop; ~*î* deep, mortal (wound); *ba ~ âmadan* to be of use, come in handy; ¶ *kâr-* → *kishtan*

کاروان *kâravân* caravan

کاس *kâs* goblet

کاسب *kâsib* tradesman

کاستن *kâst-/kâh-* to diminish (trs)

کاسه *kâsa* cup, goblet; ~*-i sar* skull

کاشانه *kâshâna* nest

کاشکی *kâsh-kî* would that...

کافر *kâfir, kâfar* infidel, giaour; ~*î* infidelity

کافور *kâfûr* camphor; ~*gûn* pure white

کام *kâm* desire; palate

کان *kân* mine; ¶ *k'ân = ki ân*

کاو *k'û = ki û*

کاوش *kâvish* digging, drilling, hollowing out

کاه *kâh* straw; ¶ *kâh-* → *kâstan*

کای *k'ay* cont of *ki ay*

کی *kay* when?; in rhetorical questions, "how?"; ¶ *k'ay = ki ay*

کاین *k'în* contraction for *ki în*; ¶ *kâyin = kâ'in*

کائن *kâ'in* a being; ~*ât* beings, those things that exist

کباب *kabâb* roast, roasted; ~*kardan* to roast

کبر *kibr* pride, haughtiness

کبریا *kibriyâ* divine grandeur

کبک *kabk* partridge

کبوتر *kabûtar* pigeon, dove

کبود *kabûd* blue, dark blue

کتابه *kitâba* inscription

کتف *kitf* shoulder

کج *kaj* crooked, awry; ~*ravî* deviation

کچل *kachal* bald, mangy

کدخدا *kadkhudâ* elder, lord

کدیور *kadîvar* farmer, peasant

کر *kar* deaf

کرامت *karâmat* saintly miracle

کران *kirân* shore, boundary

کربلا *Karbalâ* Kerbela, town in Iraq where Husayn was slain

کرته *kurta* shirt, chemise

کردار *kirdâr* manner; *ba ~-i* like, as, in the manner of

کردگار *kirdigâr* the Maker, God

کردن *kard-/kun-* to do, make; see first element for compounds

کرشمه *kirishma* amorous gesture

کرگدن *kargadan* rhinoceros

کرکس *kargas* vulture; ~*-i vâqi'* the constellation Lyra

کرم *karam* generosity

کرمان *Kirmân* Kirman, city in Iran

کره *kara* butter

کریم *karîm* generous, noble; ~*î* generosity, nobility

کز *kaz = ki az*

کزو *kazû = ki az û*

کژ *kazh = kaj*; ~ *u mazh* staggering

کس *kas* person; ~*ân* people

کسب *kasb* acquisition; ~*-kardan* to acquire

کسوت *kisvat* garment, raiment

کسوف *kusûf* solar eclipse

کش *k'ash = ki-ash*; ¶ *kash-* → *kashîdan*; ¶ *kush-* → *kushtan*

کشت *kisht* field; ~*zâr* field; ~*ukâr* planting, sowing

کشتن kisht-/kâr- to sow; ¶ kusht-/kush- to kill

کشتی kushtî wrestling; ~-giriftan to wrestle; ¶ kashtî boat, ship; ~bân pilot, captain

کشف kashf-shudan to be discovered

کشمش kishmish raisins

کشمیر Kashmîr Kashmir

کشور kishvar country

کشیدن kashîdan to draw, pull; gulp

کعبه ka'ba the Kaaba in Mecca

کف kaf(f) hand, palm; foam, froth; ~-andâkhtan to slap the hands in distress

کفر kufr unbelief, infidelity

کفن kafan winding sheet, burial shroud

کفیدن kafîdan to burst

کل kal bald

کلاف kalâf pinned, trapped

کلاله kulâla ringlets over the forehead

کلان kalân big

کلاه kulâh hat; crown

کلبه kulba hut

کلف kalaf blemishes on the moon

کلك kilk pen

کله kulah = kulâh; ~dâr crowned head

کلی kullî altogether, in general

کلید kilîd, kilêd key

کلیسا kalîsâ church

کم kam little, little bit; less; ~-shudan to be less; ~sipâh with a small army; ¶ k'am = ki-am

کمال kamâl perfection

کمان kamân bow; ~khâna bow

کمر kamar waist

کمند kamand lasso

کمین kamîn ambush; ~gâh place of ambush

کن kan- → kandan; ¶ kun- → kardan

کنار kinâr limit, boundary; edge, shore; embrace; lap

کنان kanân → kandan; ¶ -kunân see first element of compound with -kardan

کنج kunj corner

کنجد kunjud, kunjid sesame-seed

کندن kand-/kan- to tear out (hair); to dig up (earth); to strike, take down (tent)

کنشت kinisht church, synagogue

کنعان Kan'ân Canaan

کنگره kungara battlement, parapet

کنون kunûn now, henceforth

کنیز kanîz girl, maid; ~ak young girl

کو kû where?; ¶ kû = kûy; ¶ k'û = ki û

کواکب kavâkib pl of kawkab heavenly body, star

کوبیدن kôbîdan to stamp, stomp; pâ-~ to dance

کوتاه kûtâh short; ~-kardan az to shorten, cease; ~î deficiency

کوته kûtah = kûtâh

کوثر Kawsar Cawthar, a river in paradise

کوچ kûch migration; ~gah route traversed in migration

کودك kûdak child

کور kôr blind; ~î blindness; ~vash like a blind man

كوزه *kûza* pot, jug; ~*furôsh* pot seller; ~*gar* potter; ~*khar* pot buyer

كوس *kôs* battle drum, kettle drum

كوشيدن *kôshîdan* to strive, endeavor

كوفه *Kûfa* Kufah, city in Iraq

كوفى *kûfî* Kufan

كوكب *kawkab* pl *kavâkib* star, heavenly body

كوكبه *kawkaba* steel ball carried on a pole as royal ensignia

كون *kawn* world, being; ~*u fasâd* generation and corruption, the sublunar world; ~ *u makân* time and space; *du* ~ this world and the next; ¶ *kûn* the backside; ~*î*, ~*kun* sodomite, bugger

كوه *kôh* mountain; ~-*i tûr* Mt. Sinai; ~*paykar* enormous; ~*sâr* mountain; ~~ mountain-like; ~~*ân* with a hump like a mountain (camel)

كوى *kûy* lane

كوير *Kavîr* the Dasht-i-Kavir Desert

كه *ki* (subordinating conj) that; (relative conj) which, that; introduces direct quotation; *ki* (interrogative pronoun) who?; ¶ *kah* = *kâh*; ¶ *kuh* = *kôh*

كهتاب *kahtâb* hot herbs laid on a swelling

كهربا *kahrubâ* amber; ~*rang* amber-colored

كهسار *kuhsâr* mountainous

كهستان *Kuhistân* Kuhistan, any of several mountainous regions by this name

كهكشان *kahkashân* the Milky Way

كهن *kuhan* old

كهنه *kuhna* old

كى *kay* when?; (in rhetorical questions) how?; ¶ *kay* king, royal title of the Kayanids; ¶ *k'ay* = *ki ay*

كيانى *kayânî* royal, regal

كيسه *kîsa* purse

كيش *kêsh* faith, religion; ~-*âvurdan* to profess a religion

كيفيت *kayfiyyat* quality

كيكاوس *Kay-Kâûs* Kay-Kaus, one of the shahs of Iran

كيميا *kîmiyâ* the philosopher's stone

كين *kîn* vengeance, revenge; rancor; ¶ *k'în* = *ki în*

كينه *kîna* = *kîn*

گام *gâm* foot, pace

گاو *gâv* cow, ox

گاه *gâh* time, period of time; ~~ sometimes; ~-*î* sometimes, betimes

گدا *gadâ* beggar

گداختن *gudâkht-/gudâz-* to melt (trs)

گداز *gudâz* melting, suffering; *gudâz-* → *gudâkhtan*

گذار *guzâr* placement, path; *guzâr-* → *guzâshtan*

گذاشتن *guzâsht-/guzâr-* to place

گذر *guzar* pass; ~-*kardan az* to pass by, chance upon; ~*gâh* passageway; *guzar-* → *guzashtan*

گذشتن *guzasht-/guzar-* to pass (int); to break (promise, oath)

گر *gar* = *agar*

گرازان *gurâzân* walking stately, pompously

گران *girân* heavy; ~*î* heaviness; ~*jânî* pride; ~*mâya* precious; ~*sar* proud

گربه *gurba* cat

گرچه *garchi* = *agarchi*

گرد *gard* dust; ~*âlûd* covered with dust; ¶ *gird* round; ~*âmadan* to gather around; ~*i* around (prep); ¶ *gurd* warrior; ~*zâd* of heroic lineage; ¶ *gard-* → *gashtan*

گردان *gardân* turning, spinning

گردش *gardish* revolution; promenade, stroll

گردن *gardan* neck; ~*-bastan* to tie up by the neck; ~*zadan* to decapitate, trim the wick (candle); ~*kash* bravado, refractory, unruly

گردون *gardûn* the celestial sphere

گردیدن *gardîdan* to turn (int), go about

گرز *gurz* mace, battle ax

گرسنه *gurusna, gursuna* hungry

گرفتار *giriftâr* taken, held, captive; ~*î* predicament

گرفتن *girift-/gîr-* to seize, snatch; to be eclipsed (moon, sun); *gîram* I take it that, I assume

گرگ *gurg* wolf

گرم *garm* warm, hot; ~*î* heat, briskness (of market); ~*-gashtan* to wax angry; ¶ *gurm* sorrow, grief

گرما *garmâ* heat

گرنه *garna* were...not, if it were not for the fact that; otherwise

گره *girih* knot; ~*gîr* tangled, knotted

گری *giry-* → *girîstan*

گریان *giryân* weeping

گریبان *girîbân* collar; ~*châk* with collar rent (in grief); ~*vâr* amount of cloth necessary to make a collar

گریختن *gurêkht-/gurêz-* to flee

گردون که *garaydûn-ki* since

گریز *gurêz* flight, escape; *gurêz-* → *gurêkhtan*; ~*ân* in flight, fleeing

گریستن *girîst-/giry-* to weep

گریه *girya* weeping; ~*kardan* to weep; ~*khêz* tear-producing

گز *gaz-* → *gazîdan*

گزاردن *guzârd-/guzâr-* to pass (trs), spend (time)

گزیدن *guzîd-/guzîn-* to choose, select; ¶ *gazîdan* to bite

گزین *guzîn-* → *guzîdan*

گساردن *gusârd-/gusâr-* to drink, quaff

گستردن *gustard-/gustar-* to spread

گسستن *gusast-/gusil-* to break

گسل *gusil-* → *gusastan*

گشادن *gushâd-/gushây-* to open, spread, uncover

گشاده *gushâda* opened, uncovered; ~*mûy* with uncovered hair, a sign of grief

گشای *gushây-* → *gushâdan*

گشتن *gasht-/gard-* to turn, become; to go

گشودن *gushûdan* = *gushâdan*

گفت *guft* speech, talk; ~*âr* speech, what is said; ~ *u gû* = *guftugû*

گفتگو *guftugû(y)* talk; conversation

گفتن *guft-/gû(y)-* to say; *guftanî* that which can or should be said

گل *gil* mud, clay; ¶ *gul* flower, rose; ~*-i âtash* type of red rose; ~*âb* rose-water; ~*âriz* rosy-cheeked; ~*bâng* shout, war-cry; ~*bun* rose bush; ~*chîn* rose-plucker; ~*gasht* garden, park; ~*gasht-kardan* to stroll; ~*gûn* rose-colored; ~*istân* rose garden; ~*nâr* pomegranate blossom; ~*rang* rose-colored, red; ~*rukh*, ~*rukhsâr* rosy-cheeked; ~*shan* rose garden; ~*sitân* rose-plucker; ~*zâr* garden

گله *gila* complaint; ~*-kardan* to complain

گلو *gulû, galû* throat

گم *gum* lost; ~*gashta* lost

گمار *gumâr-* → *gumâshtan*

گماشتن *gumâsht-/gumâr-* to set, place, assign

گمان *gumân* suspicion

گناه *gunâh* crime, sin

گنبد *gumbad* dome, arc

گنبذ *gumbaz* = *gumbad*

گنج *ganj* treasure, riches; ¶ *gunj-* → *gunjîdan*

گنجایش *gunjâyish* capacity

گنجه *ganja* closet

گنجیدن *gunjîdan* to fit, have room for

گندآور *gundâvar* hero; leader

گندم *gandum* wheat; ~*gûn* golden, wheat-colored

گنگ *gung* dumb, mumbling

گنه *gunah* = *gunâh*; ~*kâr* sinner; ~*kârî* sinfulness, crime

گو *gav* = *gâv*; ~*-i pîltan* "elephant-bodied ox," one of Rustam's epithets

گوا *guvâ* = *guvâh*

گواه *guvâh* witness

گود *gawd* pit

گور *gôr* wild ass; grave

گوژ *gûzh* crooked; ~*pusht* hunchback; ~*raftâr* one whose conduct or path is crooked

گوش *gôsh* ear; ~*mâl* a box on the ear, chastisement; ~*vâr* earring

گوشت *gôsht* meat; ~*khwâr* meat-eater

گوشه *gôsha* corner; ~*nishîn* one who sits in a corner, withdrawn

گونه *gûna* manner; *bar ân* ~ in that manner

گوهر *gawhar* pearl, gem

گوی *gûy, gôy* polo ball

گویا *gûyâ* speaking; = *gûî*

گوینده *gûyanda* speaker, narrator; reciter, singer

گوئی *gûî* one would say; one would think that; it is as though

گوئیا *gûîâ* = *gûî*

که *gah* = *gâh*; ~~ sometimes, betimes; ¶ *guh* excrement

گهر *guhar* = *gawhar*

گیا(ه) *giyâ, giyâh* plants, shrubs, scrub

گیتی *gîtî* the world

گیر *gîr-* → *giriftan*

گیسو *gêsû* lock (of hair), braid

گیلان *Gêlân* Gilan, the province on the Caspian

لا *lâ* the Arabic negative "no," the first word of the Muslim profession of faith (*lâ ilâha illâ 'llâh*)

لابد *lâbud* of necessity, therefore

لابه *lâba-kardan* to pray

لاجرم *lâjaram* of necessity, consequently

لاجورد *lâjavard* azure, lapis lazuli

لاغر *lâghar* skinny; ~*miyân* thin-waisted

لاف *lâf* boasting; ~*i zabân* idle talk; ~*-zadan* to boast, brag

لالا *lâlâ* shining (pearl); tutor

لاله *lâla* tulip; ~*rukh* with cheeks as red as tulips

لآلى *la'âlî* pl of *lu'lu'* pearl

لايق *lâyiq* worthy

لب *lab* lip; edge

لباس *libâs* guise, garb

لجه *lujja* abyss

لحد *lahad* tomb

لحظه *lahza* moment

لحن *lahn* pl *alhân* melody

لخت *lakht* a bit, a little

لذت *lazzat* pleasure, enjoyment

لرزان *larzân* trembling (adj)

لرزه *larza* trembling, commotion

لشكر *lashkar* army, camp; ~*î* soldier

لطف *lutf* grace; ~*rasân* doer of good, gracious

لطيف *latîf* fine, subtle; ~*a* a subtle point; ~*î* fineness, refinement

لعاب *lu'âb* saliva, mucus

لعبت *lu'bat* plaything, doll

لعل *la'l* ruby

لفظ *lafz* utterance

لقا *liqâ* encounter

لقمه *luqma* morsel

لگن *lagan* candlestick

لنگ *lang* lame

لنگر *langar* anchor

لوا *livâ* banner

لوح *lawh* tablet

لولو *lu'lu'*, *lâlâ* pl *la'âlî* pearl

لولى *lûlî* gypsy

لون *lawn* color, aspect

ليك *lîk* but, however; ~*an* but

ليل *layl* (Ar.) night

ليلى *Laylî* Layli, beloved of Majnun

ليمو *lîmû* lemon, citron; ~*i um-mân* lime

مابقا *mâbaqâ* everything else, all the rest, all that remains

مات *mât-i...âmadan* to be stupified by...

ماتم *ma'tam*, *mâtam* mourning assembly, wake; ~*î* mourner, bereaved; ~*zada* grief-stricken, bereaved

ماجرا *mâjarâ* adventure

ماحضر *mâhazar* possessions, worldly goods

مادت *mâddat* matter, substance, material

ماده *mâda* female

ماديان *mâdiyân* mare

مار *mâr* snake, serpent; ~*pêch* writhing, slinking

ماست *mâst* yoghurt

مال *mâl* possessions, wealth; ¶ *mâl-* → *mâlîdan*

مالك *mâlik* Malik, the warden of hell

ماليدن *mâlîdan* to rub

مام *mâm* old crone, witch; mama

مان *mân-* → *mândan*, *mânistan*

ماندن *mând-/mân-* to remain; to place, put (trs)

مانستن *mânist-/mân- ba* to resemble

مانع *mâni'* hindering, preventing

مانند *mânand-i* like, as; ~-*kardan* to liken

ماه *mâh* moon; ~ *girift* the moon was eclipsed; ~*chihr*, ~*paykar*, ~*rukhsâr*, ~*rûy* one whose face is as beautiful as the moon; ~*tâb* moonlight, moonbeams

ماهى *mâhî* fish

مايه *mâya* substance; *chi*~ how much, how many a

مبارز *mubâriz* warrior

مباركباد *mubârakbâd* congratulations

متاع *matâ'* (commercial) goods, commodities; ~-*i asar* goods cast off by passing caravans, the traces of which can be followed

متفق *muttafiq* in agreement

متفكر *mutafakkir* worried, concerned

مجاز *majâz* metaphor; irreality

مجاور *mujâvir* resident (at a shrine), pilgrim

مجره *majarra* the Milky Way

مجلس *majlis* assembly, assembly hall

مجمر *mijmar* brazier

مجنون *Majnûn* Majnun; possessed, crazy

محبت *mahabbat* love, affection

محبوب *mahbûb* beloved

محتاج *muhtâj* in need, needy

محترز *muhtariz* cautious, avoiding

محراب *mihrâb* the niche in a mosque indicating the direction of Mecca

محرق *muhraq* inflamed

محرم *mahram* intimate, confidant; ¶ *muharram* Muharram, the first lunar month of the Islamic year

محروم *mahrûm* deprived; ~*î* deprivation

محشر *mahshar* Resurrection Day

محفل *mahfil* party, festive occasion

محل *mahall* place, position

محمل *mahmil* camel litter, howdah

محمود *Mahmûd* Sultan Mahmud of Ghazna (r. 998–1030)

محنت *mihnat* trial, tribulation; ~*âbâd* place of trial and tribulation; ~*î* sorely tried, afflicted

محيط *muhît* ocean

مخالف *mukhâlif* adverse, opponent

مختصر *mukhtasar* lacking, deficient, abbreviated

مخزن *makhzan* treasury

مخفى *makhfî* hidden

مخلع *mukhalla'* clad in a robe of honor

مخمس *mukhammas* pentagonal

مخمور *makhmûr* hungover

مدام *mudâm* continual(ly)

مداين *Madâyin* Ctesiphon (near Baghdad), capital of the Sassanian empire

مدت *muddat* period of time; ~*î* for a long time

مدد *madad* aid, assistance

مدرسه *madrasa* school

مدعی mudda'â design, purpose; complaint; ¶ mudda'î plaintiff, claimant, suitor

مدفون madfûn buried

مدهوش madhûsh dazed, stupified

مدینه Madîna Medina

مذاق mazâq taste, palate

مر mar a pleonastic particle that accompanies -râ

مراد murâd desire

مربع murabba' quadrilateral, square

مرتبه martaba degree, rank; time

مرتضی Murtazâ epithet of Ali ibn Abi-Talib

مرجان marjân coral

مرحبا márhabâ welcome, marvellous (interjection)

مرحله marhala stage

مرد mard man; ¶ murd death; ¶ mirad = mîrad (see murdan)

مردم mardum people; ~-i chashm pupil of the eye; ~ak pupil of the eye; ~î manliness

مردن murd-/mîr- to die

مردود mardûd rejected

مرده murda dead; ~rêg useless, worthless

مرسله mursala necklace

مرصع murassa' gem-studded

مرض maraz disease, illness

مرغ murgh fowl; ~-i havâî bird of the air; ~-i-havâî-shikâr that which preys on birds of the air; ~ak little bird

مرغزار marghzâr meadow

مرغوا murghuvâ ill omen

مرکب markab mount, vehicle

مرگ marg death

مروا murvâ omen

مروارید murvârîd pearl; ~bâr pearl-raining; ~gûn pearl-colored

مرهم marham ointment

مرید murîd disciple

مزاج mizâj temperament

مزار mazâr tomb

مزد muzd wages, allotment

مزیدن mazîdan to smack the lips

مژ mazh → kazh

مژده muzhda good news

مژه muzh(zh)a eyelash

مساعد musâ'id favorable, auspicious

مساله mas'ala pl masâ'il problem

مسام masâm(m) holes, chinks

مسائل masâ'il pl of mas'ala

مسبع musabba' septagonal

مست mast drunk, intoxicated; ~âna drunk-like

مستعجل musta'jil in haste, in a hurry

مستغنی mustaghnî az not in need of, able to dispense with

مستقر mustaqar(r) residing (adj)

مستمع mustami' listener

مستور mastûr veiled, hidden

مسجد masjid mosque

مسح mas'h-kardan to wipe

مسدس musaddas hexagonal

مسطر mistar writing guide

مسکن maskan dwelling

مسکین miskîn poor, unfortunate, miserable; ~î need

مسلمان musalmân Muslim; ~î being a Muslim

مسمار mismâr nail

مسیحا masîhâ the Messiah, the Christ

مشارق *mashâriqul'anvâr* the dawning of lights

مشاركت *mushârakat* cooperation, forbearance

مشاعل *mashâ'il* → *mash'al*

مشام *mashâm(m)* sense of smell

مشت *musht* handful, heap

مشتاق *mushtâq* yearning, longing

مشتری *mushtarî* customer

مشتعل *mushta'al* kindled, lit

مشرب *mashrab* sect

مشرق *mashriq* the orient, place where the sun rises; ~*ayn* the East and West

مشروطه *mashrûta* Iranian constitutional movement

مشعبد *musha'bid* sleight-of-hand artist, con man

مشعشع *musha'shi'* sparkling, glistening

مشعل *mash'al* pl *mashâ'il* torch

مشق *mashq* lesson

مشك *mishk, mushk* musk; ~*bûy* musk-scented; ~*în* musky; ~*înmûy* with musk-scented hair; ~*înnafas* with musk-scented breath; ~*zulf* with musky-scented locks

مشكات *mishkât* niche in a wall where a lamp is placed

مشكل *mushkil* difficult

مشكوة *mishkât* niche in a wall where a lamp is placed

مشهد *mashhad* shrine

مشهور *mashhûr* famous, renowned

مصاف *masâf* battle

مصالحه *musâlaha* truce

مصباح *misbâh* lamp, lantern

مصر *Misr* Egypt

مصطفی *Mustafâ* the Chosen, epithet of the Prophet Muhammad

مصلی *musallâ* open area outside a town where the entire population can gather for festival prayers

مصلحت *maslahat* prudence; ~-*âmêz* prudent

مصیبت *musîbat* calamity

مصور *musavvir* painter

مضار *mazârr* harm, hurt

مضایقه *muzâyiqa-kardan* to refuse

مضرت *mazarrat* detriment, harm

مضرس *muzarras* uneven, jagged

مضلع *muzalla'* striped; geometrical figure

مضمر *muzmar* concealed

مضمون *mazmûn* contents, meaning

مطبخ *matbakh* kitchen

مطرب *mutrib* musician, minstrel, entertainer

مطرف *mitraf* veil

مطلب *matlab* goal, intent

مطلع *matla'* place of rising (sun, stars); first line of a poem

مطمئن *mutma'in(n)* at rest, quiet

مظالم *mazâlim* redress of grievances

مظلوم *mazlûm* wronged, having suffered injustice

معاصی *ma'âsî* sins, acts of disobedience

معتكف *mu'takif* on retreat, withdrawn

معتوه *ma'tûh* delirious

معجر *mi'jar* head-scarf

معدن *ma'dan* mine; mineral

معده *mi'da* stomach

معذور *ma'zûr* forgiveable

معراج mi'râj heavenly ascent of the Prophet Muhammad

معريد mu'arbid quarrelsome, pugnacious

معرفت ma'rifat internal knowledge, gnosis

معركه ma'rika tumult, battle

معشوق ma'shûq beloved

معظم mu'azzam exalted

معلق mu'allaq hung, hung high; ~bâz puppet, marionette

معما mu'ammâ riddle, enigma

معنبر mu'ambar scented with ambergris; ~zulf with ambergris-scented tresses

معنى ma'nâ, ma'nî meaning; subtle point; substance, matter

مغ mugh Magian; ~bachcha Magian boy; pîr-i ~ân the old man of the Magi, a Mazdaean tavern keeper

مغز maghz brain, kernel

مغلوبه maghlûba rout

مغيلان mughaylân thorn bush

مفت muft free, gratis, worthless

مفخر mafkhar pride

مفلس muflis broke, bankrupt

مقام maqâm station; ¶ muqâm dwelling

مقبول maqbûl acceptable, received

مقترن muqtaran in conjunction (stars)

مقتول maqtûl killed, murdered

مقدار miqdâr quantity, length

مقدس muqaddas sacred

مقر maqar(r) residence

مقراض miqrâz scissors, shears; ~rândan to wield scissors

مقرر muqarrar an agreed-upon amount, tribute; ~-gashtan to be settled, agreed upon

مقصد maqsad destination

مقصود maqsûd object, goal

مقعد maq'ad crippled, lame

مقلموت maqalmawt (for malaku'l-mawt) the angel of death

مقيم muqîm resident

مكان makân place

مكتب maktab grammar school

مكحل makhal pot for kohl, collyrium bottle

مكر makr trick

مكلس mukallas calcinated

مكمن makman ambush

مكيدن makîdan to suck

مگر magar except; perhaps

مگس magas fly

ملا mullâ mulla, priest

ملاحت malâhat goodness, beauty

ملازمت mulâzimat, mulâzamat service to, or belonging to, a retinue

ملل malâl languor, ennui

ملامت malâmat censure; ~-kashîdan to attract censure

ملايك malâyik pl of malak angel

ملت millat sect, nation

ملك malak pl malâyik angel; ~khûy angelic in temperament; ¶ malik pl mulûk king; ~î royal; ¶ mulk possession, kingship

ملكوت malakût kingdom of heaven, the spiritual realm

ملوك mulûk pl of malik king

ملول malûl weary, languid

ممتاز mumtâz separate, distinct

متحن *mumtahan* sorely tried

ممكن *mumakkan* stable, powerful

ممنوع *mamnû'* forbidden, deprived of

مناظره *munâzira* discussion, disputation

منافق *munâfiq* hypocrite, hypocritical

منبر *mimbar* pulpit

منت *minnat* obligation, debt; ~-*kashîdan* to be obliged

منتظر *muntazir* waiting, expecting

منجم *munajjim* astronomer, astrologer

منجنيق *manjanîq* catapult

منديل *mandîl* turban cloth

منزل *manzil* stopping place, station; ~-*kardan* to halt, dismount; ¶ *munzal* sent down

منصور *mansûr* victorious

منضم *munzam(m)* added, admixed, joined

منظر *manzar* belvedere, watch tower; perspective

منظور *manzûr* object of one's gaze, object of affection

منظوم *manzûm* in poetry, versified

منقار *minqâr* beak

منقسم *munqasim* divided

منقل *manqal* brazier, chafing dish

منكر *munkir* disavowing; ~-*shudan* to disavow

منوچهر *Minûchihr* Minuchihr, a king of Iran

منور *munavvar* illuminated

منی *manî* conceit, egotism; ~-*kardan* to boast

منير *munîr* radiant, luminous

موافق *muvâfiq* agreeable, harmonious

مويد *môbad* Magian priest

موج *mawj* wave

مودت *mavaddat* affection

مؤذن *mu'azzin, mu'zin* muezzin

مور *môr* ant

موسم *mawsim* season

موسی *Mûsâ* Moses

موش *mûsh* mouse; ~*ak* mouseling

موقع *mawqi'* opportunity; ~*shinâsî* opportunism

موقف *mawqif* halting place

موقوفه *mawqûfa* legacy

موكشان *mû-kashân* dragging by the hair

مولا *mawlâ* mulla

موليان *Mûliyân* Mulian, name of a river in Bukhara

موم *mûm* wax

مؤمن *mu'min* believer

مونس *mu'nis* familiar, companion; that which causes intimacy

موی *mûy* hair; edge (of sword); ~-*i sar guzâshtan* to let the hair grow long; ~*shikâf* hair-splitting; ~*îna* woolen; ~*îna-pôsh* wearing a woolen garment, Sufi

مويه *môya* lamentation; ~-*kardan* to lament

مه *mah = mâh*; ¶ *mih = mihtar*

مهتاب *mahtâb* moonlight

مهتر *mihtar* elder, lord

مهجور *mahjûr* separated

مهر *mihr* love, affection; the sun; ~*bân* affectionate, kind; ~*bânî* kindness; ¶ *muhr, ~a* bead

مهرگان mihragân Mihragan, the Zoroastrian festival of the autumnal equinox

مهستی Mahsatî Mahsati (female name)

مهمان mihmân guest

مهندس muhandis geometer, geometrician

مهی mihî greatness

مهیا muhayyâ ready, prepared

مهین mihîn, mihîna great, old, aged

می may wine; ~furôsh wine seller; ~gûn wine-colored; ~kada wine house; ~kash wine quaffer; ~khâna tavern; ~parast worshipper of wine

میان miyân middle, midst; waist, girth; ~-bastan to gird the loins, be prepared; ~a middle

میدان maydân square; open space; arena, battlefield

میر mîr lord, prince; ¶ mîr- → murdan

میز mêz desk

میسر muyassar possible

میل mayl inclination; ~-i chîz-î kardan to incline to something, have an inclination to do something

مینا mînâ enamel; blue; an enameled cup

مینو mînû heaven; ~sifat of heavenly quality

میوه mêva fruit

میهمان mêhmân = mihmân

ناامید nâum(m)êd in despair, desperate

ناب nâb pure, unadulterated

نابود nâbûd nonexistence

نابینا nâbînâ blind

ناپدید nâpadîd not visible

ناپروا nâparvâ fearless

ناتمام nâtamâm incomplete, deficient

ناتوان nâtavân impotent, weak

ناجنس nâjins ignoble

ناچخ nâchakh battle-axe

ناحق nâhaqq unrightful

ناخن nâkhun fingernail

ناخوانده nâkhwânda uninvited

ناخوش nâkhwash unpleasant, ill; ~î unpleasantness, illness

نادان nâdân foolish

نادر nâdir rare

نادیدنی nâdîdanî what cannot be seen

نار nâr fire; = anâr pomegranate; ~dân(a) grain of pomegranate

نارامیدن nârâmîdan to be upset, excited

نارون nârvan tall, shady tree

ناز nâz pride; coquetry; ~nîn coquettish; ~ u niyâz supplication, entreaty

نازك nâzuk delicate; ~jigar faint-hearted

ناشده مدفون nâshuda madfûn unburied

ناصح nâsih advisor

ناطقه nâtiqa possessed of speech and reason

ناظر nâzir viewer, onlooker

ناف nâf navel

نافه nâfa musk bag

ناقابل nâqâbil unacceptable, unbelievable

ناقص nâqis decreasing; deficient

ناقوس *nâqûs* clapper used in Oriental churches instead of bells

ناكس *nâkas* nobody

ناگاه *nâgâh,* ~*ân* suddenly, all of a sudden

ناگوار *nâguvâr* foul-tasting

نالان *nâlân* complaining, moaning; ~*tan* quivering

ناله *nâla* wail, moan; complaint, lament

ناليدن *nâlîdan* to wail, moan, complain

نام *nâm* name, good name, renown, repute; ~*-nihâdan* to name; ~*dâr* renowned; ~*var* renowned

نامدن *n'âmadan* cont. for *nayâmadan,* negative of *âmadan*

ناموس *nâmûs* good repute; ill repute, shame

نامه *nâma* letter, epistle, book

نان *nân* bread, food (in general)

ناوك *nâvak* small arrow, dart

نای *nây* flute

نایاب *nâyâb* unavailable, not to be found

نایژه *nâyzha* windpipe

نبات *nabât* plants

نبرد *nabard* battle

نبرده *nabarda* warrior, experienced in battle

نبض *nabz* pulse

نبی *nabî* prophet

نبید *nabîd* wine

نتیجه *natîja* conclusion, result

نثار *nisâr* anything scattered over or strewn before a person, particularly at a wedding feast

نجم *najm* pl *anjum, nujûm* star

نجوم *nujûm* stars

نجیب *najîb* noble

نخچیر *nakhchîr* hunt

نخست *nukhust, nakhust* first; at first; prime; ~*în* first

نخل *nakhl* date palm

نخوت *nakhvat* haughtiness, pride

ندامت *nidâmat* penitence

نر *nar* male

نردبان *nardbân* ladder

نرگس *nargis* narcissus; ~*ak* little narcissus

نرم *narm* soft, gentle; ~*ak* softly, gently

نزار *nizâr* emaciated

نزد *nazd-i* near, in the opinion of

نزول *nuzûl-kardan* to descend, stop, camp

نژند *nizhand* terrible, horrible

نسترن *nastaran* white rose, wild rose

نسرین *nasrîn* jonquil; ~*tan* slender; ¶ *nasrayn* Vega and Altair

نسیم *nasîm* breeze

نشاط *nishât* pleasure

نشان *nishân* sign, trace; ~*-justan* to seek out; ¶ *nishân-* → *nishândan*

نشاندن *nishând-/nishân-* to make someone sit down; to quell, quench

نشانی *nishânî* = *nishân*

نشاه *nash'a* pleasure, tipsiness

نشستن *nishast-/nishîn-* to be seated, endure, bear with

نشور *nushûr* resurrection

نشیمن nishîman perch

نشین nishîn- → nishastan

نصیب nasîb lot, portion

نصیحت nasîhat advice

نطع nat' leather placed under the chopping block at an execution; chessboard

نطفه nutfa seed, sperm; ~-si-tadan to receive sperm

نظارگی nazzâragî spectators, audience

نظاره nazâra glimpse

نظر nazar sight, speculation; ~-kardan bar to look upon; ~-bâzî playing at amorous glances

نظم nazm poetry; poetical composition

نعایم na'âyim ostrich

نعره na'ra cry; ~-zadan to cry out, shout

نعمان Nu'mân Nu'man III, king of Hirah ca. A.D. 580–602

نعمت ni'mat ease, luxury, the good things of life

نعیم na'îm luxury

نغز naghz beautiful, nice

نغم nagham low voice

نغمه naghma melody

نفاق nifâq hypocrisy

نفخ nafkh blow; ~-i sûr blow on trumpet (signal for doomsday)

نفرت nifrat, nafrat aversion

نفرین nifrîn curse, malediction

نفس nafas breath; moment; ~-î for a moment

نفور nafûr averse

نفیر nafîr shrill sound

نقاب niqâb veil

نقد naqd cash, ready money

نقره nuqra silver; ~-gûn silvery

نقش naqsh pl nuqûsh picture, painting; line, circle; ~-kar-dan to paint, draw; ~ bar âb zadan to draw on water, to "build castles in Spain"

نقصان nuqsân deficiency; decrease

نقطه nuqta dot, point

نقل naql narration; nuql sweets passed out at social gatherings

نقم niqam punishments

نقوش nuqûsh pl of naqsh line, circle

نکته nukta point

نکو nikû = nêkû

نگار nigâr picture, portrait; beautiful, beauty; ~-kardan to paint a portrait; ~istân picture gallery, Bahram Gor's gallery; ¶ nigâr- → nigâshtan

نگاشتن nigâsht-/nigâr- to paint, draw, write

نگاه nigâh glance; ~-kardan dar to look at, regard

نگر nigar- → nigarîstan

نگریدن nigarîdan dar to look at

نگریستن nigarîst-/nigar- to look, watch

نگون nigûn, ~-sâr upside down; ~-î being upside down

نگردار nigardâr keeper, watchman

نگ nigah-kardan to look at; to keep, maintain

نگین nigîn signet, seal

نم nam wet

نماز namâz prayer; ~-burdan to show reverence

نمای numây- → numûdan

نمایان numâyân visible

نمرود *Namrûd* Nimrod

نمك *namak* salt; ~*sûd* salted

نمو *namû* growth, vegetation

نمودن *numûd-/numây-* to show (trs); appear (int)

ننگ *nang* shame

نو *naw* new; ~~ again and again; ~*'arûs* in the bloom of youth; ~*bahâr* the beginning of spring; Buddhist monastery; ~*khêz* newly-sprouted; ~*rusta* newly sprung up; ~*rôz* Nawroz, Persian New Year; ~*shikufta* newly-blossomed

نوا *navâ* tune, strain; sound, voice; ~*sanj* musician, singer

نوبت *nawbat* large drum; the kettle drums beat at a sultan's gates; turn

نوح *Nûh* Noah

نوحه *nawha* lament; ~*gar* mourner

نور *nûr* light, splendor, aura

نوردیدن *navardîdan* to traverse

نوش *nôsh* agreeable, pleasant to the palate; ~*în* sweet, delicious; ~*înlab* sweet-lipped; *bâd-at* ~ cheers; ¶ *nôsh-* → *nôshîdan*

نوشتن *nivisht-/nivîs-* to write, ascribe

نوشته *nivishta* written, fated

نوشروان *Nûshravân, Nûshirvân* Anushirvan the Just, Sassanian king

نوشیدن *nôshîdan* to drink, quaff

نوع *naw'* kind, sort; ~*î ki* in such a manner as

نوکر *nawkar* servant

نومید *nawmêd* desperate, without hope

نوید *navêd* good news

نه *nih-* → *nihâdan*

نهادن *nihâd-/nih-* to put, place; *dar-*~ to place, insert

نهار *nahâr* daytime

نهان *nihân* secret, hidden; ~*khâna* secret chamber

نهفتن *nihuftan* to hide, keep within, conceal

نهفته *nihufta* hidden, in secret

نهنگ *nahang, nihang* crocodile

نهی *nahy, nahî* prohibition; *sar-i* ~ head hung on city gate as an example

نهیب *nahêb, nahîb* anxiety; terror

نی *nî* no, not; ¶ *nay* reed, reed flute; ~*istân* reed bed

نیاز *niyâz* supplication, need; poverty

نیایش *niyâyish* blessing, praise; ~*kardan* to praise, worship

نیت *niyyat* intention

نیران *nîrân* fires

نیرم *nîram* brave, heroic

نیرنگ *nayrang* sorcery, incantation, spell

نیرو *nîrû* power, might, strength; ~*mand* strong, powerful

نیز *nîz* also

نیزه *nayza* spear

نیسان *nîsân* April

نیست *nîst* (verb) is not; (noun) nonexistence; (adj) nonexistent; ~ *bâd* may it not exist; ~*-u-hast* entirety, sum total

نیستان *nayistân* reed bed

نیش *nêsh* sting, lancet; fang

نیك *nêk* good, well; ~*î* goodness; ~*û* good, beautiful

نیل‌ nîl indigo; ~fâm, ~gûn indigo-colored; ~î indigo blue; ¶ nayl acquisition

نیلوفر nîlûfar water lily

نیم nîm half; ~shabân at midnight

نیوشیدن niyûshîdan to listen, hear

وا اسفا vâ'asafâ alas

وادی vâdî valley

وار -vâr (suffix) -like

وارهاندن vâ-rahândan to deliver, set free

واسطه vâsita means

واصل vâsil arriving, maturing; coming into union

واقع vâqi' for vâqi'an actually, really

واقعه vâqi'a calamity

واقف vâqif donator of an endowment; ~ az aware of, acquainted with

والسلام vassalâm ...and goodbye

والله vallâh by God

وام vâm loan; ~-giriftan to borrow

واماندن vâ-mândan to be left behind, straggle

وای vây woe

وجد vajd ecstasy

وجود vujûd existence

وجه vajh means; bi-~-i by means of

وحدت vahdat unity, oneness

وحشت vahshat dread, terror

وحشی vahshî wild

وداع vidâ' farewell

ور var = va agar

ورای varâ-yi beyond

ورد vird rosary, supererogatory prayer

ورداشتن var-dâshtan (modern colloquial) = bar-dâshtan

ورزیدن varzîdan to experience, try out

ورطه varta precipice, predicament

ورق varaq paper

ورمالیدن var-mâlîdan to knead

ورنه varna were it not that; otherwise

وزیدن vazîdan to blow (wind)

وزیر vazîr vizier, advisor, minister; ~-i lashkar minister of the army

وسط vasat middle

وسن vasan sleep

وشی vashî type of silken fabric

وصال visâl union

وصف vasf description

وصل vasl union, state of union

وصلت vuslat union, communion

وضع vaz' condition, situation

وطن vatan homeland; ~gâh homeland, native land

وعده va'da promise

وعظ va'z admonition, sermon

وفا vafâ faithfulness

وقار viqâr dignity

وقت vaqt time

وقف vaqf endowment, mortmain

وکیل vakîl parliamentary representative

وکر vagar cont. for va agar

ولایت vilâyat province, realm

ولی الابصار valîl'absâr one who has "eyes to see"

وهم vahm imagination, illusion

وی *vay* he, she, it

ویران *vayrân, vîrân* ruined, destroyed; ~-*kardan* to destroy; ~*a* ruined place

هاله *hâla* halo, ring around the moon

هامون *hâmûn* plain

هان *hân* beware, behold; intensifies imperatives

های‌وهوی *hây-u-hûy* uproar, tumult

هبا *habâ-kardan* to annihilate

هجر *hajr* separation

هجران *hijrân* separation

هدایت *hidâyat* right guidance

هدر *hadar-kardan* to shed blood with impunity

هدف *hadaf* target

هدهد *hudhud* hoopoe

هدیه *hidya* gift, present

هذا *hâzâ* (Ar.) "this is..."

هذیان *hazayân* delirium

هراسان *harâsân* afraid

هرانچش *harânchash* = *har ânchiash*

هرچ *harch'* cont. for *har chi*

هرگز *hargiz* ever, (+ neg.) never

هرمز *Hurmuz* Hormizd Ardasher

هزار *hazâr* thousand; nightingale

هست *hast* existent; ~*î* being, existence

هش *hush* = *hôsh*

هشت *hasht* eight; ~*pây* eight-legged

هشتن *hisht-/hil-* to let go of, turn loose

هشیار *hushyâr* aware, awake; sober

هشیوار *hushîvâr* herald

هفترنگ *haftrang* multicolored, variegated

هل *hil-* → *hishtan*

هلا *halâ* hey!

هلاک *halâk* destruction, death

هلال *hilâl* crescent (moon)

هم *-ham* (enclitic) too, also, even

هما *humâ* Huma, a mythical bird

همان *hamân* that very

همانا *hamânâ* certainly, assuredly

هم‌آوا *hamâvâ* for *hamâvâz* harmonious, in agreement

همپا *hampâ* companion, fellow-traveller

همت *himmat* ambition

همچشمی *hamchashmî* competition

همداستان *hamdâstân* in agreement

همدم *hamdam* confidant

همراز *hamrâz* one with whom secrets are shared, confidant

همراه *hamrâh* companion

همرنگ *hamrang* of the same color

همره *hamrah* = *hamrâh*

همزبان *hamzabân* one who speaks the same language

همسال *hamsâl* contemporary, of the same age

همسایه *hamsâya* neighbor

همسر *hamsar* spouse

همنشین *hamnishîn* companion, intimate

همنفس *hamnafas* intimate

هموار *hamvâr* smooth; continually, continuously; ~*a* smooth, level; ~*î* smoothness

همی *hamî* particle that indicates repeated action

هنجار hanjâr way, rule, custom

هند Hind India

هندسه handasa geometry, engineering

هندو hindû Hindu, Indian; slave

هنر hunar art, craft

هنگام hangâm time

هنگامه hangâma commotion, riot

هنيالك hanîyan lak (Ar.) cheers

هوا havâ air; love, passion, romance; ~dâr infatuated

هوام havâmm insects

هوس havas desire, desiring; love

هوش hôsh consciousness, sobriety, awareness; ~mand intelligent; ba~, bâ~ conscious; ba ~ âmadan to come to, awake

هويدا huvaydâ apparent

هی hay ho, hark; construed with verb, "to keep on..."

هیاهو hayâhû ado

هیبت haybat awe, awesomeness

هیزم hîzum kindling

هیکل haykal skeleton, form

هین hîn behold, lo

یاب yâb- → yâftan

یاد yâd memory; ~-dâshtan to remember; ~-kardan to mention, describe; ~gâr memento, souvenir; -am ~ âmad, ~-am âmad I remembered; ~ bâd may (it) live in memory, may it be remembered

یار yâr friend, comrade, beloved; ¶ yâr- → yâristan

یارا yârâ power, ability

یا رب yârab(b) (Ar.) O Lord

یارستن yârist-/yâr- to be able

یاره yâra gauntlet

یازان yâzân stretching out

یازیدن yâzîdan to unsheathe

یاسمن yâsiman = yâsimîn; ~tan jasmine-bodied

یاسمین yâsimîn jasmine; ~bar jasmine-breasted

یافت yâft-shudan to be found

یافتن yâft-/yâb- to find, get

یاقوت yâqût ruby

یال yâl mane

یدبیضا yad-i bayzâ "white hand," sign of prophecy

یراق yarâq arms

یزد Yazd Yazd, city in Iran

یزدان Yazdân Yazdan, God; ~parast God-fearing

یسر yusr difficulty, hardship

یعقوب Ya'qûb Jacob, Joseph's father; ~vâr like Jacob

یغما yaghmâ plunder, pillage; ~gar plunderer

یقین yaqîn certainty, certain

یك yak one; ~â~ suddenly; ~bâr, ~bâra all at once; ~fan specialist, master of one craft; ~î oneness; ~ka unique, alone; ~rah once, suddenly; ~rân steed; ~rôza sufficient for a day; ~sân altogether, alike, in one manner; ~sar completely, totally, at once; ~sara all at once

یگانه yagâna one (adj.), only

یمن Yaman the Yemen; ¶ yumn prosperity, ease

یوسف Yûsuf Joseph

SOURCES

Rûdakî: Âsâr-i manzûm, ed. I. S. Braginskii (Moscow: Nauk, 1964): Ay ânki ghamginî u sazâvârî, p. 108f.; Zindagânî chi kûtah, p. 64; Bôy-i jûy-i Mûliyân, p. 108.

Daqîqî: Daqîqî u ash'âr-i û, ed. Muhammad Dabîr-Siyâqî (Tehran: 'Ilmî, 1342): Shab-i siyâh, p. 99; Barkhêz u barafrôz, p. 97.

Munjîk: Zabîhullâh Safâ, ed., Ganj-i sukhan, vol. 1 (4th ed., Tehran: Ibn-i Sînâ, [1339]): Ay khûbtar zi paykar-i dêbâ-yi armanî, p. 50f.

Kasâ'î: Muhammad-Amîn Riyâhî, Kasâyî-i Marvazî: Zindagî, andîsha u shi'r-i û (Tehran: Tûs, 1367): Nîlûfar-i kabûd nigah kun miyân-i âb, p. 85; Gul ni'matîst hidya firistâda az bihisht, p. 90; Nargis nigar chigûna hamî âshiqî kunad, p. 78.

Firdawsî: Shâhnâma, ed. Ye. E. Bertels et al., 9 vols. (Moscow: Nauk, 1966–71): Chu Rustam zi chang-i vay âzâd gasht, vol. 2, p. 235ff. (with variants); Chu khwarshêd-i tâbanda shud nâpadîd, vol. 1, p. 171–74 (with variants).

Farrukhî: Dîvân, ed. 'Alî 'Abdul-Rasûl (Tehran: Majlis, 1311): Shahr-i Ghaznî na hamânast, p. 92; Chun parand-i nîlgûn, p. 177.

Unsurî: Dîvân, ed. Muhammad Dabîr-Siyâqî (Tehran: Sanâ'î, 1342): Ba gird-i mâh bar, p. 305; But ki butgar kunad'sh, p. 12; Sada jashn-i mulûk-i nâmdârast, p. 14.

Minûchihrî: Dîvân, ed. Muhammad Dabîr-Siyâqî (Tehran: Zuvvâr, 1338): Ay bâ adû-yi mâ guzaranda, p. 213; Âmad shab, p. 6f.; Jahân-i mâ sag-i shôkhast, p. 138.

Azraqî: Dîvân, ed. Sa'îd Nafîsî (Tehran: Zuvvâr, 1336): Jâ ba jâ abr-i sipêd andar havâ bîn, p. 79, lines 1960–65; Bin'gar în abr-i girân, p. 79, lines 1943–53.

Hujjat, Nâsir-i Khusraw: Dîvân-i qasâyid u muqatta'ât, ed. Mujtabâ Mînuvî (Tehran: Dunyâ-yi Kitâb, 1347): Dar dilam tâ ba sahargâh, p. 341; Bâz-i jahân têzparr, p. 50; Rôz-î zi sar-i sang uqâb-î ba havâ khâst, p. 499.

Mas'ûd-i Sa'd-i Salmân: Dîvân-i ash'âr, ed. Mahdî Nûrîân (Isfahan: Kamâl, 1364): Chunân bigiryam k'am dushmanân bibakhshâyand, p. 606.

Mu'izzî: Dîvân, ed. 'Abbâs Iqbâl (Tehran: Islâmiyya, 1318): Ay sârbân, manzil makun, p. 597.

181

Khayyâm: E. H. Whinfield, *The Quatrains of Omar Khayyám* (London: Kegan, Paul, Trench, Trübner and Co., 1901): *Pésh az man u tu*, p. 25, N° 33; *În yak du si rôza*, p. 19, N° 26; *Dar kârgah-i kûzagar-î raftam dôsh*, p. 191, N° 283.

Sûzanî: *Dîvân*, ed. Nâsiruddîn Shâh-Husaynî (Tehran: Amîr Kabîr, 1338): *Shikasta zulfâ*, p. 311; *Darîn jahân ki sarây-i ghamast*, p. 18.

Anvarî: *Dîvân*, ed. Muhammad-Taqî Mudarris-Razavî, Majmû'a-i Mutûn-i Fârsî, 1 (Tehran: Bungâh-i Tarjuma u Nashr-i Kitâb, 1347): *Chu shâh-i zang bar-âvurd*, p. 368; *Bâz în chi javânî*, p. 9.

Khâqânî: *Dîvân*, ed. Ziyâ'uddîn Sajjâdî (Tehran: Zuvvâr, [1338]): *Hân, ay dil-i 'ibratbîn*, p. 358.

Nizâmî: *Kulliyyât-i khamsa-i Hakîm Nizâmî-i Ganjaî* (Tehran: Amîr Kabîr, 1351): *Shart ast ki vaqt-i bargrêzân*, pp. 587–90; *Angushtkashân sukhansarâyân*, p. 593f.

Sanâ'î: *Qissa-î yâd dâram az pidarân: Hadîqatu'l-haqîqat u sharî'atu'l-tarîqat*, ed. Muhammad-Taqî Mudarris-Razavî (Tehran: Sipihr, n.d.), p. 454f. *Bas ki shinîdî sifat-i Rûm u Chîn*: 'Abdul-Hamîd Gulshan-Ibrâhîmî, ed., *Gulshan-i shi'r-i fârsî* (Tehran: Îrânmihr, n.d.), p. 243.

Attâr: *Dîvân-i ghazaliyyât u qasâyid*, ed. Taqî Tafazzulî (Tehran: Châp-i Bahman, 1341): *Gum shudam dar khwad*, p. 183; *Ay hamnafasân*, p. 358; *Pagah mîraft ustâd-i mihîna*, Zabîhullâh Safâ, ed., *Ganj-i sukhan*, vol. 2 (4th ed., Tehran: Ibn-i Sînâ, 1969), p. 116f.

Mawlavi: *Dîvân-i kâmil-i Shams-i Tabrîzî*, ed. Badî'uzzamân Furûzânfar et al. (Tehran: Jâvîdân, 1362): *Man mast u tu dêvâna*, p. 393 (with variants); *Bin'mây rukh*, p. 175; *Ay qawm*, p. 258; *'Aql âmad*, p. 513. *Masnavî-i ma'navî*, ed. R. A. Nicholson (Tehran: Amîr Kabîr, 1341): *Bish'naw az nay*, Book One, lines 1–18, p. 1; *Châr hindû*, Book Two, lines 3027–34, p. 343; *Chun guzasht ân majlis*, Book One, lines 101–16, p. 6.

Irâqî: *Kulliyyât*, ed. Sa'îd Nafîsî (Tehran: Sanâ'î, 1338): *Nukhustîn bâda k'andar jâm kardand*, p. 193; *Khânahâ-yi tan az darîcha-i jân*, p. 328.

Sa'dî: *Kulliyyât-i Sa'dî*, ed. Muhammad-'Alî Furûghî (Tehran: Amîr Kabîr, 1363): *Shab-î yâd dâram*, p. 295; *Bakht-i âîna nadâram*, p. 614; *Yak rôz ba shâydâî*, p. 559; *Ay sârbân âhasta rân*, p. 508; *Kâravân-î shikar az Misr*, p. 514.

Amîr Khusraw: *Dîvân-i kâmil-i Amîr Khusraw-i Dihlavî*, ed. M. Darvîsh (Tehran: Jâvîdân, 1343): *Chu turk-i mast-i man*, p. 146; *Abr mîbârad*, p. 3; *Ay chihra-i zêbâ-yi tu*, p. 543; *Ay pîr, khâk-i pây-i tu*, p. 104.

Hasan Dihlavî: Zabîhullâh Safâ, ed., *Ganj-i sukhan*, vol. 2 (4th ed., Tehran: Ibn-i Sînâ, 1969): *Chandîn chi nâẓ âmôkhtî*, p. 227f.; *Bâ man namîsâẓî dam-î*, p. 229f.

Ubayd Zâkânî: *Kulliyyât-i 'Ubayd-i Zâkânî*, ed. 'Abbâs Iqbâl Âshtiyânî (Tehran: Iqbâl, [1332]): *Mûsh u gurba*, p. 169–73.

Awhadî: *Kulliyyât*, ed. Sa'îd Nafîsî (Tehran: Amîr Kabîr, 1340): *Ay sârbân ki ranj kashîdî*, p. 227f.; *Dilkhasta hamîbâshad*, p. 33.

Khwâjû: *Ghaẓaliyyât-i Khwâjû-yi Kirmânî* (Kirman: Intishârât-i Khidamât-i Farhangî-i Kirmân, 1370): *Sham'-i mâ sham'-îst*, p. 100f.; *Zi chashm-i mast-i tu ânhâ ki âgahî dârand*, p. 172; *Pêsh-i sâhibnaẓarân mulk-i Sulaymân bâdast*, p. 56.

Imâd: Zabîhullâh Safâ, ed., *Ganj-i sukhan*, vol. 2 (4th ed., Tehran: Ibn-i Sînâ, 1969): *Shinîdam aẓ malakkhûy-î parîchihr*, p. 278–80; *Mâ ba sît-i karamat aẓ rah-i dûr âmadaîm*, p. 286f.

Salmân: Zabîhullâh Safâ, ed., *Ganj-i sukhan*, vol. 2 (4th ed., Tehran: Ibn-i Sînâ, 1969): *Suhbat-î khwash dargirift imshab miyân-i sham' uman*, p. 291f.; *Dar aẓal 'aks-i may-i la'l- tu dar jâm uftâd*, p. 296f.

Hâfiz: *Dîvân-i Khwâja Hâfiẓ-i Shîrâzî*, ed. Sayyid Abû'l-Qâsim Injuvî Shîrâzî (Tehran: Jâvîdân, 1367): *Agar ân turk-i shîrâzî*, p. 1; *Dôsh dîdam*, p. 77; *Yûsuf-i gumgashta bâz âyad*, p. 133; *Zulf âshufta u khôy karda*, p. 33; *Sâlhâ dil talab-i jâm-i Jam*, p. 87; *Biyâ ki qasr-i amal*, p. 18.

Ni'matullâh Valî: *Kulliyyât-i dîvân-i qadrtaw'amân-i Sayyid Nûruddîn Shâh Ni'matullâh Valî*, ed. Mahmûd 'Ilmî (Tehran: Châpkhâna-i 'Ilmî, 1333): *Manzil-i jân-i jahân bar dar-i jânâna-i mâst*, p. 78; *Jân chi bâshad*, p. 533.

Qâsim-i-Anvâr: *Kulliyyât*, ed. Sa'îd Nafîsî (Tehran: Sanâ'î, 1337): *Rah biyâbân ast u shab târîk u pâyam dar gilast*, p. 52; *Zi chashm-i gôshanishînân nishân-i sawdâ purs*, p. 184f.

Shâhî: Zabîhullâh Safâ, ed., *Ganj-i sukhan*, vol. 2 (4th ed., Tehran: Ibn-i Sînâ, 1969): *Gar namîsôẓad dilam*, p. 338; *Ba yak kirishma ki bar jân ẓadî ẓi dast shudam*, p. 339.

Ibn-i Husâm: Zabîhullâh Safâ, ed., *Ganj-i sukhan*, vol. 2 (4th ed., Tehran: Ibn-i Sînâ, 1969): *Har subhdam musavvir-i în charkh-i akhẓarî*, pp. 347–50.

Jâmî: *Masnavî-i haft awrang*, ed. Âqâ-Murtazâ Mudarris-Gîlânî (Tehran: Sa'dî, 1361): *Yakî khâd*, p. 929; *Sûfiyî râh-i yaqîn*, p. 553. *Dîvân-i kâmil-i Jâmî*, ed. Hâshim Razî (Tehran: Pîrûz, 1341): *Khâst har sû fitna*, p. 389; *Partaw-i sham'-i rukhat*, p. 226; *Rêzam ẓi muẓha*, p. 138.

Hilâlî: *Dîvân-i Hilâlî-i Jaghatâ'î*, ed. Sa'îd Nafîsî (Tehran: Sanâ'î, 1337): *Yâr-i mâ hargiz nayâzârad dil-i aghyârrâ*, p. 57; *Shîsha-i may dûr az ân labhâ-yi maygûn mîgirîst*, p. 31.

Ahlî: *Kulliyyât-i ash'âr*, ed. Hâmid Rabbânî (Tehran: Sanâ'î, 1344): *Aknûn ki tanhâ dîdamat*, p. 342, N° 1163; *Ân sham'-i gulrukhân*, p. 101, N° 333.

Vahshî: *Dîvân-i Vahshî-i Bâfqî*, ed. Husayn Nakha'î (Tehran: Amîr Kabîr, 1366): *Dôstân, sharh-i parêshânî-i man gôsh kunîd*, p. 293.

Muhtasham: *Dîvân*, edited by the Muhtasham Brothers (n.p.: Châp-i Muhtasham, 1337): *Bâz în chi shôrishast ki dar khalq-i 'âlamast?* pp. 24–33.

Fayzî: Zabîhullâh Safâ, ed., *Ganj-i sukhan*, vol. 3 (4th ed., Tehran: Ibn-i Sînâ, n.d.): *Falak, z'în kajravîhâyat*, p. 58f.

Urfî: *Kulliyyât*, ed. Ghulâm-Husayn Javâhirî (Tehran: Muhammad-'Alî 'Ilmî, n.d.): *Jahân bigashtam u dardâ ba hîch shahr u diyâr*, p. 43; *Khêz u sharâb-i hayratam z'ân qad-i jilvasâz dih*, p. 425.

Tâlib: *Kulliyyât-i ash'âr*, ed. Tâhirî Shihâb (Tehran: Sanâ'î, [1346]): *Hamânâ turk-i mast-î*, p. 437.

Kalîm: *Dîvân-i Abû-Tâlib Kalîm-i Kâshânî*, ed. H. Partaw-Bayzâî (Tehran: Khayyâm, [1336]): *Pîrî rasîd*, p. 123; *Dijla-i ashk az bahâr-i shawq*, p. 154; *Na hamîn mîramad ân naw gul*, p. 294.

Sâ'ib: *Kulliyyât-i Sâ'ib-i Tabrîzî*, ed. Amîrî Fîrûzkûhî (Tehran: Khayyâm, [1333]): *Bazêr-i charkh dil-î*, p. 335 (with variants); *În nâkasân*, p. 339; *Bâ kamâl-i ihtiyâj*, p. 262.

Bêdil: *Kulliyyât*, 4 vols. (Kabul: Pohnî Matba'a, 1341–44): *Az talab tâ chand*, vol. 1, p. 72; *Matlab-î gar bûd az hastî*, vol. 1, part 2, p. 642.

Hazîn: *Ay vây bar asîr-î*: Shaykh Ahmad-'Alî Khân Hâshimî Sandîlavî, *Makhzanu'l-gharâyib*, ed. Muhammad Bâqir, vol. 1 (Lahore: Panjab University, 1968), p. 817. *Man ân ghâratgar-i jân mîparastam*: *Dîvân-i Hazîn* (Karachi: National Publishing House, 1971), p. 255 (margin).

Âzar: Lutf-'Alî Bêg Âzar Bêgdilî, *Âtashkada-i Âzar*, ed. Ja'far Shahîdî (Tehran: Mu'assasa-i Nashr-i Kitâb, 1337): *Darîn manzil ki kas-râ nîst ârâm*, p. 449; *Ba shaykh-i shahr faqîr-î*, p. 462.

Hâtif: *Dîvân*, ed. Vahîd Dastgirdî (Tehran: Furûghî, 1349): *Tarjî'band*, pp. 24–29.

Visâl: Zabîhullâh Safâ, ed., *Ganj-i sukhan*, vol. 3 (4th ed., Tehran: Ibn-i Sînâ, n.d.): *Gashtîm khâk*, p. 198; *Agar kushî*, p. 199f.

Furûghî: *Dîvân-i kâmil*, ed. Husayn Nakha'î (Tehran: Amîr Kabîr, 1336): *Imrôz nadâram gham-i fardâ*, p. 32, N° 50.

Yaghmâ: *Nigâh kun ki narêzad: Kulliyyât-i Yaghmâ-yi Jandaqî*, ed. I'timâdu's-Saltana (Tehran, 1339), p. 174; *Sûfiyân-râ digar imrôz na hâyast*: Zabîhullâh Safâ, ed., *Ganj-i sukhan*, vol. 3 (4th ed., Tehran: Ibn-i Sînâ, n.d.), p. 218f.

Ghâlib: *Kulliyyât-i Ghâlib* (Lahore: Shaykh Mubârak 'Alî, 1965): *Dil burd*, p. 472; *Ay zawq-i navâsanjî*, p. 545f.

Qâ'ânî: *Dîvân-i kâmil-i Hakîm Qâ'ânî-i Shîrâzî*, ed. Nâsir Hîrî (Tehran: Gul-shâ'î, 1363): *Bahâr âmad*, p. 192; *Bâz bar-âmad ba kôh*, p. 677.

Îraj: *Dîvân-i Îraj Mîrzâ* (Tehran: Muzaffarî, n.d.): *Shinîdam man ki Ârif jân-am âmad*, pp. 120–23; *Shinîda-am ki ba daryâ*, p. 266; *Nadânam dar kujâ în qissa dîdam*: Zabîhullâh Safâ, ed., *Ganj-i sukhan*, vol. 3 (4th ed., Tehran: Ibn-i Sînâ, n.d.), p. 267f.

Parvîn: *Dîvân-i qasâyid u masnaviyyât u tamsîlât u muqatta'ât* (Tehran: Majlis, 1954): *Ghuncha-î guft ba pizhmurda gul-î*, p. 174; *Lâla-î bâ nargis-î pizhmurda guft*, p. 108.

Bahâr: *Dîvân-i ash'âr* (Tehran: Amîr Kabîr, 1344): *Tarsam man az jahannam*, pp. 165–67; *În dûd-i siyahfâm*, p. 261f.

FOR FURTHER STUDY AND REFERENCE

Anthologies

Gulshan-Ibrâhîmî, 'Abdul-Hamîd. *Gulshan-i shi'r-i fârsî*. Tehran: Îrânmihr, n.d.

Haqîqat, 'Abdul-Rafî'. *Nigîn-i sukhan*. 6 volumes. Tehran: Âfrâb-i Haqîqat, 1363–67.

Musaffâ, Mazâhir. *Qand-i Pârsî: Nimûnahâ-yi shi'r-i darî*. Tehran: Safî-'Alî-shâh, 1348/1970.

Safâ, Zabîhullâh. *Ganj-i sukhan: Shâ'irân-i buzurg-i pârsîgûy u muntakhab-i âsâr-i ânân*. 3 volumes. 4th revised ed. Tehran: Ibn-i Sînâ, 1969.

Literary histories

Bertel's, E. É. *Izbrannye trudy: Istoriya persidsko-tazhikskoy literatury*. Moscow, 1960.

Browne, Edward G. *A Literary History of Persia*. 4 volumes. 1902–24; reprinted. Cambridge: At the University Press, 1964.

Humâ'î, Jalâluddîn. *Târîkh-i adabiyyât-i Îrân*. 2nd ed. Tehran, 1340.

Rypka, Jan. *History of Iranian Literature*. Dordrecht: D. Reidel, 1968.

Safâ, Zabîhullâh. *Târîkh-i adabiyyât dar Îrân*. 5 volumes. 6th printing. Tehran: Firdawsî, 1363.

A LITERARY HISTORY OF PERSIA / EDWARD G. BROWNE
The classic history of Persian literature
ISBN 978-0-936347-66-0

A DICTIONARY OF COMMON PERSIAN AND ENGLISH VERBS
ISBN 978-1-58814-030-2

LEARNING PERSIAN: BOOK ONE
Includes an audio CD
ISBN 978-1-58814-052-4

LEARNING PERSIAN: BOOKS TWO & THREE
Includes two audio CDs
ISBN 978-1-58814-069-2

THE POEMS OF HAFEZ BY REZA ORDOUBADIAN
ISBN 978-1-58814-019-7

THE POEMS OF ABU SAID BY REZA ORDOUBADIAN
ISBN 978-1-58814-039-5

SELECTED POEMS FROM THE DIVAN-E SHAMS-E TABRIZI
ISBN 978-0-936347-61-5

THE DIVAN-I HAFIZ / H. WILBERFORCE CLARKE
Complete literal translation of Hafez's divan with copious notes.
ISBN 978-0-936347-80-6

THE HAFEZ POEMS OF GERTRUDE BELL
ISBN 978-0-936347-39-4

PERSIAN COOKING: A TABLE OF EXOTIC DELIGHTS
ISBN 978-1-58814-087-6

To order the above books or to receive our catalog, please contact us
Ibex Publishers / Post Office Box 30087 / Bethesda, MD 20824
301-718-8188 / www.ibexpublishers.com